LIBERTY OR DEATH

DEATH

WARS THAT FORGED A NATION

LIBERTY OR DEATH

WARS THAT FORGED A NATION

Carl Benn & Daniel Marston
Foreword by Fred Anderson

First published in Great Britain in 2006 by Osprey Publishing,
Midland House, West Way, Oxford OX2 0PH, UK.
443 Park Avenue South, New York, NY 10016, USA.
Email: info@ospreypublishing.com

Previously published as Essential Histories 41: *The War of 1812*,
Essential Histories 44: *The French-Indian War 1754–1760*, and
Essential Histories 45: *The American Revolution 1774–1783*.

A CIP catalog record for this book is available from the
British Library

ISBN 1 86403 022 6

Page layout by Ken Vail Graphic Design, Cambridge, UK
Index by Alison Worthington
Maps by The Map Studio
Originated by Grasmere Digital Imaging, Leeds, UK
Printed in China through Bookbuilders

06 07 08 09 10   10 9 8 7 6 5 4 3 2 1

For a catalog of all books published by Osprey please contact:

NORTH AMERICA
Osprey Direct, c/o Random House Distribution Center,
400 Hahn Road, Westminster, MD 21157, USA
E-mail: info@ospreydirect.com

ALL OTHER REGIONS
Osprey Direct UK, P.O. Box 140, Wellingborough, Northants,
NN8 2FA, UK
E-mail: info@ospreydirect.co.uk

www.ospreypublishing.com

Front cover: Virginia State Library, Richmond.
Title page: 'Washington entering New York City, 1783', Topfoto.

Contents

Foreword
by Fred Anderson

The decision to combine these three excellent books in a single volume is a most welcome one, for the wars they describe, while they are seldom treated together, were intimately interrelated. Because the connections between them become apparent when they are seen in juxtaposition, I would like to suggest, by way of introduction, a context in which these three conflicts can be seen together.

The American phase of the Seven Years' War – here called by the name traditionally used in the United States, the French and Indian War – erupted when colonists from Virginia tried to extend Britain's sway beyond the Allegheny Mountains, and New France and its Indian allies struck back to keep them from doing so. In ways completely unforeseeable at its outset, the war began a six-decade-long process by which native peoples who had been critical players in the great game of imperial competition found themselves overwhelmed by an Anglo-American expansionist juggernaut. Certainly George Washington had no way of knowing that his attempt to take control of the headwaters of the Ohio in 1754 would trigger a war that eventually engaged the forces of Britain and its allies in a titanic struggle with France and its allies by land and sea from the Virginia frontier to India and even the Philippines. Neither Washington nor any of his contemporaries dreamed that the war would end more decisively than any European conflict in three centuries, erasing the North American empire of France and compelling Spain (France's ally in the final year of the war) to surrender its imperial claims east of the Mississippi. It was an outcome no less welcome among Britons on both sides of the Atlantic for being so unanticipated. To many this unexampled victory seemed to herald an age in which their nation's glory would surpass that even of Rome.

Britain's victory, however, severely destabilized a longstanding balance of power by diminishing the capacity of native Americans to influence military outcomes in North America. By dividing the continent along the axis of the Mississippi River into a British east and a Spanish west, the Peace of Paris effectively deprived those Indian groups in closest contact with the British of an ally to help them, as the French traditionally had, to resist Anglo-American incursions onto their lands. Indian power was not yet, of course, at an end. As native peoples formerly allied with France demonstrated in Pontiac's War (1763–64) they could still deal powerful blows to British garrisons too small and dispersed to exert effective control in the American interior. Despite spectacular initial successes, however, the Indians found themselves compelled to make peace – not by British military might, but rather because the absence of an external source of arms, ammunition, and food deprived them of the capacity to carry on.

After 1763, both victorious Britain and defeated Spain attempted to strengthen metropolitan control over their colonies. The Spanish succeeded best in reforming their empire, which survived for more than a half-century thereafter. The British, by contrast, imposed reforms that only alienated their colonists to such a degree that a dozen years after the Peace of Paris colonists from New Hampshire to Georgia took up arms against the empire. In justifying resistance against the King and Parliament, colonial leaders stressed what had been called the rights of Englishmen, stressing the centrality of political freedom, the protection of property, and the rule of law. Because the colonists were an ethnically diverse, geographically divided, and mutually suspicious lot, however, the leaders of the resistance took care to couch their explanations and appeals in universalistic language – as defenses of natural rights, not merely English liberties.

The War for American Independence (1775–83) broke apart the British Empire and made those universalized ideas the foundation of American political identity. It took another dozen years after the end of the war in 1783, however, to produce the complex of institutions and compromises centering on the Constitution, the Bill of Rights, and the Northwest Ordinance that became the basis for the survival and success of the United States. By the end of 1795 Americans had succeeded where the British Empire had failed in exerting control beyond the Appalachians in the upper Ohio Valley, Kentucky, and Tennessee. Imperial and republican elements combined to form an American political culture that the instinctive expansionists of the frontier – men like Andrew Jackson – used to justify the subordination of native peoples whenever they encountered resistance to white appropriation of their lands. Seen in this light, the American Revolution of 1775–89 appears as the institutionally creative heart of a much longer era in which a monarchical empire expanded into the trans-Appalachian west, only to disintegrate and be replaced by an imperial republic capable of exerting control over the interior of the continent.

By the 1810s, bands of white citizens on the marches of the republic had succeeded in defining the American political community as a brotherhood of white Protestant men like themselves. Finding no place in their new world for native peoples, Americans treated suddenly vulnerable Indians as obstacles to be removed – or extirpated. In the War of 1812, Americans conjoined their defiance of British efforts to dictate their commercial and diplomatic policy with a war to conquer all of eastern North America. The first object of their attention, naturally enough, was Canada, from which the British had supplied arms and provisions to Indians on the western frontier, enabling a great pan-Indian movement to flourish before 1811. While the Americans failed to conquer Canada, the end of the War of 1812 signaled in the withdrawal of British support for Indians south of the Great Lakes, effectively destroying the power of Native Americans east of the Mississippi River. The conquest of the Southwest, begun by Andrew Jackson in his campaigns against the Creeks in 1813–14 and continued in 1818 when he invaded and occupied Florida, ended in 1819 with the annexation of Florida and the subsequent removal of most Indians to lands west of the Mississippi.

As important as these aspects of the War of 1812 were, the war's most significant legacy was the distinctively American just-war ideology that proponents of war with Britain first articulated in 1811. Unlike the Revolutionaries, who justified taking up arms to defend a fragile liberty against Britain's seemingly unlimited power, the so-called War Hawks argued that offensive warfare could be justified if it liberated the oppressed and hence expanded the sphere of freedom. Americans would invoke this argument again in 1845–46 to justify war against Mexico. In 1861 white Southerners used liberty to justify (ironically, it would seem in retrospect, although those who made the argument were unaware of any irony at the time) taking up arms against the United States. Later in the resulting war, Abraham Lincoln would invoke the same principle, with less irony and more reluctance, to destroy slavery. So too would Americans invoke liberty as the ultimate rationale for war in 1898, in the many Caribbean interventions that followed, in World War I, World War II, Korea, Vietnam, and beyond.

In this sense the three wars so well described in this volume can be seen as the crucible in which Americans forged their enduring attitudes toward the justification and practice of war. It may not be too much to argue that nearly two centuries after the Treaty of Ghent we live with the consequences of these three critical conflicts, even now.

Chronology

1754   **27 March** Skirmish at Great Meadows
3 July Battle at Fort Necessity

1755   June British siege and capture of Fort Beausejour
6–9 July Braddock's Defeat
17 August British force arrives at Oswego
8 September Battle of Lake George

1756   **17 May** Formal Declaration of War between France and Britain
14 August British forts Ontario, Pepperell, and George at Oswego capitulate

1757   **9 August** British Fort William Henry capitulates

1758   **8 July** Battle at Fort Carillon (Ticonderoga)
1 August French port of Louisbourg capitulates
27 August French Fort Frontenac is sacked
14 September Grant's Battle outside Fort Duquesne
12 October French repelled at Fort Ligonier
24 November French Fort Duquesne is abandoned

1759   **24 July** Battle of La Belle Famille
26 July French Fort Niagara capitulates, Fort Carillon abandoned
31 July French Fort St. Frederic (Crown Point) is abandoned
31 July British attack on Montmorency Falls
August Countryside around Quebec laid waste by British
13 September First battle of the Plains of Abraham
17 September Surrender of Quebec

1760   **28 April** Second battle of the Plains of Abraham (Sainte-Foy)
Early September Montreal surrounded by three British columns
8/9 September Montreal surrenders

1761–62   War continues in the Caribbean, India, and Europe

1763   **10 February** Treaty of Paris
15 February Treaty of Hubertusburg
10 May–15 October Indian siege of Fort Detroit
End of June All British forts in the west captured except for forts Detroit, Niagara, and Pitt
31 July Battle of Bloody Run
5/6 August Battle of Bushy Run
10 August Fort Pitt relieved by British forces
7 October Royal Proclamation of 1763

1764   **December** End of the Indian Uprising
5 April Sugar Act passed

1765   **22 March** Stamp Act passed

1767   **29 June** Townshend Revenue Act enacted

1770   **5 March** "Boston Massacre"

1773   **10 May** Tea Act enacted
16 December Boston Tea Party

1774   Quebec Act

1775   **19 April** Skirmishes at Lexington and Concord
17 June Battle of Bunker Hill (Breed's Hill)
31 December Battle of Quebec

1776   **28 June** British attack on Fort Moultrie, Charleston, South Carolina
4 July Declaration of Independence issued

27 August Battle of Long Island, New York
28 October Battle of White Plains, New York
8 December British capture of Newport, Rhode Island
25–26 December American surprise attack on Trenton, New Jersey

1777
3–4 January American attack on Princeton, New Jersey
16 August Battle of Bennington, Vermont
11 September Battle of Brandywine, Pennsylvania
19 September Battle of Freeman's Farm, New York
4 October Battle of Germantown, Pennsylvania
7 October Battle of Bemis Heights, New York

1778
6 February Treaty of alliance signed between France and the United States (Thirteen Colonies)
28 June Battle of Monmouth, New Jersey
July–August American siege of Newport, Rhode Island
7 September French seize island of Dominica, West Indies
29 December British seize Savannah, Georgia

1779
May British coastal raids, Virginia
8 May Spain declares war on Great Britain
May–end of war Franco-Spanish siege of Gibraltar
June–September Naval stand-off, English Channel
July–August British defense of Castine, Massachusetts (Maine)
29–30 August Battle of Newtown, New York
September–October American siege of Savannah, Georgia

1780
14 March Spanish seize Mobile, Florida (Alabama)
February–May British siege of

Charleston, South Carolina
July French forces arrive in Newport, Rhode Island
16 August Battle of Camden, South Carolina
6 September Battle of Pollimore, India
7 October Battle of King's Mountain, North Carolina
20 December Great Britain declares war on the Dutch Republic

1781
17 January Battle of Cowpens, South Carolina
3 February French seize St Eustatius, West Indies
15 March Battle of Guilford Court House, North Carolina
9 May Fall of Pensacola, Florida
1 July Battle of Porto Novo, India
6 July Battle of Greenspring Farm, Virginia
27 August Battle of Polilur, India
27 September Battle of Sholingur, India
30 September–19 October Franco-American siege and capture of Yorktown, Virginia
November Fall of St Eustatius, St Martin, and St Bartholomew, West Indies

1782
February Fall of Minorca
13 February French seize St Kitts, West Indies
12 April Battle of the Saintes, West Indies
30 November First peace treaty signed in Pari

1783
13 June Battle of Cuddalore, India
3 September Peace of Paris signed

1786–87 Shays' Rebellion
1787 US Constitution Convention
1790 US Constitution ratified
1790–94 US military expeditions to the Northwest
1791 Creation of Upper and Lower Canada provinces

1793–1815 Anglo-French war, except briefly
in 1802–03, 1814–15

1794 **August 20** Battle of Fallen
Timbers
19 November Jay's Treaty

1806 **November** French Berlin Decree

1807 **January/November** British
Orders-in-Council
June HMS *Leopard* attacks USS
Chesapeake
December French Milan Decree
December US Embargo Act

1809 **March** US Non-Intercourse Act

1810 **May** US Macon's Bill Number 2
November French outwardly
appear to repeal their decrees

1811 **March** US imposes non-
importation on Britain
May USS *President* vs HMS *Little
Belt*
September British Order-in-
Council restricts US–West
Indian trade
November Battle of Tippecanoe
November US Congress begins
to debate war

1812 **18 June** US declares war
23 June Britain repeals Orders-
in-Council
23 June First naval encounter:
escape of HMS *Belvidera* from
a US squadron
12 July American army invades
Canada from Detroit
16 July Skirmish at the Canard
Bridge
17 July Capture of Fort Mackinac
17 July Capture of USS *Nautilus*
by a Royal Navy (RN) squadron
5 August Engagement at
Brownstown
9 August Engagement at
Maguaga
13 August Capture of HMS *Alert*
by USS *Essex*
15 August Engagement at Fort
Dearborn
16 August Capture of Detroit
19 August USS *Constitution* vs
HMS *Guerrière*

3–16 September Siege of Fort
Harrison
5–9 September Action at Fort
Madison
5–12 September Siege of Fort
Wayne
October RN begins blockading
US Atlantic coast
9 October Capture of HMS
Caledonia, HMS *Detroit* burned
12–13 October Battle of
Queenston Heights
18 October USS *Wasp* vs HMS
Frolic
18 October Capture of USS
Wasp and *Frolic* by HMS *Poictiers*
25 October USS *United States*
vs HMS *Macedonian*
19–20 November Action at
Lacolle
22 November HMS
Southampton vs USS *Vixen*
28 November Action at Red
House/Frenchman's Creek
17–18 December Engagement
at Mississenewa
29 December USS *Constitution*
vs HMS *Java*

1813 **January** RN blockades
Chesapeake and Delaware rivers
17 January Capture of USS
Viper by HMS *Narcissus*
22 January Battle of
Frenchtown (Raisin River)
February RN blockade
extended between the Delaware
and Chesapeake
February British begin raiding
US Atlantic coast
22 February Attack on
Ogdensburg
24 February USS *Hornet* vs HMS
Peacock
March RN blockade extended
north to New York, south to
Georgia
27 April Amphibious assault
at York
28 April–9 May First siege of
Fort Meigs

3 May Attack on Havre de Grace
25–27 May Amphibious assault at Fort George
29 May Amphibious assault at Sackett's Harbour
1 June HMS *Shannon* vs USS *Chesapeake*
3 June Capture of USS *Growler* and *Eagle*
6 June Battle of Stoney Creek
7 June Action at Forty Mile Creek
June–October Blockade of US-held Fort George
22 June Attack on Craney Island
24 June Attack on Hampton
24 June Battle of Beaver Dams
11 July Raid on Black Rock
21–28 July Second siege of Fort Meigs
29 July Raid at Burlington Beach
31 July Raids at Plattsburgh and York
2 August Engagement at Fort Stephenson
6 August Occupation of Kent Island
7–10 August Engagement on Lake Ontario (Burlington Races)
14 August HMS *Pelican* vs USS *Argus*
3 September Americans burn and abandon Fort Madison
5 September USS *Enterprise* vs HMS *Boxer*
10 September Naval Battle of Put-in-Bay (Lake Erie)
5 October Battle of Moraviantown (Thames)
6 October Battle of Châteauguay
November RN blockade extended from New York to Narragansett Bay
1–2 November Action at French Creek
6 November Bombardment at Prescott

1814

11 November Battle of Crysler's Farm
10–11 December Americans evacuate Fort George, burn Niagara and Queenston
19 December Capture of Fort Niagara
25 December Capture of USS *Vixen II* by HMS *Belvidera*
29–30 December Burning of Lewiston, Tuscarora, Fort Schlosser, Black Rock, Buffalo
16–24 January Raids on Franklin County, NY
14 February Capture of HMS *Pictou* by USS *Constitution*
5 March Engagement at Longwoods
28 March HMS *Phoebe* and *Cherub* vs USS *Essex* and *Essex Junior*
30 March Action at Lacolle
20 April Capture of USS *Frolic* by HMS *Orpheus*
29 April USS *Peacock* vs HMS *Epervier*
May Napoleon abdicates; British resources freed for the American war
May RN blockade extended to New England
5–6 May Amphibious assault on Oswego
14–15 May Raid on Port Dover and other villages
30 May Engagement at Sandy Creek
2 June Occupation of Prairie du Chien
22 June Capture of USS *Rattlesnake* by HMS *Leander*
28 June USS *Wasp* vs HMS *Reindeer*
3 July Capture of Fort Erie
5 July Battle of Chippawa
11–12 July Occupation of Eastport
12 July Capture of USS *Syren* by HMS *Medwa*

17–20 July Siege of Fort Shelby/Prairie du Chien
21 July Engagement at Campbell Island (Rock Island)
25 July Battle of Lundy's Lane
August Peace negotiations begin in Ghent
August–September Blockade of Fort Erie
2–3 August Battle of Conjocta Creek
4 August Battle of Mackinac Island
8 August Capture of USS *Somers* and *Ohio*
14 August HMS *Nancy* destroyed
14 August Assault on Fort Erie
22 August Skirmish at Pig Point
24 August Battle of Bladensburg; Washington occupied; navy yard burned
27–28 August Destruction of Fort Washington; occupation of Alexandria
August–September Actions against British squadron on the Potomac
1 September Occupation of Castine and Belfast
3 September Battle of Hampden
3–6 September Capture of USS *Tigress* and *Scorpion*
5 September Occupation of Bangor
5–6 September Battle of Rock Island Rapids (Credit Island)
7 September USS *Wasp* vs HMS *Avon*
10–11 September Occupation of Machias
11 September Battle of Plattsburgh
12 September Battle of North Point
13–14 September Bombardment of Fort McHenry

15 September Engagement at Fort Bowyer
15 September Sortie from Fort Erie
19 October Engagement at Cook's Mill
October–November Raids on the Lake Erie region of Upper Canada
5 November Americans evacuate and blow up Fort Erie, retire to Buffalo
December–January Hartford Convention
13–14 December Engagement on Lake Borgne
23–28 December Actions outside New Orleans and battle of Villeré Plantation
24 December Treaty negotiations conclude in Ghent
27 December Prince Regent ratifies Treaty of Ghent

1815
1 January Action outside New Orleans
8 January Battle of New Orleans
9–12 January Siege of Fort St Philip
14 January RN squadron vs USS President
11 February Capture of Fort Bowyer
16 February US ratifies Treaty of Ghent
20 February USS *Constitution* vs HMS *Levant* and *Cyane*
11 March Recapture of HMS *Levant* by an RN squadron
23 March USS *Hornet* vs HMS *Penguin*
24 May Skirmish at the Sink Hole
30 June USS *Peacock* vs East India Company Ship *Nautilus*

1815–16   Indian tribes negotiate peace

This contemporary illustration shows Ticonderoga in 1759 after Amherst's capture. The view is from the summit of Rattlesnake Mountain, the same vantage point Rogers' Rangers had used to study enemy activity at the fort over the previous four years. (National Archives of Canada, C-010653)

Part I
The French-Indian War
1754–1760

Introduction

The French-Indian War is the name commonly given to the conflict which arose in North America in 1754–55, between the British Thirteen Colonies (and Nova Scotia) and New France (comprising Louisiana, the Ohio River Valley, Quebec [known as Canada], and Cape Breton and St. Jean Islands). Following the War of the Austrian Succession, which was officially concluded by the Treaty of Aix-la-Chapelle, Great Britain and France continued their disputes over land boundaries in North America. The fighting chiefly took place along the frontier regions of the northern Thirteen Colonies and in the Quebec and Cape Breton regions of New France. New France was at a numerical disadvantage due to a disparity in population:

New France had 75,000 settlers, while the Thirteen Colonies had 1.5 million people.

The frontier skirmishes of 1754 propelled both France and Great Britain to seek Continental allies. With Europe firmly divided into two camps – France, Austria and Russia on one side and Prussia and Great Britain on the other – conflict was inevitable. By 1756, the frontier skirmishes had developed into a fully-fledged war in North America and spilled over into conflict in Europe itself. While it was connected to the larger, worldwide campaign known as the Seven Years' War, the French-Indian War anticipated that conflict by a year and served as one of the spurs to the eventual outbreak of hostilities in Europe and on the Indian

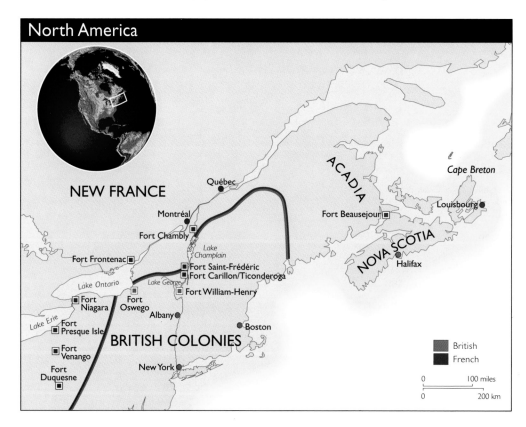

George II, King of Great Britain. (Ann Ronan Picture Library)

subcontinent. (For more detail on the war in the rest of the world, please see the Essential Histories *The Seven Years' War*.)

The French-Indian War was fought in the forests, open plains, and forts of the North American frontier. The French Army, supported by allied Indian tribes and local colonial forces, initially benefited from a superior understanding of how to operate in the forests of North America, although throughout the conflict it was numerically inferior to the British Army. The British Army was also bolstered by colonial forces and allied Indian tribes, but in the early days of the war suffered from lack of experience and tactical knowledge of fighting in forest terrain. The British learned the lessons of their early defeats, however, and their subsequent tactical and training reforms ultimately enabled them to outperform French forces, both in skirmishes in the forests of the frontier and in continental-style battles at Louisbourg and Quebec.

Great Britain was to emerge from the French-Indian War as the dominant European power on the eastern seaboard of North America. As with the War of Austrian

Louis XV, King of France. (Ann Ronan Picture Library)

Succession, however, the French-Indian War did not signal the end of conflict in the region. Within 13 years of its conclusion, Great Britain was at war with the colonists she had sought to protect in North America.

The war strained relations between the mother country and her colonial subjects. France, seeking to reverse the misfortunes of the French-Indian War, was only too happy to undermine British superiority in the region, and threw her support behind the fledgling United States in 1778.

Tension in the Ohio River valley

The conflict in North America had its formal beginnings in 1754. Following the end of the War of the Austrian Succession (1740–48), French and British colonists, motivated by desire to expand their domains into the rich Ohio River valley, edged closer to armed conflict. The area along the Ohio River was considered to be uncharted, and thus formally unclaimed by either side. The British contended that the area should be open to both sides for trade, and followed this claim with the establishment of the Ohio Company. The French, however, viewed this as a British attempt to claim the entire area, and responded by sending both militia and regular troops into the region to build forts and eject any British settlers or traders found there.

Tensions had also risen in Acadian Nova Scotia, particularly along the Bay of Fundy. The French had established several new forts whose locations the British colonial governments considered to be in violation of the Treaty of Aix-la-Chapelle (1748). Both sides claimed large areas of present day New Brunswick, and considered the other the transgressor. The insult offered by these encroachments was compounded by the French government's relations with the Acadians, a French-speaking population who, as a result of treaty agreements, had become subjects of the British Crown. The French authorities deliberately stirred the Acadians' aspirations to independence, incensing the British governors. The establishment of Fort Beausejour in the disputed area was the last straw, as this made it apparent to the British colonists that the French had them surrounded. They were not being paranoid; the French did in fact intend to construct a series of forts from Louisbourg to New Orleans, enclosing the British colonies. The

hostility between the two countries was near to breaking point.

Governor Robert Dinwiddie of Virginia decided to make a move against the French in the Ohio River valley, while Governor William Shirley of the Massachusetts Bay Colony was to organize a move against the French in the Bay of Fundy. (This second campaign will be discussed later, as it took place in 1755.)

The British had begun to build a fort at the forks of the Ohio River in 1754. A Virginia militia officer, Lieutenant Colonel George Washington, then 23 years old, was ordered to march into the Ohio River valley with 200 men, to assist with and protect the

George Washington as an officer in the Virginian Provincials. (Ann Ronan Picture Library)

fort's construction. Washington and his men left on 2 April. News arrived on 20 April that the French had already moved against the British at the forks of the Ohio and forced them from the area. The French seized the fort and renamed it Fort Duquesne, after the Governor of New France, Marquis Duquesne. After a council of war at Wills Creek, Washington decided to continue to move towards the region, after establishing Fort Cumberland at Wills Creek.

Various other colonies decided to send reinforcements to the region. A Regular Independent Company from South Carolina moved into Virginia. Militia troops from North Carolina marched north to provide support, while Pennsylvania decided to grant money towards the cost of the expedition. These were helpful gestures, but the reinforcements were small and inadequate to the task that they potentially faced: undertaking the defense of the frontier. Washington continued marching towards an enemy that vastly outnumbered him, when he should have remained at Wills Creek and waited for reinforcements.

On 7 May Washington and his small force reached Little Meadows. Ten days later, on 17 May, the force reached the Great Crossing of the Youghiogheny. By 24 May, Washington reached an area named Great Meadows where, after receiving intelligence that a party of French troops was moving against him, he began to build fortifications, naming the structure Fort Necessity. On 27 May, Washington and 40 militia soldiers moved 9 km (six miles) distant to ambush the French detachment. Washington hoped to surprise the French camp, but the alarm was sounded. The battle was short but brisk. The French commander, Ensign Coulon de Jumonville, was killed, along with nine French soldiers, and 21 French soldiers were taken prisoner. One French soldier escaped and reported back to Fort Duquesne. The Virginia troops lost one killed and three wounded. This skirmish signified the opening of armed hostilities.

Washington decided to remain in the area, to build up the defenses of the fort and the road towards Fort Duquesne. On 9 June, a further reinforcement of 200 Virginia militiamen arrived, followed by reinforcements from the Independent Companies of South Carolina on 12 June. Welcome as fresh troops were, their arrival sparked an immediate tussle over the politics of command. The Independent Companies were on the British Establishment, which meant that their commander, Captain James MacKay, was senior to Washington. While MacKay did not attempt to assume command, he refused any orders from Washington for his men.

On 16 June, Washington moved out towards Fort Duquesne with his Virginia troops, while the Independent Companies remained at Fort Necessity. Reports from scouts claimed that the French garrison was reinforced by more than a thousand men, and that the Shawnee and Delaware Indians had sided with the French. Less than 32 km (20 miles) from Fort Duquesne, Washington stopped to hold a war council with the Delawares and Shawnees, hoping to convince them to switch their allegiance. On 28 June reports arrived that the French, with their Indian allies, were moving towards him.

The Independent Companies caught up with Washington on 29 June, and MacKay and Washington agreed to withdraw towards Wills Creek and then on to Fort Necessity. The withdrawal to Fort Necessity was hard going, due to the number of horses and wagons that had to be left behind. The exhausted troops arrived at Fort Necessity on 1 July and began to prepare the area for battle.

A French detachment of 500 soldiers and allied Indian warriors, led by Captain Coulon de Villiers, brother of Jumonville, marched on the heels of Washington's force. The French came upon the Great Meadows area on the morning of 3 July. Villiers decided to fan out his troops to draw fire and locate the enemy forces. The French and Indian forces immediately drew heavy fire, so Villiers kept the majority of his men in the forests to the west and south of the British positions. Villiers advanced cautiously as the British troops withdrew into the entrenchment surrounding the fort. The French and Indian troops fired into the British positions from the edge of the woods. The fighting lasted for nine hours, and the British suffered not only losses under fire but also from a considerable number of desertions. The rainy weather also played a significant role in the outcome of the battle. The British trenches became waterlogged and, as one British observer noted: 'by the continued Rains and Water in the trenches, the most of our Arms were out of order' (Gipson, VI, p. 39). At around 8.00 pm on 3 July, Villiers called for a possible negotiated settlement. Villiers emphasized that he had carried out his attack not because a state of war existed, but to avenge the death of his brother. He also promised that he would allow the British troops to march back to Virginia without harassment from the Indians. Two British officers, Captains Van Braam and Stobo, were to serve as hostages in return for the French prisoners taken on 27 May.

The terms were agreed and on the morning of 4 July, the French marched in to take possession of Fort Necessity. During this transition, the Indians decided to attack the British troops, scalping and killing several men. The French officers and men did little to stop them. While this incident was minor compared to the outrages that were to follow at Fort William Henry in 1757, it clearly demonstrated the problems inherent in promising protection from the Indians following surrender.

The British force marched slowly but in good order towards Wills Creek. The French had effectively forced them out of the Ohio River valley, and Villiers finished the job by destroying Fort Necessity and withdrawing to Fort Duquesne. This defeat galvanized the British government, prompting the decision to deploy British Regular regiments to the Ohio River area. Regular regiments were already stationed in Nova Scotia, and the Fort Duquesne incident convinced British leaders that their presence was required elsewhere. As a result, this engagement was one of the last waged against the French without a sizable British Regular Army presence.

The French and British armies in North America

Warfare in the mid- to late-18th century was characterized by two dissimilar fighting styles, commonly known as linear warfare and irregular or frontier-style warfare. The first was the traditional style in which battles were fought in Europe, whilst the second arose in response to the particular demands of fighting on the North American frontier.

Soldiers of all armies were armed with the flintlock musket, but how they were used differed depending on the style of warfare employed. In any situation, the weapon's range was only 200–300 paces, so no style was developed that was based on the need for accurate fire. Extending the usefulness of the musket during this period was the development of the socket bayonet, which permitted firing with the bayonet already fixed on the musket barrel. The socket bayonet could be attached before troops went into battle, permitting troops to go directly from short-range firing to hand-to-hand combat.

Linear warfare

Given the relative inaccuracy of the flintlock musket, the linear or continental style was designed to maximize its effectiveness. Troops were intended to deploy in a line and deliver a synchronized volley of fire against the opposing line of enemy troops. By training soldiers to fire simultaneously, leaders hoped to offset the musket's inaccuracy with sheer volume of coordinated fire. To accomplish this quickly and effectively required intensive training, not only in firing techniques, but also to enable troops to march overland in column formation, and then rapidly deploy into lines using a series of complicated maneuvers.

The deployment of the front line of troops, or frontage, was determined by the terrain of the battlefield and the position of the enemy. As armies came within sight of one another, each side attempted to maneuver to flank the enemy's position, enabling them to deliver a devastating fire on the enemy, either when they were already in line or attempting to deploy. The battalion deployed in either two, three, or four lines, depending upon the army. The idea was that the forward line fired, then moved back to reload their muskets. They would be replaced by the second line, which would repeat the process and then be followed by the third line and so on.

The French Army deployed its battalions into four lines, with a frontage of 162 men. French battalions were drawn up into 10 companies, consisting of eight fusilier, one grenadier, and one light company. The British Army deployed its battalions into three lines, also with 10 companies of soldiers. The British deployed nine line companies and one grenadier company. As the war progressed they switched to eight line companies, one grenadier company, and one light infantry company. The British frontage was 260 men; some experts argue that this gave the British an advantage by providing a bigger volley, while others claim that the French system was more compact and more maneuverable, and thus superior. In 1758, the British expanded their frontage even further by deploying their battalions in only two lines.

The line of fire was also varied, depending on the situation. The officers would assess the battle situation and order the men either to fire one synchronized volley from the entire line, or a series of volleys from the end of the wings to the center (or vice versa), known as platoon firing. The British Army, for example, divided the men into

This image of the Battle of the Plains of Abraham shows the two different styles of warfare. (National Army Museum, Chelsea)

companies that would fire as one unit. The men in each company were then divided into two platoons, which could fire either as two individual units or one larger one. As described above, battalion firing would begin either in the center or on the wings, hitting the enemy at different locations. It was common for both sides to fire at least one or two coordinated volleys before the battle deteriorated into men firing at will. This was partly due to the fact that the powder and noise of battle often made the soldiers deaf. Fire commands were normally communicated by the battalion drummers, but the escalation of battle made the drums difficult to hear.

The ability to deliver a coordinated heavy volley, and preferably more than one, on the main body of the enemy line was paramount to an army's successful performance. The main intention of this tactic was to create havoc and disorder within the enemy's ranks. A successful volley could break enemy lines, and the firing side would attempt to capitalize on the confusion by advancing on the enemy position. The infantry advance would force the other side to attempt to withdraw, while the advancing side closed in with bayonets to engage in hand to hand fighting. Often units failed to hold the line in the face of a bayonet charge, escalating the disorder and confusion in the ranks of the side under attack.

Troop discipline was critical. Soldiers were drilled exhaustively in the complex procedures involved in deployment, firing, and reloading. In addition to mastering the various techniques, discipline also required troops to stand to attention under enemy fire, retaining a cohesive line while being shot at close range, and returning fire only when ordered to do so. The opposing sides viewed one another as single, massive targets, and soldiers were expected to behave accordingly, functioning as parts of a whole. It was common for a soldier to require 18 months of training to perform the various drills required, and most generals felt it took five years to create a well-trained soldier capable of withstanding the rigors of battle. Contrary to popular perception, the regular soldier of the 18th century was highly trained and proficient; in fact, some rulers' tactics to avoid battle when they were

Rogers' Rangers Officer by Gerry Embleton.

prohibited the use of cavalry. If there had been engagements in the south, cavalry might have been required, but the heavily forested frontier made operating on horseback both difficult and dangerous. Some senior officers rode to battle on horseback, but tended to dismount before leading a charge.

Irregular warfare

The French-Indian War was instrumental in the further development of a new style of fighting, known as irregular warfare. This approach was characterized by the use of lightly armed troops who could march easily in heavily wooded terrain and fight in small, flexible units. This system was not an entirely North American phenomenon; the Austrians, British, French and Prussians had employed light troops in the European theater of the Seven Years' War. However, the majority of the fighting in North America took place in woodlands, and this necessitated the development and deployment of light troops and other specialists, such as bateaux men (pilots of whale boats and canoes) and Indian scouts, in much greater numbers than had ever been used before.

outnumbered or outmaneuvered was due to their unwillingness to risk losing costly and valued regular soldiers.

Artillery was also used in linear warfare of this period, principally as siege weaponry, although smaller pieces were used in infantry battles. These were employed as fire support and also served as markers to indicate divisions between battalions drawing up in linear formation. During the French-Indian War, artillery was used during the small number of linear-style battles, but not to the same extent as in Europe. It was more likely to be used in a conventional manner during sieges of the forts in the North American interior, as these engagements operated in more traditional Continental fashion.

The terrain where most of the North American engagements were fought

The Indians of North America were excellent woodsmen; their warriors were skilled not only in fighting one another in forested terrain, but also in hunting in the same woodlands. The frontier populations of both the French and British colonies had also grown adept at maneuvering and fighting in the woods; frontiersmen had extensive contact, both positive and negative, with local Indian populations. In addition, many men were traders or hunters, used to marching overland into harsh territory. Not everyone was an expert however; in fact, a large proportion of people in North America, both recently-arrived Europeans and colonists living in the more developed areas, were utterly unfamiliar with woodland operations.

The North American terrain and conditions dictated not only the strategies of the war but also its progress. Roads and tracks were minimal and poorly developed, and the armies had to take the time (and possess the capability) to build roads as they progressed, as well as forts to protect the roads once completed. Given these conditions, lakes and rivers were ready-made conduits for the movement of men and supplies, and both sides made use of them whenever possible. The ability to move troops and re-supply forward units efficiently was critical to success in the field. The French forces were able to rely on a supply network that operated largely over waterways. The British more often had to build new roads and forts to secure their supply lines, and over time their skills increased through repeated employment. Despite limited opportunity, the British military also performed well in moving both troops and supplies over waterways.

While both France and England had a core of woodland expertise among their fighting men, each side perceived that the war was not going to be won solely on familiarity with the ways of the woods and the Indians. Strategy for both sides involved deploying large numbers of regular troops from Europe who would be able to wage a traditional linear-style battle when terrain permitted. The senior commanders of both armies recognized, to varying degrees, the usefulness of the irregular troops, but preferred linear-style engagements to provide a decisive conclusion to the conflict. In the end, however, the ways in which each side attempted to reform its army to adapt to new conditions in North America proved to be the critical factor in determining a victor.

The following section is an examination of the two military forces involved in the French and Indian War. This will include consideration of the regular forces: their assets, weaknesses, and attempts to reform. The local colonial, militia, and provincial forces will also be discussed. Finally, the fighting capabilities of the Indian

Light Infantryman, 1759 by Gerry Embleton.

participants, as well as their alliances with both sides, will be assessed.

Great Britain

The British Army had four different Commanders-in-Chief over the course of the war in North America. Some, such as Major General Jeffrey Amherst, were successful in battle, while others, such as Lieutenant General John Campbell, Earl Loudon, made a less obvious but more profound organizational impact upon the army. Loudon, while not as successful as Amherst, deserves credit for laying the foundations that gave the Army victory in the campaigns of 1758–60. Although he was only in command during 1756–57, his tenure was marked by significant reforms in methods of supply and tactical development of the regular army.

Loudon centralized the system of supplies for British regular and provincial soldiers to a degree previously unheard of in the Thirteen Colonies. As a result of his restructuring efforts, soldiers were consistently able to receive adequate uniforms and arms – the minimum required for undertaking active service. Main storehouses were created at Halifax, New York, and Albany.

Loudon also recognized that transportation of supplies to troops in the field was necessary for success, and set out to reform the army's systems accordingly. The army had previously relied upon local wagoneers to move supplies forward. This system was unreliable and forced the army to rely upon civilians who were often unwilling to venture very far into the woods. Loudon replaced this system with a corps of army wagons, and undertook a road improvement program. He also appreciated the potential advantages of using waterways for transportation, and delegated John Bradstreet, a leader of armed boatmen, to investigate alternative plans of moving material. This led to an initiative to build a fleet of standardized supply boats piloted by armed and experienced boatmen. A program of creating portages was also undertaken to facilitate the forward movement of supplies. The army and navy also built sloops to move supplies from coastal cities upriver to the Army's major staging areas.

Following the defeats of 1755 and 1756, British Army leaders realized that the troops, in their present state of training and equipment, were not capable of effective operation in the forests of North America. It would be necessary to train and equip men specifically for these conditions; troops would be so equipped as to enable them to maneuver more efficiently in difficult terrain, and would be trained to move in formations other than the large columns used in the linear-style of warfare. Soldiers trained in these unconventional methods were commonly known as rangers.

The concept of rangers did not originate with the onset of the Seven Years' War; ranger troops are recorded as being raised as early as 1744, when a unit named Gorham's Rangers (after its founder, John Gorham), was raised in Nova Scotia. When war broke out in North America in 1754, the number of rangers in Nova Scotia was increased, at the expense of the British government. In 1755, a second group of rangers was organized, consisting of men from the frontiers of New York and New England. This group, raised and commanded by Major Robert Rogers, took their name, Rogers' Rangers, from him. The ranger corps quickly demonstrated their value in both skirmishes and scouting expeditions on the frontier, but some members of the military establishment remained skeptical, considering the ranger units too expensive to justify their continued existence.

During his tenure as Commander-in-Chief, Loudon, encouraged regular soldiers and officers to attach themselves to the ranger corps to learn methods of forest fighting. He set up a training cadre of 50 rangers at Fort Edward to support this suggestion. Despite attempts such as this to curb the numbers of rangers by creating 'regular' light infantry, the numbers of Rogers' Rangers continued to rise. By 1759 there were six companies of rangers, comprising more than 1,000 men, all financed by the British government.

Loudon decided to create units that would be made up of regulars who would receive special ranger-type training as well as instruction in traditional linear methods. He expected, with this initiative, to manage cost and discipline issues simultaneously: the first by training the same men for different types of warfare, and the second by instilling the 'regular' discipline that was thought to be lacking in rangers. In the event, Loudon's scheme took shape in two different forms. The 60th Regiment of Foot was raised initially from the frontier peoples of Pennsylvania and Virginia, with the intent that the regiment would embody the spirit and abilities of the frontiersman, tempered by the discipline of the regular soldier. Four battalions of the 60th were raised; the 1st and 4th were deployed more often in frontier fighting situations, and fought in successful engagements in Pennsylvania and New York. The 2nd and 3rd battalions served most of

British soldier of the 60th Royal American Regiment
(Osprey Publishing)

discusses the specifics involved in waging
war in North America, including operating
in the forest:

*[I]n passing through close or wooded country …
I would have the regiment march two deep, in four
columns … having small parties of light infantry
advanced [one] hundred paces in their front; but
the main party of the light infantry should be on
the flanks … [I]f the front should be attacked, the
grenadiers and light infantry will be sufficient to
keep the enemy in play till the regiment is formed*
(Military Treatise, pp. 66–67).

In the second account, William Amherst,
brother of Jeffrey, notes in his journal a typical
training day for two regiments in 1758,
including a description of a new firing
sequence to be used by British columns if they
were attacked on the march in the woods:

*the advanced party if attacked, the two platoons
marching abreast, the left platoon fires singly,
every man, the right platoon keeps recovered,
both platoons moving on very slowly and inclining
to the right* (William Amherst, pp. 40–41).

The aim of such exercises was to accustom
the soldiers to wooded conditions, and so
neutralize the fear of Indian tactics.

The innovations made in training and
equipment improved British performance in
the forest but it did not make them invincible.
On several occasions during both the French-
Indian War and the subsequent Indian
uprising of 1763–64, British troops were
ambushed and suffered accordingly. The
British regular soldier became the equal in
the forest of his French equivalent, although
the Indian remained, for the most part, the
master of forest operation. This expertise,
however, was offset by a lack of discipline and
coordinated command and control expertise,
which benefited the regulars on both sides.
Most important, the average British soldier
had, by 1759, largely lost his fear of operating
in the forest, having received the training
required to cope with most situations.

The average British battalion numbered
from 500–900 men. Numbers fluctuated due

their time as regular linear soldiers, and saw
action at Louisbourg and Quebec.

Two other regiments were raised under a
different interpretation of Loudon's initiative,
and these were to have a greater influence on
the army as a whole. The 55th and 80th
Regiments of Foot were raised specifically as
light infantry. They were trained in the tactics
used by the ranger corps, but were also
subjected to the discipline imposed upon
regular troops. (Rangers were not expected to
conform to the same standards of discipline as
other Army units.) As a result of this successful
development, by 1759 all regular British Army
regiments, including the 60th, had adopted
a light infantry company. These could be
deployed as needed in specific situations;
their uniforms, weaponry, and tactical
training were adapted for marching in the
woods, fighting skirmishing actions, and
carrying out ambushes in the manner of
Indians and rangers.

Two accounts demonstrate the range and
effects of these reforms. The first is a manual,
published in Philadelphia in 1759, which

to battle casualties, illness, and desertion. In 1754 there were no British line regiments stationed in the Thirteen Colonies, only in Nova Scotia and the Caribbean. The Thirteen Colonies had seven regular units named Independent Companies, which were posted along areas of the South Carolina and New York frontiers. By 1757, more than 14,000 regulars had been deployed to the Thirteen Colonies as a result of the conflict in North America. By 1759, the peak of regular establishment in North America, nearly 24,000 men were under arms. The British Army included mostly regular line regiments with 10 companies (eight line, one grenadier and one light infantry). There were also dedicated ad hoc light infantry and grenadier battalions.

British military officials had an additional reserve force to draw upon for the French-Indian War: the colonial provincials. These were units whom the Colonies were requested to raise, to serve alongside the regular forces. Some military officials considered them more of a burden than an asset, principally because, unlike regular soldiers, provincial soldiers were only called for one campaign season at a time, and then returned to their homes. This created the impression that because provincial soldiers were not professionals, they were not subjected to the same harsh discipline and rules that the regulars endured, and that they were not, therefore, true soldiers. The provincials, on their side, considered regular soldiers ignorant of how to operate in the forest and the conditions of the frontier. Such beliefs created a rivalry that persisted throughout the war period, each side regarding the other as unfit to fight in various combat situations.

During the first years of the war, relations between provincials and regulars were further strained. The first article of the Rules and Articles of War of the British Army of this period stated that 'a provincial soldier serving with regulars ceased to be governed by colonial disciplinary measures but became subject to the mutiny act' (Pargellis, p.84). This stipulation was created by British military

authorities who envisioned no more than a few provincial companies serving with the regulars. It meant, in theory, that provincial soldiers serving alongside regulars were subject to the same strict regulations and discipline. In practice, however, there were likely to be discrepancies in treatment. Loudon reported one instance where 'a private of the 60th found guilty of mutiny received 1,000 lashes whereas a private of a Massachusetts [provincial] regiment got 500 for the same offence' (Loudon, 3 September 1757). Braddock's defeat in 1755 changed the situation considerably by demonstrating the immediate need for a large number of soldiers. As a result, the number of provincial soldiers required also increased dramatically.

The increased need for provincial troops brought about one beneficial change in their situation. Previously, commissioned officers in the provincial forces, even as high as the rank of General, were degraded to the level of senior captain when serving alongside regular forces in the field. This was a major source of resentment for the provincial forces. Loudon was uninterested in resolving this issue with the colonial governments, and no changes were made until after he was removed from command. William Pitt, Secretary of State (with control of the war and foreign affairs and later the leader of the British government), amended the ruling so that provincial officers retained their rank, but were junior to regular officers of equivalent and higher rank. Pitt considered this necessary to appease the colonial governments and convince them to recruit more men for the campaigns. Even though the British government ultimately funded colonial units, they had to rely on the colonial governments' efforts to fill the ranks. In the event, his tactic was successful; the colonial governments provided more soldiers in 1758 and 1759, after the ruling was changed, than they had previously.

Despite this initiative and the rising number of provincial troops, regular soldiers continued to distrust their fighting abilities, and only grudgingly would they concede that provincials made a contribution. It was true that provincials were unlikely to have the stamina to sustain the rigors of a linear-style battle, since they did not have the same level of training or discipline as regular troops. There was the occasional compliment; as noted by a regular officer in 1759 :

the provincial regiments, under arms today, to be perfected in the manoeuvres contained in the regulations of the 20th of June … [T]hey [provincials] made a good performance, performed well, and gave great satisfaction (Knox, p. 486).

Major General Amherst gave a reluctant-sounding compliment when speaking of the provincials in 1759 at Fort Edward:

[they] began to grow sickly and lose some men; they are growing homesick but much less so than ever they have been on any other campaigns (Amherst, 22 September 1759).

France

On the other side of the conflict, the French were spending comparable time arguing over strategy and the abilities of their regulars to wage war along the frontier. Major General Louis-Joseph Montcalm, who commanded the French regular forces from 1756 until his death in 1759, disagreed firmly with the governor-general of New France, Pierre Francois de Rigaud Vaudreuil on issues of strategy. There was often considerable antagonism between colonial-born (such as Vaudreuil) and French-born officials (such as Montcalm); the colonials perceived visitors as high-handed interlopers who did not understand the issues particular to the colonial setting. The French government had clearly established the lines of command – Vaudreuil was unquestionably senior to Montcalm – but in practice this had no effect on mitigating tensions or resolving proposals of conflicting strategies. Unlike Loudon in the British Colonies, neither man was removed from service when tensions flared, and the situation escalated. Each man

accused the other of interfering in issues of strategy. Marquis de Vaudreuil favored a guerilla campaign along the frontier, and dismissed the ability of the French regulars to adapt to the necessities of waging war in the forest. Montcalm recognized the value of militia and Indians in forest operations, but still believed that the war would ultimately be decided by regular troops.

Montcalm did understand the issues of supply and scouting involved in fighting in the woods. A master strategist, he recognized early that the British were going to outnumber his forces, and decided upon a defensive strategy that would allow him to launch pre-emptive strikes whenever opportunity permitted. Having decided on this plan of action, he implemented it early in the campaign with surprise attacks on the British forts at Oswego and Fort William Henry in 1756 and 1757. He succeeded in overwhelming the troops guarding all the forts, and forced them to surrender. He did not stay put, but destroyed the forts and moved. It was

Marquis de Vaudreuil. (Public Archives of Canada)

Louis-Joseph Montcalm. (Ann Ronan Picture Library)

a bold strategy, and effectively knocked the British off balance for a time early on. In 1758, however, the situation changed dramatically. The British had begun to learn the art of war in the forest and had created a supply network that could carry their armies over difficult terrain. On the other side, the

French forces received no reinforcements after 1757, thanks to the Royal Navy blockade. Montcalm was forced to guard a vast frontier with less than one-third of the regular troops that the British had at their disposal. He continued to take gambles; some of them paid dividends, such as the decision to deploy most of his regulars to Fort Carillon in 1758 as described below. But from 1758, Montcalm

Fusilier, Compagnies Franches de la Marine by
Michael Roffe. (Osprey Publishing)

Grenadier, Regiment de Languedoc by Michael Roffe.
(Osprey Publishing)

was constantly on the defensive, attempting to
stem the rising tide of British attacks.

The French and British forces were
organized along similar lines – a mixture of
regulars, militia, and Indian allies. The first
group of regulars that served in New France
was the *troupes de la marine* or marines. When
war broke out between France and Britain in
1754, no French regular line infantry units
were initially deployed to North America. The
marines had been serving under the command
of the French Navy in New France for many

years before the outbreak of hostilities. The
men and officers were recruited in France
for colonial service, and encouraged to remain
in North America after their terms of
enlistment ended. The marines served along
the frontiers of New France, as well as in the
trading centers, and were organized along

lines similar to those of the British Independent Companies; their detachments were organized into company sized units. Numbers within companies fluctuated from 50–75 men, and as of 1750, there were 30 companies deployed in New France. By 1757, 64 companies had been deployed in Quebec and Cape Breton, with another 30 companies stationed in the Louisiana territory. Companies from Louisiana were involved in fighting in the Ohio River area during the course of the war. Marines, while commonly considered regular soldiers in the colonial administration, also had considerable experience of operating in the woods based upon years of deployment on the frontier.

By 1757, only 12 battalions of French regulars, known as the *troupes de terre* and numbering just over 6,000 men, had been shipped to North America. Eight of the battalions saw service with Montcalm in the Canada and Western theaters, and four were sent to Louisbourg to bolster its defenses. French regular soldiers were generally willing to learn some of the bush fighting tactics used by the Canadian militia and Indians and, like their British counterparts, often attached themselves to small raiding parties to learn the tactics of the woods.

During the first years of the war, the French regulars performed very well in battle. Discipline was very good; Montcalm cited only two courts martial during the period from 1756–58. Montcalm also commended the condition and performance of his troops, describing the Royal-Roussillon regiment as 'well supplied and well disciplined' (Sautai, p. 23). However, as French strategy changed in the wake of the effective British naval blockade and troops were increasingly left to fend for themselves in New France, discipline and desertion became greater problems. The performance of the French regulars at the Battle of the Plains of Abraham indicated that fire discipline had deteriorated noticeably from previous standards. To their credit, the French regulars continued to perform very well, particularly considering that they were

vastly outnumbered by the British, suffered from unreliable provision of supplies, and became increasingly aware that grand strategy in the larger conflict had shifted attention and resources away from them. In light of these obstacles, American historian Francis Parkman commended the French Army in North America 'for enduring gallantry, officers and men alike deserve nothing but praise' (Parkman, p. 215).

The Canadian militia was a major asset to the French commanders. Unlike provincial troops in the Thirteen Colonies, the Canadian militia was geared for war. Montcalm, apparently recognizing their value, described Canadians as

born soldiers, from the age of 16 … on the rolls of militia. Boatmen and good shots, hunters … [T]hey excelled in forest war and ambushes (Sautai, p. 16).

This idea of a citizenry geared for war was not unique to New France and occurred often in Europe; notably similar to the Canadians were the Croat populations along the Austrian/Turkish borderlands. While militiamen were not sufficiently trained to rebuff a full-scale linear-style attack, they were more than proficient in wilderness fighting and scouting. Militiamen in New France were generally assigned to protect forts and remote outposts, a practice that was also common in the Thirteen Colonies. They were also assigned flank and scouting activities, either performed alone or as part of a larger regular column.

The number of militiamen raised in New France throughout the war period never exceeded 15,000 men per year. Similar to British provincials, they returned home after each campaigning season; many men returned to the militia year after year, as the threat to New France increased. The Thirteen Colonies provided a larger number of provincial soldiers, but they were not of the same quality as Canadian militiamen. Montcalm claimed that relations between his regulars and the militia and Indians were very cordial; in 1757 he declared that 'our troops ... live in perfect union with the Canadians and savages' (Sautai, p. 26). Some of his junior officers disagreed with this assessment; one officer noted in 1758 that:

> when the French had won the battle, confidence returned ... [T]hey regained their Canadian spirits and busied themselves only in ways of taking away from the French [Regular] troops the glory of an action which it appeared difficult to attribute to anyone else (Bougainville, p. 239).

There was tension between French and Canadian officers, principally on questions of tactics. Some French officers preferred to use linear-style tactics, and believed that the Canadian soldiers and officers were no better than the Indians. The Canadian officers, for their part, felt on more than one occasion that French troops were not suited for frontier warfare. This caused friction, as it did within the British forces.

Indians

Both Great Britain and France sought the allegiance of the numerous Indian tribes living along the frontiers of the European colonies in North America. Indian warriors were expert forest fighters, unsurpassed in their skill at both ambushing and scouting. Their reputation as warriors struck fear into the hearts of civilians and soldiers alike. A British grenadier reported outside Quebec in 1759 that 'all the grenadiers crossed over to the island of Orleans ... [T]he Indians attacked us very smartly' (*Journal of the Expedition to the River St. Lawrence*, 21 July 1759). This was only intensified by their willingness to shift their alliances from one side to the other as the fortunes of each waxed and waned. Many Indian warriors would disappear from a campaign if they felt their side was losing or there was a chance of plunder in another part of the frontier. They were considered untrustworthy by European troops, and criticized for their opportunistic decisions to side with the strongest power.

Of course, both Britain and France also tried to use such opportunism to their own advantage, trying more than once to undermine existing treaties between the enemy side and its Indian allies. In battle, Indians excelled in gaining intelligence for their European commanders, as well as setting ambushes. However, when faced with continental-style fighting in the open they tended to break very easily. They also lacked the stamina and planning skills to carry out a siege of a small post. The Indian Uprising of 1763–64 is an example.

The French tended to be more successful in winning the allegiance of Indians. This is partly due to the fact that the French

Colonel William Johnson, Superintendent of Indian affairs for the British Crown. (Albany Institute of History and Art)

Huron by Michael Roffe. (Osprey Publishing)

Indian lands along the frontier. Tension was thus correspondingly greater. The French formed alliances with five major Indian tribes: the Hurons, Ottawas, Wyandots, Miamis, and Algonquins. The principal British-Indian alliance was with the members of the Five (later Six) Nations of the Iroquois. The original five nations were the Oneidas, Mohawks, Senecas, Onondagas, and Cayugas, and were subsequently joined by the Tuscaroras. The French repeatedly attempted to win over one of the Iroquois nations to their cause throughout the course of the war, but were consistently thwarted by the efforts of Lieutenant Colonel William Johnson, chief Indian agent for the British Crown. The Senecas did later become dissatisfied with the British alliance, but this was later and for other reasons; the dispute will be covered in the Indian Uprising section.

On the whole both sides tended to accept their Indian allies as a necessity, and tried to regulate their behavior by imposing harsh penalties for failure to follow orders. One characteristic situation happened in 1757, when the French-allied Indians killed a number of the British civilians who had surrendered at Fort William Henry. French regulars had to restrain their allies with the threat of violence if they did not stop the killing. Some senior British commanders loathed using Indian allies against European soldiers or civilians. In the end, warfare increasingly utilized more conventional methods, and both sides relied less upon the services of Indians. Equally significant, following the French defeat at Quebec in 1759, many Indians decided to leave French service, fearing British reprisals upon their villages.

presence in North America was smaller than the British presence. Many Indians only came in contact with Canadian traders, who they did not consider to be encroaching upon their territory. British colonists, however, were a larger population, seeking land as well as trading opportunities in the

Entry of the regular soldiers

Although formal declarations of war were not exchanged between France and Great Britain until 1756, the deployment of two British Regular regiments toward Fort Duquesne and the operations against Fort Beausejour in Nova Scotia, Fort Niagara, and Crown Point marked the formal outbreak of the war in North America. The narrative describing the progress of the conflict will be divided into years and subdivided into regions. The fighting that took place in the Ohio River region and Pennsylvania will be referred to as the Western theater. The fighting in the Lake George, Lake Champlain, and western New York regions will be referred to as the New York theater. The Canadian theater will cover operations in Nova Scotia, Cape Breton, and Quebec.

In October 1754, the British government, headed by Thomas Pelham-Holles, Duke of Newcastle, ordered the reinforcement of the Thirteen Colonies with regular troops in response to increasing tension in the Ohio River valley. The orders called for the transportation of the 44th and 48th Regiments of Foot to Virginia, under the command of Major General Edward Braddock, who was to be in overall command of all troops in North America. The two regiments were below strength and officials decided to fill the companies with locally recruited men upon reaching the American colonies. Two additional regiments, the 50th and 51st Foot, were to be raised in their entirety in North America.

The dispatch of British regulars only alerted the French to follow suit. Beyond the companies of marines (regulars) already deployed in New France, the French dispatched 3,000 regulars from the line regiments of La Reine, Artois, Guienne, Languedoc, and Bearn. They were all under the supreme command of Baron de Dieskau. These regulars were unable to reach Fort Duquesne in time to support its defense, but were deployed to protect other vulnerable positions afterwards.

The British strategy for 1755 was that General Braddock and his two regiments, along with provincial units, would march on and seize Fort Duquesne from the French. Meanwhile, the second-in-command in North America, Governor Shirley of Massachusetts, was to march with the 50th and 51st regiments, as well as various provincial units, to seize the French fort at Niagara. Colonel Johnson was to march from Albany against the French Fort St. Frederic at Crown Point. Finally, Lieutenant Colonel Robert Monckton, a British Regular, was to lead a force of 2,000 militia and 200 regulars against Fort Beausejour in Nova Scotia.

War of the forest and fortress

Western theater

Braddock, along with the 44th and 48th Foot, arrived in Virginia in March 1755. By May, the force, regulars, provincials, and Royal Artillery, was assembling at Fort Cumberland, Wills Creek. They were delayed from leaving on schedule by the lack of supplies forthcoming from the various colonial governments and the need for additional recruits for both regular and provincial units. The British expedition, finally fully assembled and provisioned, marched out from Fort Cumberland on 10 June.

The British government was confident that the infusion of regular troops would ensure victory, but failed to recognize that a different type of war was in store. Braddock's only experience of warfare was on the European Continent, and he was not fully aware of the potential pitfalls involved in waging war over difficult, hilly, and forested terrain. His French adversaries had a better understanding of how to effectively mix the discipline and training of French regulars (marines) with the more unorthodox methods of the Canadian militia and allied Indians.

The British expedition averaged only 6 km (four miles) a day on the march, slowed down by the wagons and the condition of the road. On 18 June, the force reached Little Meadows, where Braddock decided to split his force. He would lead 1,200 picked men ahead of the baggage and rest of the men, the vast majority of whom were provincial troops. A specialist unit of rangers was put under the command of Lieutenant Colonel Thomas Gage to advance forward of the column and protect it from surprise attack. Braddock and Gage set off, and were soon set upon by French scouts and Indians. The rangers and other flank troops successfully subdued repeated French and Indian ambush attempts. Braddock, Gage,

and 1,200 men reached the remains of Fort Necessity on 25 June.

The French garrison at Fort Duquesne numbered more than 100 regulars, 200 Canadian militia, and nearly 1,000 allied Indians. The British column crossed the Monongahela River about 32 km (20 miles)

east of the fort in early July, but shortly had to cross back, frustrated by the terrain. In the meantime, Captain de Beaujeu assembled an attack force of most of the French regulars, plus 100 Canadians and a sizeable Indian force, and led them out of Fort Duquesne. On 6 July forward elements of both armies met and skirmished. On 8 July, Braddock's column crossed the river for the second time just below Fort Duquesne. The crossing went without difficulty, one British observer describing how the 'main body cross with colours flying, drums beating and fifes playing' (*JSAHQR*, 61, p. 202).

The French force came within sight of the advance guards of the British column, and fighting broke out at midday. The British formed a skirmish line and opened fire on the French, killing Captain de Beaujeu in the opening volley. A Captain Dumas assumed command and decided to deploy the troops along the sides of the British column in the woods, trapping the advance guard of Gage's force in a cross-fire from the French and Indian troops. Gage, instead of pushing forward, decided to

Braddock's march to Fort Duquesne. (Ann Ronan Picture Library)

Braddock's column under attack. The image is viewed from the positions of the French and allied Indians firing into the British positions. (State Historical Society of Wisconsin)

fall back. The French and Indians had seized the crucial high ground, and as the British troops withdrew, the French and Indians continued to pour fire into their ranks. A Royal Artillery officer described the scene:

the first fire the enemy gave was in front and they likewise attacked the piquets in flank, so that in a few minutes the grenadiers were nearly cut to pieces and drove into great confusion … [When t]he main body heard that the front was attacked they instantly advanced … [T]he enemy attacked the main body … [The British] engaged them but could not see whom they fired at [as] the trees were thick … [S]oldiers [were] encouraged to take the hill but they had been intimidated and many officers declared they never saw above 5 of the enemy at one time … [Braddock] divided the men into small parties but the main part of the officers were either killed or wounded and in short the soldiers were totally deaf to the command of the few officers

that were left unhurt (JSAHQR, 61,
pp. 202–203).

After three hours of fighting, the British column began to fall back to the river. More than 800 of their men and officers were killed or wounded, including General Braddock, who had been mortally wounded. The French lost three officers killed and four wounded, plus 10 regulars and Canadians killed. It is estimated that the Indians lost between 20 and 100 warriors. The remains of the British

column reached Fort Necessity on 17 July, and from there the army made a further withdrawal to Fort Cumberland. The immediate threat to Fort Duquesne had been nullified, at least for 1755.

It is true that Braddock lacked knowledge of warfare in North America, but as he undertook very good flank protection on the march, his inexperience was only part of the reason for the crushing British defeat. The battle was, effectively, a collision between the two armies. The French and Indians had the advantage of the high ground, which Gage should have seized. Braddock attempted to seize the high ground by force, but the French and Indians were too well established and the troops were beaten back mercilessly. Any British general of the period would have had a difficult time attempting to rectify the situation, and there is nothing to indicate that a provincial commander would have fared any better. Captain Dumas, the French commander, deserves full credit for sound and innovative action at the right moment.

New York theater

Following General Braddock's death, Governor (Major General) Shirley became commander-in-chief of the British forces in North America. Shirley was designated to lead the expedition against Fort Niagara, primarily using the two newly raised regular regiments filled with raw recruits and various provincial units. He assembled his force in late July. The plan called for the column to travel overland and by river to Oswego, a British–Indian trading center situated on Lake Ontario. It was more than 321 km (200 miles) from Albany to Oswego, and a further 241 km (150 miles) to Fort Niagara via Lake Ontario.

Shirley and the major part of his expedition arrived at Oswego on 17 August. They encountered no opposition, either en route or when they arrived. The difficult passage to Oswego, followed by numerous delays in the arrival of supplies and troops once there, prevented Shirley moving on toward Fort Niagara as quickly as planned. The last troops arrived in Oswego on 2 September, but supply problems continued and desertions had begun. In the interim, the French, taking advantage of the delay, had moved troops to Fort Frontenac, on the north side of Lake Ontario, and to other posts to protect Niagara. Shirley, aware of the growing threat from the north and the decreasing time left to lay siege to the fort, decided to call off the attack until the next campaign season and build up defenses in the Oswego area instead.

At around the same time, Lieutenant Colonel Johnson headed from Albany towards Lake George with 2,000 provincial soldiers, under orders to construct Fort Edward on the Hudson River, south of Lake George. Upon completion of this task, he was to proceed to Lake George, sail north, and attack the French positions on the north side of the lake. From there, he was supposed to continue to Fort St. Frederic (Crown Point) at the southern end of Lake Champlain, just north of Lake George. Johnson reached the southern end of Lake George in late August, where he received reports from Indian scouts that the French were in position at Ticonderoga (later Fort Carillon, also at the southern end of Lake Champlain) but they had not yet constructed fortifications. Baron Dieskau had heard reports that Johnson was stationed at Fort Edward. He led 3,500 French regulars, militia, and Indians to Ticonderoga, and leaving the majority of these troops there to construct Fort Carillon, took 1,000 regulars, militia, and Indians to attack the British at Fort Edward. As the French forces moved down the lake in bateaux, they realized that Johnson was in fact encamped at the southern end of Lake George, several miles north of where they expected to find him.

The British camp was fortified against possible attack, and the two armies met on 8 September. The French regulars marched in open order towards the camp, but their fire only pounded the felled trees surrounding the British position. The provincials retaliated with musket and artillery. The French attempted to shift their fire, but were unable to inflict heavy casualties. After a few hours the Canadian and Indian troops melted away, but, as Johnson noted, the '[French regulars] kept their ground and order for some time with great resolution and good conduct' (Gipson, VI, p. 172). Eventually, however, the French began to lose ground, and the provincials seized the advantage, launched a counter-attack, and captured the wounded Dieskau. The battle ended when a relieving force arrived from Fort Edward, forcing a conclusive French withdrawal.

The British and French had each lost more than 200 men in the battle at Lake George. The British campaign towards Fort St. Frederick came to a halt when news was received that the French had begun to fortify Ticonderoga and renamed it Fort Carillon. The British were content with their victory and fortified the southern end of Lake George with the construction of Fort William Henry.

Canadian theater

Ironically, the smallest British expedition was also the most successful of the 1755 campaign season. Lieutenant Colonel Monckton led 2,000 provincials and 280 regulars against the French Fort Beausejour in Nova Scotia. The invasion force sailed from Boston on 26 May for (Fort) Annapolis Royal in Nova Scotia. Artillery and supplies were sent in from Halifax to Fort Lawrence, on the route to the expedition's final destination, in time for the arrival of the Boston contingent on 2 June. The troops stopped just long enough to re-supply, marching out on 4 June toward the fort.

British troops spent the next week clearing the areas surrounding Fort Beausejour of Acadians who were providing support to the French cause. The displaced Acadians flooded toward the fort for protection. Beausejour was manned by a few

companies of regulars, plus nearly
1,000 Acadian militia. By 14 June, most of
the area around the fort had been cleared
and the British artillery was in position to
begin the bombardment of the fort. A
French observer described how

*on the morning of the 16 [June] an enemy
bomb exploded on one of the casements to the
left of the entrance … [I]t was enough to bring
about the surrender of the fort because fire
combined with inexperience made everyone
in that place give up* (Journals of Beausejour,
p. 97).

The nearby French Fort Gapereau also
capitulated, creating a significant breach in
the French strategy of a continuous line of
forts from Louisbourg to New Orleans. Aside
from the water route toward Quebec,
Louisbourg had been utterly cut off by the
British action. One lasting, and infamous,
legacy of the fighting in Nova Scotia in 1755
was the expulsion of the Acadian population
by British authorities. This will be discussed
later in the book.

The overall British strategy for 1755 had
not been fully executed. The British had
been completely stymied in the Ohio River
area and had made limited gains in two
other campaigns. Only in Nova Scotia had
the strategy borne fruit. The fighting in the
New York and Western theaters had
additionally accelerated the deterioration of
relations between regular and provincial
troops. Numerous provincial observers were
critical of the performance of the regulars
with Braddock's expedition, especially after
some regulars accidentally mistook Virginian
provincials for French troops and fired upon
them. Lieutenant Colonel Washington, who
was present at the battle on 9 July,
commented that 'our poor Virginians
behaved like men and died like soldiers'
(18 July 1755, *The Writings of George
Washington*). The victory at Lake George, also
won by provincials, gave further credibility
to the colonial belief that British regulars
might not be suited to fighting conditions in
North America.

1756

The major fighting of 1756 occurred around
the British post at Oswego on Lake Ontario.
The British were very much on the defensive
during 1756, mainly because of their focus
on the build-up of provincial and regular
units to fight and on smoothing relations
between the two groups. The French, even
though they were outnumbered in both
regular and militia establishments for the
remainder of the war, nevertheless launched
numerous offensive operations in both 1756
and 1757.

The French command in Canada was
largely divided between Marquis de
Vaudreuil, who in theory had influence in
the deployment of the colonial regulars and
militia, and the new commander-in-chief of
the French regular forces, Marquis de
Montcalm-Gozon de Saint-Veran. The French
port of Louisbourg, however, was under the
command of neither Montcalm nor
Vaudreuil, but that of Chevalier de Augustin
Drucour.

Montcalm sailed from France for Quebec
on 3 April 1756, accompanied by a
reinforcement of two battalions of the
Royal-Roussillon and La Sarre regiments. His
two senior commanders were Brigadier le
Chevalier de Levis and Colonel le Chevalier
de Bourlamaque. As Montcalm sailed toward
Quebec, war between Great Britain and
France was formally declared on 17 May. For
the French forces in North America, this did
not mean that France would focus her
military might on North America. On the
contrary, strategy in France was divided
between colonial and Continental ambitions,
and there was strong sentiment at the
French court for devoting the largest military
effort to the conflict in Continental Europe.
By 1758, the French court had shifted almost
completely to a strategy of invading and
seizing Hannover, in the hope that it could
be used as a bargaining chip for the return of
New France, should the British succeed in
defeating Montcalm. In any case, even had
strategic plans been otherwise, the Royal
Navy undertook a very successful blockade,

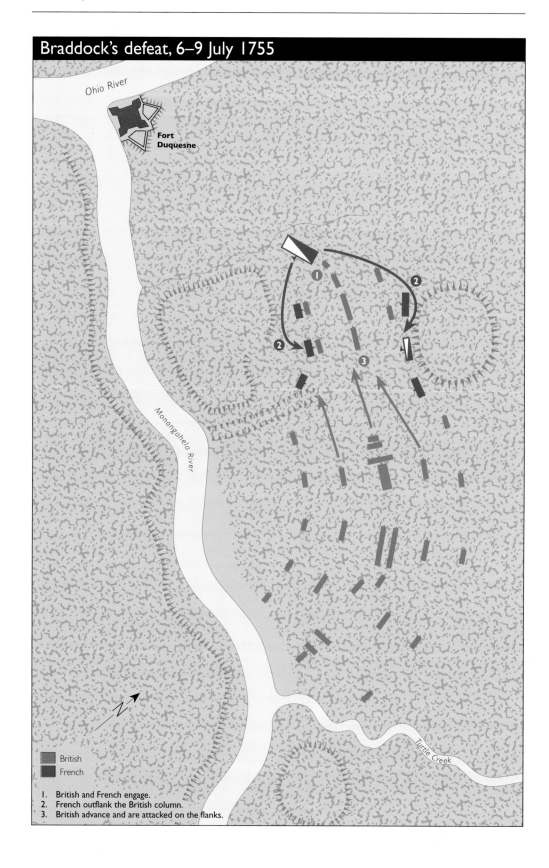

Braddock's defeat, 6–9 July 1755

Ohio River

Fort Duquesne

Monongahela River

Turtle Creek

British

French

1. British and French engage.
2. French outflank the British column.
3. British advance and are attacked on the flanks.

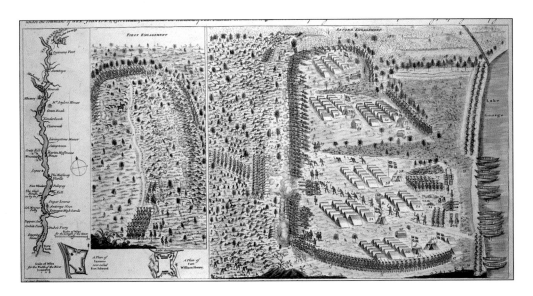

Battle of Lake George 1755. The image illustrates the British fortified camp on the right. Lake George is to the British rear. The French are attacking from the left side of the image. (Anne SK Brown Collection)

bottling up the French fleet in Toulon and Brest and denying the French the opportunity to supply North America with reinforcements. For more information regarding this strategy see Essential Histories, *The Seven Years' War*.

The British government took the opposite strategic approach following the formal outbreak of war, deciding that seizing New France would be an important strategic advantage in the larger world war that began to develop in the spring of 1756. To this end, two more regiments were sent from Great Britain in 1756, accompanied by senior generals, such as Major General James Abercromby, Major General Daniel Webb, and a new commander-in-chief, John Campbell, Earl of Loudon, with orders to rectify the situation that had developed in 1755. British regulars were still not equipped to fight effectively in the forest, and Army leaders had decided to create a new regiment of regulars. The 62nd (later 60th) Regiment of Foot was to be raised in North America from the frontier populations, and its training was designed to combine the discipline of the regulars with the frontier fighting skills of a colonial militiaman. Although not all of the recruits for this four-battalion regiment originated from the frontier population, this development marked a significant change in policy and an attempt by British regulars to get to grips with the sort of warfare particular to North America.

New York theater

Loudon, his staff, and the regular reinforcements arrived in Albany in late June, where he assumed overall command of the army in North America. As discussed earlier, he was faced immediately with the problems resulting from a Royal Order which decreed all provincial officers (including senior officers such as generals and colonels) were to revert to the senior rank of senior captain when serving alongside regular troops. Loudon met with senior provincial officers and was able to get them to agree to the new edict, but it did nothing to improve relations between the two groups.

A senior British officer, Lieutenant Colonel Burton, was sent to report on the state of the provincial forces stationed at Fort William Henry and Fort Edward. He described the camp at Fort William Henry as 'nastier than anything I could conceive ... a great waste of provisions, the men having just what they please, no great command kept up' (Parkman, p. 233). The regular

View of Fort Beausejour. (Public Archives of Canada)

officer was not being prejudiced. A Massachusetts doctor, Dr. Thomas Williams, stationed at Fort William Henry reported: 'we bury five or six a day. Not more than two thirds of our army fit for duty' (Parkman, p. 234). The plan for an attack on Fort Carillon, just beyond the north side of Lake George, would have to be delayed.

The French feared that the main British attack would come against them at Fort Carillon. Montcalm arrived at Fort Carillon in July, and decided to draw off British attention from the fort and apply pressure against Oswego instead. At first this plan only envisioned a feint attack but in the end it was to be the major campaign of the season. A column of 1,000 French regulars, Canadians, and Indians, under the command of Coulon de Villiers, was assembled to cut communications between Oswego and Albany. They arrived in the area in early July, where they encountered a column of provincial troops. The unit numbered just over 500 men, and was under the command of Captain John Bradstreet, a New Englander with a commission in the 62nd (60th) Foot. Bradstreet's men had arrived in Oswego with supplies and were returning by boat to Albany.

On the 3 July, Bradstreet was ambushed by the French troops. The skirmish lasted for most of the day, with both sides claiming victory in the end. The encounter was most likely a draw, from which both sides were able to extricate themselves with prisoners taken but few casualties. The French ambush did alert the British commanders to the precarious position that Oswego was in, but the confusion surrounding Loudon's arrival and accompanying changes in bureaucracy meant that a major reinforcement for the area was not prepared till 12 August. The 44th Regiment of Foot and provincials were assigned the task of reinforcing Oswego, where they were sorely needed. They were not, however, to arrive in time.

Montcalm was already on the move against Oswego. He had marched out from Fort Carillon in early July, leaving behind 3,000 men to defend the north end of Lake George. Montcalm reached Fort Frontenac, at the northern end of Lake Ontario, on 29 July, and from there he sent ahead a small detachment of regulars, militia, and Indians to rendezvous with Villiers near Oswego. Montcalm, meanwhile, came behind with the bulk of the force, which landed a mile from Oswego on 10 August. The French columns converged on Fort Ontario the next day.

The garrison at the three forts at Oswego – Ontario, Pepperell (Oswego), and George – were commanded by Colonel Mercer. Shirley had left two locally raised regular regiments in the area for the winter of 1755–56, and these were divided between forts Ontario and Pepperell. New Jersey provincials were stationed at Fort George, with the total garrison numbering just over 1,500 men. A river separated Fort Ontario from the other two encampments, and it stood on a height overlooking Oswego and Fort George.

The French column was carrying a large contingent of siege artillery for its assault on the three forts. After two days and nights of heavy bombardment, Fort Ontario was shattered. Colonel Mercer ordered the evacuation of Fort Ontario to the western side of the river on 13 August, and the survivors were able to get across to Oswego. Montcalm moved his artillery to the captured heights where Ontario had stood, and on the morning of 14 August, his cannon opened up on the two remaining forts. A column of French and Indian troops crossed the river unopposed under cover of cannon fire. The effect of the artillery fire was described as leaving the British: 'so much exposed that the Enemy could see the buckles in our shoes' (*Journal of the Siege of Oswego*, Military History of Great Britain, for 1756, 1757, p. 38).

After the heavy bombardment in which Colonel Mercer was killed, the remaining officers held a council of war and decided to surrender. In the end the British lost 50 men and the French forces about half that. As with other French victories, the French-allied Indians wrought havoc among the surrendered British soldiers and civilians. Montcalm had to intervene to stop the killing and pillaging after the surrender. The prisoners were transported to Montreal. Montcalm destroyed everything in the area of any value, and then withdrew. His troops redeployed to forts Niagara, Frontenac and Carillon, having decisively entered the conflict in 1756. The offensive defense had paid dividends, keeping the British off balance for another year.

The rest of 1756 passed with small bands of provincials, principally Rogers' Rangers and French Canadian and Indian troops, harassing posts along the frontier. This period became known as the partisan war. The loss of the 50th and 51st Regiments of Foot at Oswego prompted the renumbering of all British regiments listed above 51, and so the 62nd Regiment of Foot became the 60th.

1757

Similar to 1756, 1757 would be marked by only one major engagement between France and Britain, and again this was fought in the New York theater of operations. The partisan war continued along the frontier, spreading fear among both French and British settlers.

Over the course of 1757, the British reinforced their war effort with more than 11,000 regular troops shipped out from Great Britain. By the end of 1757, 21 battalions of British regulars and seven Independent companies were operating in North America. The British were also able to call upon the colonies for further provincial forces, which were used in increasing numbers to protect lines of communications with forts along the frontier. On the French side, Montcalm received his last major reinforcement in 1757, with the arrival of two battalions of the Regiment de Berry. Montcalm had only eight battalions of regulars (there were 12 in total, but four were stationed at Louisbourg) and 64 companies of colonial regulars, stationed from Louisbourg to New Orleans. He also, like his British counterparts, had a large contingent of militia and a larger number of Indian allies to draw upon for the campaign.

A change of government in Britain in 1757 caused the Newcastle ministry to be replaced, first by William Pitt and William Cavendish, and then, after a short time by a coalition government, the Newcastle-Pitt ministry, in the winter of 1757. The Newcastle-Pitt ministry changed strategy, shifting the British focus to attacking Louisbourg and Quebec, the heart of New France. In response to the new strategic plan, Lord Loudon withdrew a large number of regulars from New York in April and sailed for Halifax. He was further reinforced with

Montcalm surrounded by his men.
(Ann Ronan Picture Library)

newly arrived regular troops from Great
Britain, and was ordered to attack the French
fortress at Louisbourg, in an attempt to open
up Quebec to attack.

Poor intelligence gathering and the
French Navy's continued dominance of its
British naval opposition in the area near
Louisbourg meant that Loudon was unsure
of the size of the French forces. He hesitated
to launch an attack, and by July, the plans
had to be put aside when the Royal Navy
was unable to gain the upper hand in the
region. Montcalm was aware of these
developments, and his scouts reported that
the frontier had been stripped of many

British regulars. Montcalm decided to take advantage of the situation, and prepared to strike at Fort William Henry, at the southern end of Lake George.

New York theater

By July, Montcalm had amassed a large force in and around Fort Carillon and was planning an attack on Fort William Henry before the end of the month. The French attack column was to number 7,500 men, including six regular battalions, marines, militia, and Indians. Montcalm split his force in two; one group of 2,600 men traveled overland, while the other, some 5,000 men traveled in bateaux over the lake. The two forces met at the southern end of the lake on 2 August.

The British force at Fort William Henry comprised just over 2,000 men, half of whom were regulars, under the command of Lieutenant Colonel George Munro. The fort was a fairly strong structure, constructed of logs and earth. General Webb was stationed with 1,600 soldiers, mostly provincials, at Fort Edward, 22 km (14 miles) to the south. Webb dispatched a reinforcement of 200 regulars on 29 July to reinforce the garrison at Fort William Henry, and he also alerted the New York and New England colonies of the need for more troops. The message was received, but the reinforcements would arrive too late.

On 3 August, the first clashes occurred between scouts of the British and French armies. The road to Fort Edward was cut by a detachment of French and Indian troops, and British forces and civilians in the area began to withdraw to Fort William Henry, burning the houses and buildings that remained outside the perimeter. The British also held an entrenched camp outside the fort. British artillery fired upon the French build-up outside the fort, but the first French siege trenches were dug under heavy fire on the evening of 4 August and the siege began in earnest.

Both sides exchanged fire as the French trenches crept closer and closer to the British ramparts. A British artillery officer wrote on 7 August:

Robert Rogers. (John Carter Brown Library at Brown University)

the enemy still continue working and carrying on their approaches. The garrison kept a continual fire both of shells and cannon till night … [A]t night the garrison kept a continual watch for fear of an assault (8311-85).

Webb was unable to send more reinforcements, fearing that his small force would be decimated trying to reach the besieged British garrison. Such a loss would leave the road to Albany open and unprotected, since the provincial reinforcements had not yet arrived. To make matters worse, smallpox broke out inside Fort William Henry.

A few days into the siege, the number of killed and wounded within the fort had reached over 300. Many of the large British cannons and mortars had blown up or been destroyed. The palisades had been breached in a few locations, and the French continued to pour artillery fire into the fort. Messages sent by Munro had been intercepted by the French and Indians. Munro was advised of this state of affairs by Louis Antoine de Bougainville, a senior French officer, who warned that the likelihood of reinforcements from Webb was minimal. Munro still refused to surrender, but morale within the fort was sinking.

Following a full night of heavy bombardment Munro at last began to feel that resistance was futile. On the morning of 9 August, Lieutenant Colonel Young, was sent to Montcalm's tent to discuss terms of a surrender. The British agreed to a surrender that allowed them to march to Fort Edward with full military honors. They were also required to promise not serve in the conflict for 18 months. The French prisoners captured since 1754 were to be returned to New France within three months. The stores and artillery of the fort, or what was left of them, were retained as spoils of the French. Montcalm summoned a war council with his Indian allies and called on them to respect the conditions of the surrender. The British evacuated the fort and entrenched camp.

The French-allied Indians, disregarding Montcalm's demands, rushed to the fort as the British evacuated, attacking and killing the wounded left behind. The French guards attempted to stop the killing, but there is debate about how hard they tried. Montcalm was eventually able to restore some level of order, but on the following day, as the British column marched toward Fort Edward, they were attacked again by Indians seeking revenge and prisoners. The French guards again failed to stop the slaughter, and it is estimated that 50 men, women, and children were killed and another 200 taken prisoner by the Indians. The French finally managed to restore order and escort the remainder of the column to Fort Edward. Some of the Indians sickened and died of smallpox after their attacks on sick and wounded British.

By 11 August, the number of dead and wounded from the British side far exceeded the 300 who had been killed before the surrender of the fort and was well over 700 people killed, wounded, or missing. The French forces had lost fewer than 100 men killed and wounded. It is not known how many French-allied Indians died. However, a British prisoner of the Indians reported that 'the Indians that went from the town [to Fort William Henry] where I lived one quarter of the numbers were missing, seven killed and three died of their wounds' (King). This suggests that the toll on some small Indian villages could have been quite high.

The partisan war on the frontier continued after the British defeat. Montcalm destroyed Fort William Henry and returned to Fort Carillon. He had been ordered to proceed to Fort Edward but had decided it was not a good idea, as the Canadian militia was nervous about getting back for the harvest. The year 1757 was the high water mark for the French effort in the French and Indian War; while the British were to suffer a few more defeats, the initiative began to shift in their favor with the 1758 campaign.

1758

One of the first major changes of 1758 was to the high command of British forces in North America, with the replacement of Lord Loudon by Major General James Abercromby. The Newcastle-Pitt Ministry also made concessions to the colonial governments on disputes over command and payment, in an effort to resolve past issues of reinforcements and supplies and make the way smoother for Abercromby. Britain agreed to pay for a portion of the raising, clothing, and arming of provincial units recruited for future campaigns, and to discontinue the custom of de-ranking provincial officers.

The British strategy for 1758 envisioned a large-scale, three-pronged attack on New France. Major General Abercromby was to lead an attack on Fort Carillon; Major General James Amherst was to lead an amphibious attack and siege of Louisbourg; and Brigadier John Forbes was to try once again to take Fort Duquesne, using a different route than Braddock had taken in 1755. Some 24,000 British regulars and 22,000 provincials were deployed for these campaigns, against a French force that was spread thinly across New France.

Western theater

Brigadier Forbes's expedition towards Fort Duquesne was different from Braddock's in several major ways. For a start the route was shorter and originated in Pennsylvania. Forbes also had a highly motivated and trained second-in-command, Lieutenant Colonel Henry Bouquet of the 60th Foot. Bouquet had been actively involved in drawing up battle plans and devising tactics to fight in the woods of North America. In 1757, he had drawn up a plan of marching in the woods that highlighted the need for a secure line of communications. His order of march focused on the need for constant scouting and destruction of any ambush, stating that

the vanguard must detach small parties a mile forward, who shall march in great silence, and visit all suspected places, as copses, ditches and hallows, where ambuscades may be concealed … [I]n case of attack, the men must fall on their knees; that motion will prevent their running away (Bouquet Papers I, pp. 52–53).

Forbes's march, though slow, was designed to ensure that forts were constructed and a secure line of communication ensured.

Forbes's expedition began to gather in Sandy Hook, Pennsylvania in April. The total number of troops earmarked for the column was about 6,000. Nearly 1,800 of these were regulars and the rest provincial soldiers. The period between April and June was spent gathering the necessary supplies and provincial troops for the operation. The issue of supplies was becoming acute; a press warrant was issued for the authorization of pressing wagons, carriages and horses if the situation did not improve by late May. This action was likely to be unpopular with colonial settlers and was used as a last resort.

The forward elements of the column began to move out in late June. On 24 June, Bouquet and forward elements reached Raystown, where they began to construct Fort Bedford. The troops would remain in the area for nearly a month, building the fort and securing the surrounding area. Forbes's division followed

and met up with the forward units. Bouquet then pushed out a further 64 km (40 miles) to Loyalhannon Creek and began to build up the road and another fortified position, Fort Ligonier. By 6 September, Bouquet and his forward elements were within 64 km (40 miles) of Fort Duquesne at Loyalhannon Creek. Forbes and his large force remained further back, hampered by discipline and supply problems. The onset of autumn rains delayed progress still further.

As they progressed along the march route, the British were also in negotiation with local Indian tribes. They wished particularly to win over the Delawares, who had sided with the French. After a series of meetings many of the Indian tribes agreed to side with the British, including some that had previously been allied with the French.

The French position at Fort Duquesne was still fairly formidable, even without a large contingent of regulars. Contemporary reports estimate that the fort was garrisoned by some 1,200 militia and marines, supported by an additional 1,000 Indian warriors, under the command of Marchand de Lignery.

It was at Loyalhannon Creek that Bouquet made a major operational error. Several British provincial and regular soldiers had been captured at Fort Ligonier by Indian raiding parties, and Bouquet was considering sending out two parties of 100 men each to cut off the Indian withdrawal and rescue the troops. Major Grant, a regular officer, suggested a different plan. He said that if Bouquet gave him 500–600 men, he would push towards Fort Duquesne, make a reconnaissance, attempt to cut off the roads and generally to harass the fort. British scouts had reported that the fort was garrisoned by only 600 men, so Bouquet agreed to the plan and Major Grant set out with a force of 400 regulars and 350 provincials.

Grant's force was within five miles of Fort Duquesne by 13 September, with a plan to destroy the Indian camp outside the fort. Major Lewis and a force of 400 men went forward and destroyed some of the blockhouses outside the fort, while Major Grant was stationed on a height overlooking

Battle of Fort William Henry, 1757

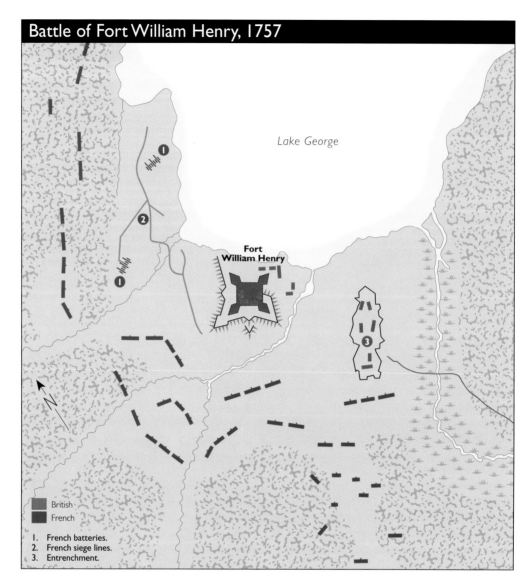

Lake George

Fort
William Henry

British
French

1. French batteries.
2. French siege lines.
3. Entrenchment.

the fort. When Lewis returned, Grant remained on the height. The following morning, 14 September, Grant divided his force into three columns. He sent Major Lewis to set up an ambush position with 100 regulars and 150 Virginian militia, while a Captain MacDonald marched to the fort with 100 regulars. Grant and the remainder of the force stayed on the heights.

As Grant reported to Bouquet, the execution of the plan went badly.

For about half an hour after the enemy came from the fort, in different parties, without much

order and getting behind forces they advanced briskly, and attacked our left where there were 250 men. Captain MacDonald was soon killed … [O]ur people being overpowered, gave way, where those officers had been killed … [T]he 100 Pennsylvanians who were posted upon the right at the greatest distance from the enemy, went off without orders and without firing a shot. In short in less than half an hour all was in confusion … [W]e were fired upon from every quarter. … [O]rders were to no purpose, fear had then got the better of every other passion and I hope I shall never see again such pannick among troops (Bouquet papers, II, p. 503).

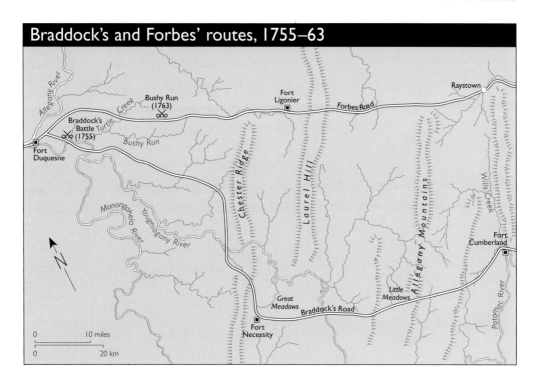

Braddock's and Forbes' routes, 1755–63

While the Pennsylvania provincials performed miserably, the Virginians acquitted themselves well. Bouquet noted: 'the Virginians who with 100 men sustained the battle with all their forces' (Bouquet, II, p. 519). In the end, Major Lewis and his detachment attempted to get back to Major Grant, but the two officers were forced to surrender to the French and Indians who had completely cut them off. More than 400 officers and men were able to escape, but some 200 had been killed or captured. It is difficult to ascertain accurate numbers of dead and wounded on the French side.

Following this victory, the French attempted to build on the advantage gained. In early October, 400 militia and marines and 100 Indians moved out to attack Fort Ligonier, arriving on the morning of 12 October. Bouquet was not in command at Fort Ligonier, having gone out on the road to make inspections. The French launched an attack at 11.00 am, pushing back two British forward reconnaissance units back toward the fort. The British commander, Colonel James Burd, counter-attacked, and after two hours of brisk

fighting the French were forced to withdraw. Although this was a relatively minor skirmish for the French, morale at Fort Duquesne began to sink in the aftermath, and the French militia from Illinois and Louisiana withdrew. Supplies due from Fort Frontenac had been destroyed by Bradstreet in August, which was probably a contributing factor.

On 5 November, the main British force was finally established at Fort Ligonier. British scouts were reporting low morale at Fort Duquesne, and on 18 November 2,500 soldiers headed out from Fort Ligonier, hoping to exploit the situation. On the evening of 24 November, forward elements reached the heights where Grant had been stationed – just in time to witness the French blowing up their own fort. The next morning, the British moved into the remains of the fort and began to rebuild it, renaming it Fort Pitt. The campaign was a success, and the regulars were sent back to Philadelphia for winter quarters, while provincial troops stationed along the newly built road and its protecting forts.

New York theater

After spending the winter in Montreal, Montcalm decided to deploy most of his regular troops to Fort Carillon, and by early summer eight regular battalions were assembled there. They were largely without support from the Canadian militia, the vast majority of which was held back in Montreal, Quebec, and other frontier areas.

General Abercromby, in preparation for the attack on Fort Carillon, had assembled 6,000 British regulars and 9,000 provincials. The British column assembled at the ruins of Fort William Henry to drill and build bateaux for the lake crossing. On 4 July, the British force was completed and ready to sail.

Montcalm had realized that the British were on the move, and in early July he ordered his troops to build an outer defensive work around Fort Carillon. A large entrenchment was constructed, with felled trees spread out in front of the dug trenches. One British observer described how the '[French] had large cut trees one laid above another a man's height and in the outside there was brush and logs for about 15 paces from it' (Black Watch, p. 24). The British would have to overcome this obstacle before they could approach the fort itself.

The British force landed unopposed on the north shore of Lake George on 6 July. As they moved to the north on 7 July, a large-scale skirmish broke out on their left flank. The French were easily pushed aside by British light infantry and rangers, but in the fracas the innovative light infantry officer, Brigadier George Augustus, Lord Howe, was killed. A French senior officer Bouganville recorded the event: '[Howe] had showed the greatest talents. ... [The skirmish] gave us twenty-four hours delay' (Bougainville, p. 229). A British captain, Charles Lee, offers another reason for the delay of the British advance, claiming that 'our troops [were] a good deal scattered and divided through ignorance of the wood' (7803-18-1).

Colonel Bouquet meeting with Indians.
(Rare Book Division, New York Public Library)

After the skirmish, Montcalm gave orders for his troops to deploy to the entrenchment. Further work was done on the works in anticipation of the British attack, and seven of the eight battalions were stationed in the entrenchment. Only one battalion remained in Fort Carillon proper. Each battalion was allotted 130 paces of frontage. Montcalm was aware that there was not an endless supply of ammunition available to his army. He specifically ordered his officers to 'see to it the soldier fires slowly and they must urge him to take good aim' (Sautai, p. 72). On the morning of 8 July, the British were in sight of the entrenchment.

At this juncture, General Abercromby made the worst command decision possible. After a forward engineer party reported that the works should be attacked immediately, Abercromby decided to make a frontal attack without artillery support. This plan made no sense, even to his own officers. One British officer noted: '[entrenchment] made it impossible to force their breastworks without cannon' (*The Black Watch*, p. 24). Captain Lee was even more scathing: 'a miscarriage maybe brought about by the incapacity of a single person I really did not think that so great a share of stupidity and absurdity could be in possession of any man' (7803-18-1). At 10.00 am Bougainville commented: 'they [British] let off a great fusillade which did not interrupt our work at all; we amused ourselves by not replying' (Bougainville, p. 232).

Sources differ on what time the main British attack began, but it was most likely sometime around 12.00 pm. Bougainville described how four main British columns attacked the entrenchment. Another French officer noted: 'our musketry fire was so well aimed that the enemy was destroyed as soon as they appeared' (Sautai, p. 77). While the British attacks were not immediately destroyed, they suffered heavy casualties as recorded by an officer of the 42nd Foot: 'had as hot a fire for about three hours as possibly could be, we all the time seeing but their hats and end of their muskets' (Black Watch, p. 24).

There are estimated to have been six major British attacks throughout the day, without a single successful breach of the breastwork. Montcalm commented that 'every part of the entrenchment was successively attacked with the greatest vigour' (Sautai, p. 85), while Charles Lee described 'attacks made with most perfect regularity, coolness and resolution' (7803-18-1). French grenadier and light companies were shifted to dangerous holes in the defense. Bougainville told of: 'their [British] light troops and better marksmen, who, protected by the trees, delivered a most murderous fire on us' (Bougainville, p. 232).

Captain Lee summarized the reasons for the defeat with his account of how the unevenness and ruggedness of the ground and height of the breastwork

… rendered it an absolute impossibility … [N]o order given to change attack … but every officer led at the head of his division, company or squadron to fall a sacrifice to his own good behaviour and stupidity of his commander [Abercromby] … [T]he fire was prodigiously hot and the slaughter of the officers was great; almost all wounded, the men still furiously rushing forward almost without leaders, five hours persisted in this diabolical attempt and at length obliged to retire (7803-18-1).

At about 7.00 pm the British began to withdraw towards Lake George. Some of the troops, after suffering such a setback, became demoralized, and Captain Bradstreet was ordered to march back to the landing place and ensure that no one stole or seized the boats. The light infantry and rangers protected the retreat as the boats were loaded, and the remaining elements of the expedition withdrew to the south end of Lake George. From there the retreat continued to Fort Edward.

The battle casualties for British were more than 1,000 regulars and 300 provincials killed. The French, by contrast, lost only 300 killed in the battle. General Abercromby's demonstration of poor leadership and decision-making skills, contrasted against Major General Jeffrey Amherst's success at Louisbourg (see below), led shortly to Abercromby's replacement as commander-in-chief by Amherst in September.

There was one bright spot in the conduct of the New York campaign. Captain Bradstreet, a regular officer, led a raid with a small waterborne force against Fort Frontenac in August. His force of 2,200 men was made up mostly of provincial soldiers, with about 500 regulars among them. Bradstreet and his men traveled by bateaux up the Mohawk and Onandaga rivers past Oswego. On 22 August, the force left Oswego and sailed due north for Fort Frontenac.

On 25 August, the flotilla arrived near Frontenac. The French garrison had been depleted in response to the need for regulars at Fort Carillon, and on 27 August, the fort and French shipping in the region were under bombardment by British artillery. The fort surrendered later the same day. Nine French ships, as well as the fort, were destroyed in the attack, and the booty gained from seizing this important trading post and its supplies was estimated to have been close to 800,000 pounds sterling. Just as important, seizing the supplies and stores

from Fort Frontenac caused major problems for the French forts in the west.

Canadian theater

The major engagement in the Canadian theater took place on Cape Breton Island, home of the French fort at Louisbourg. This structure was the strongest fortress in North America, for either side, with defenses stretching for a mile and a half on its landward perimeter. Some of the masonry was in a poor condition owing to the weather conditions of the area, which would prove beneficial to the British artillery. Defensive lines had been dug along the beaches to the south and west of the fortress, and four bastions stood within the fort itself. The governor of Cape Breton Island, Chevalier de Drucour, was in overall command of the French forces at Louisbourg. There were four battalions of regulars, 24 companies of marines, and some militia. Contemporary accounts estimate that there were 3,500 men stationed in and around the fortress. There

Battle of Fort Carillon showing the entrenchment with no felled trees in front. (National Archives of Canada)

were 219 cannons on the fortress walls and other defensive positions, as well as 19 mortars. The garrison was prepared for a long siege. A French fleet had arrived over the course of the spring to re-supply the fortress. Five ships of the line and seven frigates patrolled the harbor.

The British forces were gathered at Halifax, Nova Scotia. The Royal Navy had provided 23 ships of the line, 18 frigates and a fleet of transports, under the command of Admiral Edward Boscawen. Major General Jeffrey Amherst, was to lead the land effort. Once again, as in 1757, the expedition was made up mostly of regulars. There were 14 regular battalions earmarked for the operation, comprising just over 12,000 men with an additional 500 'Gorham's Rangers' from Halifax and Royal Artillery attached. The fleet sailed on 28 May, and arrived off the Cape Breton coast on 2 June.

There were three possible landing sites. The first was Freshwater Cove, 6 km (four miles) from the fort. Flat Point and White Point were to the east of Freshwater, closer to the fort. Royal Navy and senior army officers sailed up and down the potential landing areas to assess the best approach, then devised their plans. The army was to be divided into three divisions: Brigadier James Wolfe was to lead the main assault against Freshwater Cove, with Brigadiers Charles Lawrence and Edward Whitmore advancing towards Flat and White Points.

The fleet and army were delayed from landing for more than six days, as fog and surf denied access to the beaches. The French defenses were strongest at Freshwater Cove, where their entrenchment was ready to receive the enemy. Over 1,000 French soldiers had been deployed to throw the British back into the sea and were, as a British officer noted:

most advantageously posted behind good entrenchment, the banks very high and almost perpendicular … [W]herever there was the least probability of getting ashore it was well secured with cannon and entrenchment (7204-6-2).

Finally, on 8 June, the troops received the order to land. A British observer described 'nothing seen or heard for one hour but the thundering of Cannon and flashes of lightening' (Add Mss 45662). Wolfe's division was to see most of the heavy fighting for the day. The surf continued to be a problem – 'the surge was extremely violent … [Boats] crushed to pieces being carried away by the surf' (6807-131).

The first waves of British troops approached the beaches. An officer who landed with Wolfe's division noted:

the boats proceeded to the cove, the enemy let them come within half musket shot and gave them a warm reception from their entrenchment, with great guns and small arms (Military Affairs, p. 416).

As Wolfe's division made a foothold at Freshwater Cove, Lawrence's division also landed after making a diversion. The French were overwhelmed by the numbers of British troops landing, and began to fear that they were in danger of being cut off from the fort. A British officer recorded the attack:

the enemy's attention being quite engaged at the other cove did not perceive our men climbing rocks till a few of them got to the top who bravely maintained their guard well supported though opposed by numbers they gained the enemy's flank who feared being cut off from the garrison fled in great disorder (7204-6-2).

Each side lost about 100 men during the fight for the beaches.

Flat Point Cove became the landing place for the British artillery and stores, once the area had been secured by the troops moving from Freshwater, and a camp was built to receive troops and materiel coming ashore. General Amherst decided that the best way to deal with the fort was to surround it with batteries and slowly pummel it into submission. A formal European-style siege was planned; unlike Abercromby, Amherst decided against a frontal infantry attack.

Montcalm cheered by his men after his victory at Fort Carillon, 1758. (Fort Ticonderoga Museum)

On 12 June, Brigadier Wolfe and 2,000 men set out to seize Lighthouse battery, to the north of the fort. The British had received reports that the French had destroyed Lighthouse and Great Battery, two of the major batteries outside Louisbourg's walls. A French officer stated the reason for abandoning the batteries: 'the impossibility of maintaining this post obliged us to abandon it; for it was more than we could do to guard the batteries and ramparts of the city' (Knox, III, p. 104). Wolfe's forces reached the abandoned lighthouse battery on 20 June. They took possession and immediately opened fire on French shipping in the harbor and other French positions close by. The Island battery, opposite Louisbourg, was silenced on 25 June when the combined artillery fire from the Lighthouse and Royal Navy ships finally destroyed the will of the defenders.

On 29 June, the French sank six ships in the entrance to the harbor to deny access to the Royal Navy. Louisbourg was now completely surrounded and closed off to the outside world. The formal siege had begun. The British deployed infantry to various redoubts, set up siege batteries, and began to dig siege trenches towards the fortress.

The outcome of the siege was decided by the ability of the engineers and artillery men on both sides. The French did not sit idly in the fortress under the onslaught of British artillery. One French officer described a typical series of actions:

1st of July a detachment of our people sallied out of the wood ... [T]here was a very brisk skirmish, but at length our men were forced to retire ... [W]e made a sally on the 8th ... [W]e surprised them ... but what could 900 men do against the vanguard of the enemy who immediately flew to assistance of the sappers (Knox, III, p. 110).

Battle at Fort Carillon, 1758

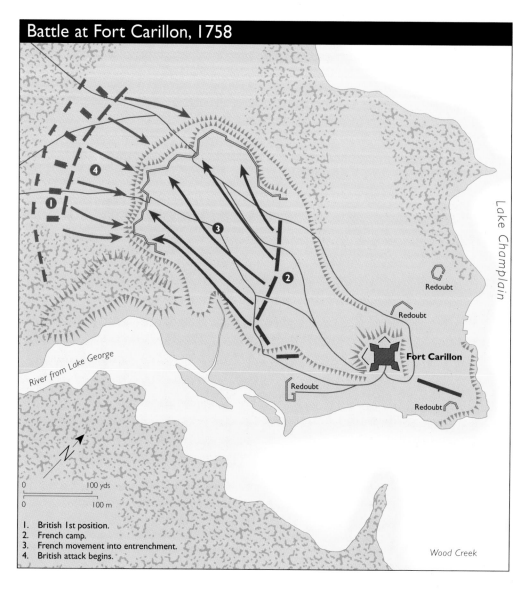

Lake Champlain

Redoubt

Redoubt

Fort Carillon

River from Lake George

Redoubt

Redoubt

N

| 0 | 100 yds |
| 0 | 100 m |

1. British 1st position.
2. French camp.
3. French movement into entrenchment.
4. British attack begins.

Wood Creek

The siege was dangerous as well for the British soldiers out in the redoubts and trenches. A British officer described what befell an overly curious fellow officer: '[a] cannon ball which cut his head off as he looked over the breastwork out of curiosity not duty' (8001-30).

By late July, the French defenders were beginning to suffer the effects of the siege in earnest. The British siege lines were continuing to close in, and a French 63-gun ship of the line had been destroyed in the harbor. A French officer described the conditions of the French batteries:

as our batteries and ramparts had been very much damaged these three days, and as the fire of the enemy's small arms made it almost impracticable for us to maintain ourselves on those ramparts which we were endeavouring to repair … a breach had been [made] in the Dauphin Bastion and West Gate (Knox, III, p. 112).

He continued 'in so melancholy a situation, there was nothing left but to capitulate; so that we suspended our fire, and sent to demand a truce, in order to regulate the articles of surrender' (Knox, III, p. 113). The French garrison surrendered on 26 July.

Lieutenant General Jeffrey Amherst. (Ann Ronan Picture Library)

The British had lost 500 killed and 1,000 wounded during the landings and the siege. The French losses are estimated at 1,000 killed and 2,000 wounded. More than 5,000 soldiers, sailors, and civilians surrendered to the British forces. The siege had taken most of the 1758 campaign season, however, and the advance towards Quebec City would have to wait until the following year. A large garrison was left at Louisbourg to rebuild the works and defend the area against potential French counter attacks. The remainder of the troops were transported to Halifax and New York for winter quarters.

The campaigns of 1758 had definitively shifted the momentum of the war in Great Britain's favor. New France was now completely on the defensive. While Abercromby had been stopped at Fort Carillon, it was only a matter of time before the British attacked it again with a different operational plan.

1759

Given their successes the previous year, the British decided once again to adopt a multi-pronged strategy for the 1759 campaign. The major thrust, against Quebec City, would be commanded by Major General James Wolfe. Wolfe's force was almost completely composed of regular troops; he had 10 battalions, plus a composite unit of grenadiers named the 'Louisbourg Grenadiers'. A small force of 300 provincial engineers and six companies of Rangers joined the force. The total number was just over 8,000 men. The force was smaller than the one that had attacked Louisbourg, since a garrison was required to remain at the Fort in case of French naval counterattacks. General Amherst was to lead a mixed force of provincials and regulars against Fort Carillon and Fort St. Frederic, with Montreal as his final objective. Amherst's force numbered just over 5,800 regulars and 5,000 provincials. A third pincer, commanded by Brigadier John Prideaux, was to originate from the re-established Fort Oswego and strike towards Fort Niagara. Prideaux' force included three battalions of regulars and two battalions of provincials. The last campaign was to be carried out by a very small force, ordered to reopen communications between Fort Pitt and Fort Ligonier, and then to establish a force at Fort Pitt to attack north against Forts Presque Isle and Venango.

Western theater

The regulars of 1/60th Foot marched from Lancaster, Pennsylvania on 31 May. After a month of undertaking repairs and ensuring security along the road, the battalion arrived at Fort Bedford. They spent June and early July carrying supplies and reinforcements to Fort Pitt, amid much skirmishing.

The 1/60th Foot received orders to march from Fort Pitt toward Fort Venango on 12 July. As the troops moved out, they received news that the French had abandoned both Venango and Presque Isle, as well as several other nearby posts, after receiving news of the fall of Fort Niagara to British troops. The 1/60th marched out to search the forts, and confirmed that they had been abandoned. The regulars returned to Fort Pitt, while provincial troops were deployed north to occupy the forts for the winter. Five companies of the 1/60th Foot remained at Fort Pitt for the winter, so that they would be in a position to move quickly if the frontier was threatened. The rest of the battalion was sent along the road to Lancaster to keep the lines of communications open for the winter.

New York theater

In March 1759, General Amherst ordered a large-scale raid on Fort Carillon. A mixed force of regulars, rangers, and Indians was ordered to observe the French and the area around Fort Carillon to assess its defenses. The raiding party destroyed French supplies outside the fort, captured five French

soldiers, and drew accurate maps of the defenses of the fort and the entrenchment, losing two men in the process.

General Amherst gathered his forces on the southern end of Lake George over the course of June. While stationed there, the forces were drilled and trained for the coming operation. A contemporary account described preparations:

the regular regiments of line will be ready formed at the head of their encampment, between four and five o'clock to-morrow morning, if a fine day, the men to be in their

waistcoats with their arms and ammunition (Knox, II, p. 486).

Amherst built part of a fort at the entrenchment constructed in 1757 and named it Fort George. He also ensured that forts were constructed between Fort Edward and Fort George to protect his rear in case a French attack originated from behind. He waited throughout June and most of July for sufficient reinforcements to arrive for his regulars and for the provincial forces to be fully mustered. On 21 July the army entered bateaux and began to sail north. They arrived at the northern end of the lake on 22 July and began to advance towards Fort Carillon.

Chevalier de Bourlamaque had reinforced Fort Carillon with 3,000 regulars and 1,000 militia troops in mid-May. However, he then received information that the British were planning to land near Quebec, only with orders to withdraw his forces from Carillon and attempt to hold the line at the north end of Lake Champlain. Nevertheless, he decided to hamper the approaching British before he withdrew.

A small but powerful French force of 400 men was left at Fort Carillon to repel the British approach. Bourlamaque decided to withdraw north to Fort St. Frederic following reports that Amherst's column was marching on the fort. The French force at Fort Carillon held up Amherst's force with artillery fire for four days, until Amherst moved his heavy artillery into range and began to pound the fort. Amherst noted on 26 July that

the artillery will be up that we may open batteries of six 24 pounders ... [A]t about 10 PM a deserter came in and said the garrison was to get off and blow up the fort ... and soon we saw the fort on fire and an explosion (Jeffrey Amherst, 26/7/1759).

The French force withdrew from Fort Carillon to meet up with Bourlamaque and his forces. The French decided to blow up

British amphibious landings at Louisbourg. The landing has a mix of British line and grenadier troops. (Aisa)

Halifax, Nova Scotia, the main staging area for the
conquest of Louisbourg and Quebec.
(National Archives of Canada)

Fort St. Frederic a few days later, fearing that
it could not withstand the powerful British
artillery train which was fast approaching.
Bourlamaque and his troops then withdrew
to Isle-aux-Noix.

Amherst decided against continuing his
advance on the French immediately. He
decided to take some time to fortify
Fort Carillon, renamed Fort Ticonderoga,
and Fort St. Frederic, now Crown Point.
Amherst also sent Robert Rogers and his
Rangers on a long-distance raid to destroy
the Indian village of St. Francis. His scouts
and rangers also sailed north from Crown
Point to the northern end of Lake
Champlain to observe and assess French
preparations for defense. Troops were further
engaged in building more bateaux and other
shipping, to contend with the small French

flotilla of armed whaleboats on the lake.
Amherst did not attempt to resume the
northward march until 11 October.

After an unsuccessful attempt to destroy
the French shipping, on 19 October Amherst
decided to withdraw for the winter to Crown
Point and Fort Ticonderoga. The advance
north on Lake Champlain, to the St. Jean
River to deal with the forts outside Montreal,
would have to wait until the next campaign
season, but the French presence on Lake
George and the southern areas of Lake
Champlain had been destroyed.

The other major offensive in the New
York theater was launched against Fort
Niagara. As mentioned previously, Brigadier
Prideaux commanded three regular and two
provincial battalions. By early spring, the
forward elements of his column had reached
Oswego, and began work to fortify the area
for future operations.

Captain M. Pouchot commanded the
French garrison at Fort Niagara. His troops

Siege of Louisbourg

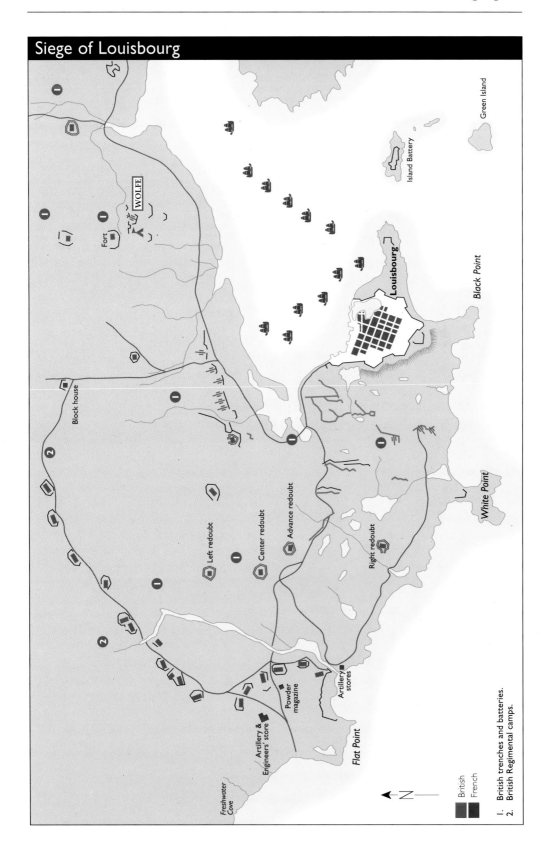

Green Island

Island Battery

WOLFE

Fort

Louisbourg

Black Point

Block house

White Point

Left redoubt

Center redoubt

Advance redoubt

Right redoubt

Artillery stores

Powder magazine

Artillery & Engineers' store

Flat Point

Freshwater Cove

N

British

French

1. British trenches and batteries.
2. British Regimental camps.

numbered 110 men from regular battalions, 180 Marines, and 100 Canadian militia. The fortifications at Niagara were quite good, however, and when Pouchot received word of the British arrival at Oswego, he set about repairing damage to the fort from weather and made other improvements to prepare for the inevitable British attack.

The British force was divided at Oswego. Eight regular companies of the 4/60th Foot and one battalion of New York Provincials remained to defend Oswego and complete work on a new fort. Two companies of the 4/60th Foot, along with the 44th and 46th Foot and one battalion of New York provincials, sailed for Fort Niagara in early July. They arrived near the fort on 7 July, and immediately prepared to lay siege. Skirmishes with the French were frequent as the British advanced.

By 16 July, the British had closed off all routes into Fort Niagara except for the water approaches. The formal siege began as both sides opened fire with artillery. The British, using trenches, moved steadily closer to the walls. Prideaux was accidentally killed by one of his own mortars during an artillery exchange, and Colonel William Johnson assumed command. He immediately called for further reinforcements from Oswego, following reports from scouts of a rumor that a French relieving force was on the march from Presque Isle and Venango.

On 24 July, the French force appeared from the south and the two sides met at La Belle Famille. There were 800 French troops present, and Johnson had deployed just over 400 regulars. The British, however, managed to surprise the French as they came within firing range. As was often the case in battles of the 18th century, the French lost any advantage their numerical superiority might have given them, when the British were able to fire into their column as they attempted to deploy into linear formation. Jeffrey Amherst noted 'Johnson had intelligence of their [French] approach and dispersed his people [so] that he beat and routed them, [and] took 160 prisoners'

(Jeffrey Amherst, p. 151). The commander of the British force, Lieutenant Colonel Eyre Massy, commented: 'The men received the enemy with vast resolution, and never fired one shot, until we could almost reach them with our bayonets' (Brumwell, p. 253).

On 25 July, Pouchot ordered a raiding party of 150 men to attack the British trenches. The attack failed, and on 26 July, the French surrendered the fort. The survivors from the battle of La Belle Famille had already withdrawn towards Fort Detroit in the west, and the surrender of Fort Niagara effectively destroyed the French presence on the western frontier. Any threat to Fort Pitt had already been removed when the forts at Presque Isle and Venango were abandoned.

Canadian theater

In May 1759, Montcalm learned that a sizeable British fleet was heading towards Quebec City from Louisbourg. Until this news was received, many in the French command had expected that the attack would come from the Lake Champlain region. The St. Lawrence River was widely considered too difficult for a full fleet to navigate. However, unknown to the French, a young Royal Navy officer, James Cook, had surveyed the St. Lawrence, giving the British the information they needed to stage a waterborne assault. Units of militia and Indians were called to Quebec to bolster the French defense, and by late May 14,000 men had been deployed to defend Quebec. These included five regular battalions, most of the Marines for New France, and militia units. A French observer described preparations:

all along the [St. Lawrence] coast as far as Montmorency Falls, redoubts, bastions and batteries were placed at a distance of a gunshot from one another, and here M. de Montcalm placed his whole army (Northcliffe Collection, p. 215).

The French regulars were stationed in the center with militia and a stiffening of marines to their left and right. The gates of

Major General James Wolfe (Roger-Viollet)

Quebec City were heavily barricaded and more than 100 artillery pieces put in place.

The British force, as mentioned previously, numbered just under 9,000 men. (French intelligence reports had consistently overestimated the actual size of the fleet.) On 21 June, the British fleet was first sighted from Quebec. After a series of reconnaissance and surveying missions, the fleet landed the British force on Isle d'Orleans on 26 June. The British troops were able to land unopposed, opposite the French lines at Beauport. Montcalm ordered fire ships to be deployed against the British anchorage, but, as an eyewitness noted, 'fire-ships were sent down to burn enemy shipping, but, instead of doing it, what was our surprise to see the fire ships ablaze two leagues away' (Northcliffe Collection, p. 216). On the evening of 29 June, a British brigade under the command of Brigadier Robert Monckton landed at Point Levi, opposite Quebec City. The brigade had cleared the area and heights by 30 June, and by 12 July had established batteries to fire on Quebec City.

The two remaining brigades, under the command of Brigadiers James Murray and George Townshend, landed opposite the left flank of the French positions stationed at Montmorency Falls on 10 July. Wolfe had decided to attempt to turn the French left flank at some point. Montcalm did not move across the Montmorency to attack Wolfe's new camp. Wolfe sent out skirmishing parties in an attempt to force Montcalm into attacking him across the river, but Montcalm did not move.

Wolfe decided to make a combined amphibious attack from the St. Lawrence and across the Montmorency River against the French left flank at Montmorency Falls. On the morning of 31 July, the Royal Navy began to bombard the Montmorency positions. This alerted the French to the possibility of a major attack, and Montcalm reinforced this position with men from the center and right flank. The landing did not take place until 5.00 pm on the 31st, when the British landed the 'Louisbourg

Grenadiers' and elements of the 60th Foot from the St. Lawrence. These troops were earmarked to seize two redoubts, the first of which was speedily completed. Reinforcements from two other regiments were then landed. What happened next destroyed any hope of a British victory. Accounts vary of exactly what happened and who was responsible, but it appears that the grenadiers rushed forward and seized a redoubt at the base of the hill, without having received orders to do so. This action undermined the British commanders' plan to launch a combined attack. A sergeant-major of the grenadiers recalled:

we fixed our bayonets and beat our grenadiers march and so advanced on, during all this time their cannon played very briskly on us, but their small arms in their trenches lay cool till they were sure of their mark then poured their small shot like showers of hail, which caused our brave grenadiers to fall very fast (Journal of a Sergeant Major, p. 10).

Other observers were more critical of the grenadiers' actions. A junior officer. Lieutenant Hamilton commented:

[t]he check the grenadiers met with yesterday will it is hoped be a diffusion to them for the future. They ought to know that such impetuous, irregular, un-soldierlike behaviour destroys all order and makes it impossible for their commanders to form any disposition for an attack and puts it out of the general's power to execute his plans … [T]he very first fire of the enemy was sufficient to repulse men who had lost all sense of order and military discipline (6707-11).

James Wolfe recorded his thoughts: 'the grenadiers landed … their disorderly march and strange behaviour necessity of calling them off and desisting from the attack … [M]any experienced officers hurt in this foolish business' (Wolfe, 31 July). A French observer noted that '[Montcalm] allowed the enemy to advance within easy musket range, when he ordered his army to fire'.

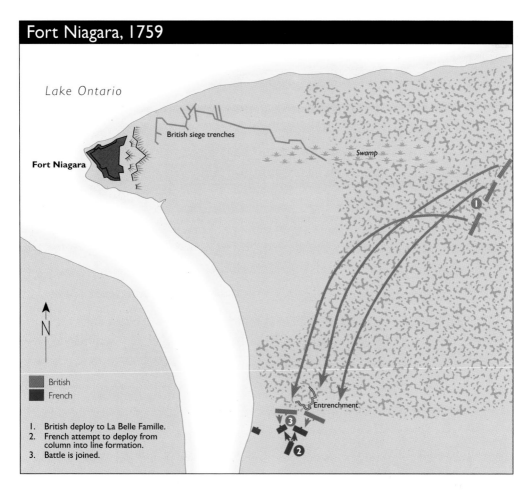

Fort Niagara, 1759

Lake Ontario

British siege trenches

Fort Niagara

Swamp

N

British
French

1. British deploy to La Belle Famille.
2. French attempt to deploy from column into line formation.
3. Battle is joined.

Entrenchment

(Northcliffe, p. 218). The outcome of the engagement was succinctly conveyed by Marquis de Bougainville: 'the enemy was repulsed with a loss of six or seven hundred men, and in the retreating they burned two of their anchored vessels' (Bougainville, p. 318). In the end the estimate of British casualties was just over 400 killed and wounded.

The French did not follow up the British withdrawal, and the British were able to leave unmolested. The main French army had not been destroyed, however, which enormously frustrated Wolfe. He continued to send detachments of light infantry, Indians, and rangers out to destroy French villages in an attempt to draw Montcalm out of his entrenchment and into open battle. As he stated on 7 August, 'large detachments sent to scour the woods

and to oblige the enemy to keep at a distance and to prepare the troops for a decisive action' (Wolfe, 7 August). He was unsuccessful in provoking Montcalm throughout the month of August. A British officer noted: 'the next attempt [post-Montmorency] will, I hope, be more practicable and more successful; if we can't beat them we shall ruin their country' (Pargellis, Military Affairs, p. 434). On 9 and 10 August, a British attempt to draw battle was sent against the French positions at Point aux Trembles. As with Montmorency, these attacks failed. The French positions were very strong, and an observer described the engagement thus: 'their loss was 100 men killed and wounded the first time, and 250 the second. Our side lost two men killed and 4 or 5 wounded' (Northcliffe, p. 219).

Quebec: Direct View. (Roger-Viollet)

By early September, Wolfe felt pressure to bring the campaign to a decisive end. Autumn was approaching and the harsh Canadian winter would put a stop to the campaign, but bring no resolution. If the British withdrew it would be a major blow to morale and to the campaign in North America. Wolfe decided to take a gamble; on 6 September, he embarked five battalions on Royal Navy transports and ships and sailed up the St. Lawrence to the bottom of the bluffs below Quebec City. Testing the resolve of Montcalm to counter his aggression, his ships sailed up and down the river, making surveys of possible landing sites, until 11 September. On 12 September, he re-embarked a division of troops and sailed for the lower end of the river. Wolfe had decided on a specific point below the cliffs which led to a large plain, known as the Plains of Abraham, which stood to the west of the city. There is some controversy as to how Wolfe gained the necessary information; some sources say that Wolfe had gathered the information himself, while others claim that a French deserter pointed out the potential weak spot in the fort's defenses.

Brigadier Townsend describes what happened next in his report of the evening and morning of 13 September:

light infantry scramble up a woody precipice in order to secure ye landing of the troops by dislodging a Captains Guard, defending a small intrenched road ye troops were to move up. After a little firing ye light infantry gained the top of the Precipice and dispersed the Captain's Guard ... by which means the troops... soon got up and were immediately formed. The boats as they emptied were sent back directly for the second disembarkation, which I immediately made ... General Wolfe thereupon began to form his army (Northcliffe, p. 419).

Montcalm thought that Wolfe's landing was a trick. A British observer recorded that 'the Marquis de Montcalm when he heard the British had ascended the hill still believed it to be a feint' (Add Mss 45662). He realized his mistake when the

British began to take to the field. Montcalm moved as many troops as he could over to Quebec in an attempt to destroy the British landing and positions that were being drawn up. The armies were in sight of one another, and Wolfe at last had the decisive battle that had eluded him since June.

Although there were periods of North American-style skirmishing throughout the battle, it was mostly fought in conventional style, with linear formations deciding the outcome. A British junior officer gives incredible detail of the developments of 13 September, describing how the British formed lines

... about two miles from Quebec. Here we lay on our arms and were very much annoyed by some Canadians who from behind the hills and from a thicket on our left kept a most galling fire ... [A]t about 9am the enemy [French] had drawn up ... [They] advanced towards us briskly and in good order. We stood to receive them. They began fire at too great a distance ... as they came nearer fired on them by divisions ... [F]ire made them waiver a bit ... [H]owever they still advanced pretty quick. We increased our fire without altering our position. When they were 60 yards gave them a full fire, fixed bayonets and under cover of smoke pushed at them. When they perceived us they immediately turned their backs and fled (7204-6-2).

A British Sergeant-Major recalled: 'in about a quarter of an hour the enemy gave way on all sides, when a terrible slaughter ensued from the quick Fire of our field guns and musketry,

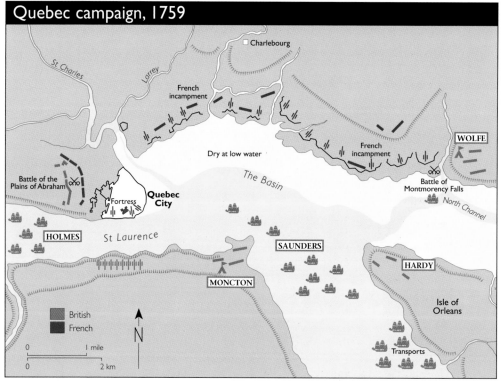

Quebec campaign, 1759

Attack at Montmorency Falls. In the foreground, the Royal Navy ships can clearly be seen giving fire support to the troops on the beaches. In the distance are British artillery firing at Quebec from the south bank of the river. (National Archives of Canada)

with which we pursued them to the walls of the town' (Sergent Major, p. 22). The British lost 50 men killed, including Wolfe, who died of gunshot wounds, and 500 wounded. The French lost more than 1,500 killed, wounded, and taken prisoner. Montcalm was mortally wounded, and died on 14 September in the city.

The battle for control of the city and fortress was far from over. The town and fortress had still not been taken, and the British began to build a camp to lay siege to the town. Reinforcements and artillery were brought over from Point Levis. Marquis de Bougainville and a large part of the French force had not yet been engaged. He reported:

I was not informed of it [arrival of British troops on the Plains of Abraham] until nine in the morning. I marched at once, but when I

came within range of the battle, our army was beaten and in retreat. The entire English Army advanced to attack me. I retreated before them and posted myself so as to cover the retreat of our army, or join with it, or to march again against the enemy if it was judged proper ... On the 18th I marched with six hundred men to throw myself into Quebec ... I was only three quarters of a league from Quebec when I learned that the city had surrendered. It had been bombarded for sixty-eight days ... [W]e spent three months in bivouac. Just the same, the English hold only the outer walls and the King [Louis XV] still holds the colony (Bougainville, pp.320-1).

While the British had been very successful in 1759, the French still had a large force stationed outside Quebec and in Montreal. The momentum that had shifted to the British in 1758 continued in 1759, but the French remained defiant in the face of defeat. The British were surrounded at Quebec. Winter was coming and the

British volunteers scaling the cliffs below the Plains of Abraham. (National Archives of Canada)

St. Lawrence would freeze, preventing the Royal Navy from delivering supplies. A major reinforcement of troops and materiel was required to contend with the encroaching French forces, and then to march to Montreal to take on the French units remaining there. The Battle of the Plains of Abraham was a critical turning point in the campaign, but it did not end the conflict. As a British observer, Lieutenant Williamson, noted: 'we are masters of the capital its true but it does not follow from thence that we have conquered the whole country, that entirely depends on our fleet' (7311-85). A second battle outside Quebec and a campaign against Montreal would need to be won before the British could claim victory in North America.

1760

The fighting in 1760 was marked by two major engagements: the second Battle of the Plains of Abraham (also known as Sainte-Foy) and the British offensive against the last remaining French post, Montreal. This section will look first at the Canadian theater of operations as this was the first, and most significant, campaign of 1760.

Canadian theater

The British garrison left in Quebec City spent the winter months in a virtual state of siege. They were holed up in the city and a few surrounding positions in the countryside, closed off from the outside world by the frozen St. Lawrence River. During the winter the British suffered due to the lack of proper winter housing. As a British observer noted: 'during the whole siege from first to last, 535 houses were burnt down, among [them] the whole eastern part of the lower town' (Sergeant-Major, p. 24). It was estimated that by March 1760, half of the garrison force was on the sick list due to scurvy

and illnesses aggravated by the weather conditions. The British, under the command of Major General Murray, were also forced to send forage parties outside the city walls to

supplement their supplies. These parties
were regularly attacked by rear guards of the
French forces. During the winter of
1759–60, the British constantly anticipated

the arrival of a large French force from
Montreal. Rumors circulated for months
that the French, under the command of
Marquis de Levis, were about to march on

Quebec, creating a sense of urgency to prepare for the worst.

The French, meanwhile, had quartered some of their regulars in Montreal, as well as in outposts near Quebec. The militia had been dismissed, ready to be called up again for duty in the spring of 1760. The French decided to attack Quebec before the ice on the St. Lawrence had broken up and the British could get reinforcements. By mid-March, orders were received to gather supplies and prepare for the march to the north, and the militia was called out once again. On 20 April, the French forces began to march. The column numbered more than 6,000 men, comprising eight regular battalions, 20 Marine companies, 3,000 militia, and 400 Indians. As the force marched north, various detachments were called in and the number rose to over 8,000 effectives.

The British received reports of a French column approaching from Montreal. One British observer recalled that 'during ye night of the 26th and 27th [a soldier] brought certain intelligence that the French were in motion to come by ye way of Lorette and St. Foy to cut off our Camp Rouge posts' (Northcliffe, p. 427). Bougainville also commented that 'the speed of [Levis'] march surprised the enemy' (Bougainville, p. 325). The French drove off any British light troops they encountered and began to build a camp at Sainte-Foy, at the western edge of the Plains of Abraham. General Murray made a critical mistake at this point; instead of assessing the situation and numbers of French forces, he decided to advance out of the city and prepare an entrenchment. He could have waited behind the walls of the city until the ice broke up and a reliving force had arrived. Instead, as one British officer, captain Knox recalled, 'about seven o'clock our army marched out to the Heights of Abraham with a respectable artillery' (Knox Journal, p. 246). A French observer, J. Desbruyeres, described '[Murray's] garrison consisting of

3,000 men ... the numbers of French appearing but small their brigades being then sheltered by the woods' (Northcliffe, p. 427).

The 10 British battalions were drawn up on the heights and as the French army was in disorder they moved to attack. The French began to deploy from column into line as the British approached. The first volleys occurred on the British right and French left flank between forward units. British light infantry engaged and

Death of James Wolfe. (National Archives of Canada)

defeated a large group of French grenadiers. British rangers engaged French advanced troops on the French right and again the French were defeated. However, the main French force arrived at this stage and overwhelmed the British light infantry, forcing them to withdraw. They then turned their attention to the British right wing, followed by an attack on the British left flank. The French began to outflank the British line, in an attempt to get between them and the city.

The British artillery was of little use because the main battle line had shifted forward. A British officer lamented that 'our cannon were of no service to us as we could not draw them through the soft ground and gulleys of snow 3 feet deep' (7204-6-2). It was during this heavy fighting that Murray realized at last how much danger his troops were in, and ordered a withdrawal to the city. The British, supported by heavy fire into the French lines, were able to retreat in good order.

Death of Montcalm. (National Archives of Canada)

Knox reported that 'this discomfirt [withdrawal] was however so regularly conducted that the enemy did not pursue with the spirit which the vast importance of their victory required' (Knox, Journal, p. 248).

The battle had lasted just over two hours. One-third of the British force had been killed, wounded, or captured, while the French had lost 2,000 men. By 29 April, the French were within 600 yards of the city and began to build trenches and siege batteries to pound the city into submission. The British responded by further reinforcing their own batteries and positions. As Bougainville noted, the deciding factor during the siege was not Levis' troops and artillery; 'the arrival of an English squadron decided the matter, it was necessary to raise the siege' (Bougainville, p. 325). On 15 May, the Royal Navy arrived

to lift the siege of Quebec. The French withdrew, except for a small force ordered to shadow the British movements from Quebec to Montreal.

Advance on Montreal

General Amherst decided to attack Montreal with another multi-pronged movement. After Murray and his troops had been re-supplied and reformed in Quebec, he was ordered to advance down the St. Lawrence from the northeast. On 2 July, Murray and 2,400 regulars embarked for Montreal, followed by a reinforcement of just over 1,000 men from Louisbourg. The second prong, under the command of Brigadier William de Haviland, was to march with 3,400 regulars, provincials, and Indians from Lake Champlain up the St. John River and then north-west towards Montreal. De Haviland began his march in August. The

Ruins of Quebec after the siege of 1759.
(National Archives of Canada)

third prong and largest force was to be under the command of General Amherst himself. Amherst, with a force of 10,000 regulars and provincials, planned to launch an attack from Fort Oswego and then Fort Frontenac up the St. Lawrence to attack Montreal from the west. He began his advance on 10 August.

Murray's force should have had to contend with French forces at Trois Rivieres, but he decided to avoid the 2,000 troops stationed there. He bypassed Trois Rivieres altogether and sailed for Montreal, landing just north at Sorel. The French forces in the area were gathering to destroy his force, but Murray sent out rangers and other units with proclamations for the militia to lay down their arms, which many did, after hearing reports that those who refused to surrender were being burned out of their houses. By the end of August most of the French forces opposing Murray had gone home.

De Haviland successfully cut off Bougainville's force of 1,000 from their lines of communication with St. Jean and

Marquis de Levis is hailed by his men after the Battle of
Sainte-Foy. (Ann Ronan Picture Library)

Fraser at Quebec. (Roger-Viollet)

Chambly, stranding them on the Isle-aux-Noix. His rangers and other forces roamed the countryside, forcing Bougainville to withdraw towards St. Jean, where he met up with additional French forces and staged a further withdrawal towards Montreal. The French forces opposing de Haviland also began to suffer from desertion losses. De Haviland continued moving towards the St. Lawrence. Forward units of Murray and de Haviland made contact in early September.

Amherst encountered and fought several small French units on his march up the St. Lawrence, but nature proved the most difficult obstacle, specifically the rapids just outside Montreal. His force was somewhat battered by their crossing, but landed at La Chine, 14 km (nine miles) from Montreal, on 6 September. Montreal was slowly being surrounded.

The Marquis de Levis recognized that his force was slowly disappearing as the British advanced. Murray had crossed the St. Lawrence and began to cut off the city from the east, while Amherst set up camp to the west. De Haviland's force was approaching the city from the south. Amherst's column was beginning to move heavy artillery from La Chine. With the French forces melting away, Vaudreuil, the

French governor, and senior French military officers held a council of war to decide the next step. Negotiations with Amherst began, and on 8 September the capitulation was signed.

One aspect of the negotiated peace was that the French soldiers were to lay down their arms and promise not to serve again during the present war. Some French officers felt that this was an intolerable condition, but the number of desertions from their ranks left them powerless to negotiate. The brother of Jeffrey Amherst, William, stated the reasons for such harsh conditions on the French:

the General's [Amherst] reason which he has given for imposing such harsh terms on he regulars that they cannot return with honour is a series of bad behaviour during this present war in the country in letting ... the Indians commit the worst cruelties (William Amherst).

Some French officers considered this reason particularly hypocritical, given the British Army's own record. The British had waged a devastating war on the civilian population during 1759 in and around Quebec with not just the help of allied Indians, but brutal force imposed by their own regulars.

Thomas Brown, a Rogers' Ranger

As noted in the section dealing with the British forces, the Ranger Corps that developed in New England and Nova Scotia was considered to be an elite force, considerably feared by its French and Indian enemies. The Rangers drew most of their men from the frontier regions, selecting those considered capable of enduring the hardships of fighting in the forest. The following is an excerpt from a narrative of a ranger from the Rogers' Ranger Corps.

Thomas Brown was born in Charlestown, Massachusetts in 1740. He decided to go to war fairly early in the conflict; while serving as an apprentice, at the age of 16 he enlisted in 'Major Rogers' Corps of Rangers', joining Captain Speakman's Company in May 1756. The way the text is written implies that this was a newly raised unit. Brown describes how he and others marched to Albany, New York, where they arrived on 1 August, and then moved on to Fort Edward.

Brown's narrative relates how, upon arrival at Fort Edward, he and other Rangers were sent out on 'Scouts', which today would be defined as patrols. He mentions that, during one of these Scouts, he managed to kill an Indian. He does not, however, provide any information about the amount or type of training that he received, and the text implies that the Rangers learned their trade of scouting and ambushing on the job.

Brown's Scouts expeditions took place during the late summer, autumn and early winter months of 1756 and 1757, during the same period that French and Indian raiding parties were operating in the area. Both sides were seeking intelligence on the preparations of the forces operating around Forts William Henry and Carillon (Ticonderoga), as well as carrying out raiding parties on convoys travelling to the forts.

Although Thomas Brown does not provide details concerning his training, he does describe, in great detail, a long distance 'Scout' to ambush French and Indian supply columns operating in the Fort Carillon and Crown Point region. This Scout, which left Fort William Henry on 18 January 1757, is very likely the Battle of the Snowshoes, which is described below in more detail. According to Brown, the Scout consisted of 60 Rangers, including Major Robert Rogers, the Corps commander. All of these, according to Brown, were volunteers: 'All were Voluntiers that went on this Scout' (p. 5). In other words, unlike other operations, the men on this Scout chose to go rather than being ordered to do so.

Brown relates how the Rangers arrived on the road leading from Fort Carillon to Crown Point. As they came in sight of Lake Champlain, Major Rogers spotted some 50 sleighs on the lake's frozen surface. He ordered the Rangers to lay in ambush and, when the French sleighs were 'near enough ... to pursue them' (p. 5). He describes his proximity to Major Rogers as the Rangers ambushed the party, as well as the Rangers' capture of seven Frenchmen in the raid. (He also notes that many men from the sleighs managed to escape, either to Crown Point or Fort Carillon, alerting the French and Indians based at both forts to the presence of Rogers and his Scout.) The Rangers interrogated the prisoners and learned that there were 500 French Regulars based at Fort Carillon. Major Rogers decided that the Scout should return to Fort William Henry and that, due to the amount of snow on the ground, they would return the same way they had come, outfitted with snowshoes. The French and Indians in the area, alerted to the Rangers' presence, set out to destroy Rogers and his men.

Within a few hours of the march, the Scout was spotted and attacked. Brown describes how:

We march'd in an Indian-File and kept the Prisoners in the Rear, lest we should be attack'd: We proceeded in this Order about a Mile and a half, and as we were ascending a Hill, and the Centre of our Men were at the Top, the French, to the number of 400, besides 30 or 40 Indians, fir'd on us before we discovered them (p. 6).

Major Rogers ordered his Rangers to advance, sending them into withering fire. Brown describes what happened to him and some of the other men, highlighting the brutal reality of eighteenth century forest warfare. He states that:

I receiv'd a Wound from the Enemy ... thro' the Body, upon which I retir'd into the Rear, to the Prisoner I had taken on the Lake, knock'd him on the Head and killed him, lest he should Escape and give Information to the Enemy (p. 6).

Brown was almost killed by two Indians as he withdrew to the rear of the column. However, he was able to form himself, with other Rangers, into a small box of men. The fighting in the area was intense, as Brown describes:

[I] got to the Centre of our Men, and fix'd myself behind a large Pine, where I loaded and fir'd every Opportunity; after I had discharged 6 or 7 Times, there came a Ball and cut off my Gun just at the Lock. About half an Hour after, I receiv'd a Shot in my Knee; I crawled again into the Rear, and as I was turning about receiv'd a Shot in my Shoulder (p. 6).

Brown speculates that the fighting lasted for five and half hours, and notes that, while they were surrounded, the Rangers were not overwhelmed during the daylight hours. Brown contends that the Rangers inflicted more than 60 casualties on the French and Indian troops, and describes what happened as night drew in:

The Engagement held, as near as I could guess, 5 and half Hours… By the Time it grew dark and the Firing Ceased on both Sides, and as we were so few the Major [Rogers] took the Advantage of the Night and escaped with all the well Men, without informing the wounded of his Design, lest they should inform the Enemy and they should pursue him before he had got out of their Reach (p. 6).

Brown was able to make it to Captain Speakman; they and another badly wounded Ranger, named Baker, were able to make a small fire. They could not hear or see any other Rangers in the vicinity; at one moment, Captain Speakman called out to Major Rogers but received no answer. The wounded men were unable to travel, and hope of escape began to dwindle as they heard the enemy approaching. The men decided to surrender to the French, at which point Brown appears to have slipped away from the other two men at the fire. Brown's account of what occurred next says:

I crawl'd so far from the Fire that I could not be seen, though I could see what was acted at the Fire; the Indian came to Capt. Spikeman [Speakman], who was not able to resist, and stripp'd and scalp'd him alive; Baker, who was lying by the Captain, pull'd out his Knife to stab himself, which the Indian prevented and carried him away (p. 7).

Speakman, who was still alive after this attack, pleaded with Brown to kill him. Brown refused, and moved off in order to avoid a similar fate. Since he had no shoes, and the snow was quite deep, he found progress difficult. (Speakman was later beheaded by the Indians). He attempted to move around various French sentry positions and at one point, came close to being seen by a French soldier. Brown survived the night in an agony of discomfort, without adequate clothing or shoes. Around 11am the next morning, he was spotted by a small group of Indians. They rushed him and he thought it would be best to be killed outright instead of being scalped alive. He describes how:

I threw off my Blanket, and Fear and Dread quickened my Pace for a while; but, by Reason of the Loss of so much Blood from my Wounds, I soon fail'd. When they were within a few Rods of me they cock'd their Guns, and told me to stop; but I refus'd, hoping they would fire and Kill me on the spot; which I chose, rather then the dreadful Death Capt. Spikeman [sic] died of. They soon came up with me, took me by the Neck and Kiss'd me. ... They took some dry Leaves and put them into my Wounds, and then turn'd about and ordered me to follow them (p. 8).

Thomas Brown served out the remainder of the war as a captive, both of French military officers and various Indians. He travelled as far as the Mississippi River, to the west, and the Montreal region, to the north. He was returned to the British forces on 25 November 1759, after more than two years of captivity, and returned to Charlestown at the beginning of January 1760.

The economic and civilian costs

In pure economic terms, the war in both North America and the rest of the world cost France and Great Britain considerably. Britain had to pay for the upkeep of major armies in North America and Germany. The expense of building naval vessels was also significant. Even with tax levies throughout the war, the debt rose annually, and the British government was forced to borrow to make good on the shortfall. Britain did have one economic bonus during this period: the Royal Navy was dominant on the seas by 1759 and thus was able both to seize war booty and to deny access to French ports. In 1756, Great Britain's national debt was 75 million pounds; by the end of the conflict it had climbed to 133 million pounds. The continuing need to maintain garrison troops after 1763 were the principal reasons for the controversial demand that the wealthy Thirteen Colonies to take on some of the costs of their own protection in the 1760s.

France was in much the same financial position as Great Britain. However, France decided to borrow more money rather than levy taxes on the population. Unlike Britain, her trade suffered heavily from the Royal Navy blockade of the French ports, causing a further loss of revenue during the conflict. In 1753 the national debt was 1,360 million livres. By the end of the conflict the national debt had nearly doubled, climbing to 2,350 million livres. It cost 24.5 million livres a year just to keep the French armies in the field; most of this was spent on the regular army in Germany.

The war also proved a major financial drain on the Thirteen Colonies and New France. Each of the Thirteen Colonies provided varying levels of support in the form of supplies, provincial troops, recruits for regular regiments, and billeting of troops. Some colonies, such as South Carolina, were not particularly willing to support the war effort; this was often linked to the level of belief in the cause of the war demonstrated by elected and appointed officials. As the fortunes of war began to turn in Britain's favor, some colonies grew less enthusiastic about committing money and men to a campaign happening far away to the north of them. Others saw the threat diminish in their own region and decided that the war was not as important as they had previously believed.

The British commander-in-chief periodically had to rely upon local merchants for specie, or borrow money to pay for supplies and provisions for the coming year. Shipments of money from Great Britain often arrived later than officers would have preferred. In 1759, General Amherst called upon the New York Assembly for a loan to pay for his campaign. In both New France and the Thirteen Colonies, many merchants and business people came to rely upon government and military clients for the main part of their business. One issue that did not affect the Thirteen Colonies was shortage of food, for either civilians or soldiers. While the soldiers may have been restricted at times during the campaigns, the civilian population did not have rationing imposed upon them, unlike New France.

The colonies were asked each year to provide provincial soldiers for campaign duty. This entailed men serving outside their respective colonies. Each year a new force was raised, and then released from duty at the end of the campaign season. The British government provided subsidies for the raising of these forces. Regardless, by 1759 assemblymen from several colonies asserted that the colonies could no longer provide the numbers needed. Considerable numbers of provincial troops had been lost to battle or sickness; other men seeking adventure or pay had also left the colonies to enlist in the Royal Navy or the British regulars. Colonial leaders feared that the constant drain would have a negative effect on colonial farming and trades. They were also angered by the British government's method of handling the issue: each year the British government provided subsidies for the past campaign season, reimbursing the Thirteen Colonies for about 40 percent of their total military expenses. As the new campaign season approached, officials would threaten not to pay the subsidies owed unless each colony provided the desired number of soldiers.

The numbers of soldiers provided and the money raised by each colony also became a sore point between the colonies. Colonies such as Massachusetts Bay, Connecticut, New York, New Jersey, New Hampshire, and Rhode Island provided considerable support to the war effort. They were resentful of the smaller amounts of support provided by other colonies such as Georgia, South and North Carolina, and Maryland. Georgia was a poor colony and was unable to raise provincial troops; the colony's security was provided for by British regulars. South Carolina only provided for three companies of provincial infantry and two of horse. North Carolina and Maryland were criticized for not providing any major support to the war effort; both of these colonies felt less threatened by the conflict than their neighbors to the north. The border colonies of Pennsylvania and Virginia provided sufficient men and support for the war effort as long as they felt directly threatened, but as the war in the west dwindled and the focus shifted to the invasion of Canada, their support began to dry up as well.

This constant need for soldiers and supplies from the colonies was an ongoing source of friction between British military officials and colonial assemblymen. Each side accused the other of not carrying its share of the load or of being autocratic. The debate became so acrimonious that even the end of the war did not resolve it and argument, continued through the financial crises of the postwar period. It eventually led

to more drastic demands by the British government and, eventually, war between Britain and the Thirteen Colonies.

The situation in New France was overall more difficult. One of the major problems was the food supply, which proved to be insufficient on more than one occasion. One possible reason for this was the fact that only a small portion of the province had been cultivated properly. This level of cultivation was satisfactory during the peace years, but when war broke out demand increased. The crop yield, which had been sufficient for the population as well as supplies to the Marines, militia, and allied Indians, could not stretch to accommodate the 6,000 regular soldiers who were shipped to New France during the war. The plan was that soldiers would be shipped with their own provisions, and that each year a large supply convoy would arrive from France to support the offensive operations of the campaign season.

The reality, however, was that due to the successful Royal Navy blockade, the number of ships that arrived each year dwindled steadily. The situation reached crisis point in 1757. A large flotilla arrived with stores, but it was still not enough to support both the soldiers and citizens of New France. Montcalm recorded that 'provisions fail the people, reduced to a quarter pound of bread. Perhaps the rations of the soldiers must be reduced again' (Sautai, pp. 38–39). In June 1757, all grain was centrally stored and made into bread by the colonial government. Daily allowances were allocated to all the people within the colony. Nature also had a role to play in the colony's plight; the harvests for 1756 and 1757 were poor, followed by the unusually severe winter of 1757–58. The population was forced to consume the seed crop of wheat for the following year. France responded and three ships were sent with seed, which reached their destination.

The results of the harvest had an additional effect on the army: the composition of the colonial militia. The militia, as described previously, was drawn from all sectors of the French community, including farmers. If the threat to New France did not subside for a significant period of time and the men could not be released, the yield of the harvest might be adversely affected. As a result, at times militiamen took matters into their own hands and returned to their farms without having been discharged. Widespread desertion, in turn, put French commanders in a precarious position. The two conflicting priorities created an apparently insoluble dilemma.

Corruption was another major issue for New France. The colony's chief colonial administrator, Francois Bigot, had created a monopoly on goods sold within the colony to benefit himself and some of his friends. With the advent of war, the principal products sold in New France were no longer furs, fish, or skins, but military provisions and supplies. Bigot was in charge of the contracts for military stores supplied to the troops, and he and his cronies were lining their pockets. When food was rationed, the sale of bread also came under Bigot's control, when the French Crown bought the grain and made it into bread. The prices that the Crown paid for the flour were set and controlled by Bigot, as was the price of bread sold to colonists.

Paper currency in New France was steadily devalued over the course of the war. French attempts to send specie to the colony only sped up the process. Farmers only sold to soldiers who had been paid in specie, and both civilians and soldiers hoarded the coins. New France was paying over 12 million livres a year by 1757 for the upkeep of New France. By 1758, the British blockade and the shift within the French court to a Continental strategy had left New France almost abandoned. Ships with food, supplies, soldiers, or currency were diverted to other regions, and New France was left to defend itself.

Portions of the civilian populations of both sides suffered directly as a result of the war, and there were examples of outright 'cruelty' by both sides. One of the most famous cases is the expulsion of the Acadian (French) population from Nova Scotia by the British. After the capture of Fort Beausejour in 1755, the question arose of what to do

with the Acadians. Many colonial governors, such as William Shirley of Massachusetts, considered them a nuisance and a risk to the security of Nova Scotia. The situation came to a head when the British produced an oath of allegiance to the British Crown, and required Acadians to adhere to it. Many of the Acadians, however, preferred to remain neutral. They had no desire to swear allegiance and wished to be exempt from military duty. British commanders reported that their mood changed from neutral to hostile when rumors began to circulate of a French fleet arriving in the Bay of Fundy.

The British were in a difficult position. The Acadians lived on a particularly strategic piece of land, and the war had just begun in earnest. There were also British land speculators waiting to cash on the excellent lands occupied by the Acadian farms.

British military and colonial officials met in Halifax, and determined that the Acadians should be forcibly removed from their homes and transported to the Thirteen Colonies. They decided against sending them to Quebec or Louisbourg because in either place they would provide valuable reinforcements for the militia. The Acadian villages were emptied and the settlers marshaled towards the Bay of Fundy where, over the course of autumn 1755, ships arrived from the Thirteen Colonies to transport the people. The British authorities did their best to keep villages and families together, so as not to cause further psychological damage to the uprooted Acadians.

In the end more than 6,000 men, women and children were transported. Some Acadians, upon receiving word of the British plan, escaped to Quebec. Other groups of people withdrew into the woods of Nova Scotia. Some of the men in these groups carried out a guerrilla campaign over the coming years. Many of the Acadian homes and farms were burned to prevent escaped refugees returning to their homes. The British government also hoped that people would surrender to British authorities after they realized their position was hopeless. Many of the Acadians who were sent to the

Exile of the Acadians. (National Archives of Canada)

Thirteen Colonies eventually made their way to Louisiana. Some returned to Acadia after the Treaty of Paris and continue to live in the same districts today. The story of the Acadians was later made famous in Longfellow's poem 'Evangeline'.

The British continued this policy for most of the war. Following the seizure of Louisbourg in 1758, General Amherst decided to round up and transport the civilian populations in and around Louisbourg, as well as the French colonists on St. Jean Island (Prince Edward Island). All colonists who took up arms were considered prisoners of war and were subsequently transported to Great Britain along with the French soldiers. Colonists who did not take up arms were transported to France. More than 8,000 people were transported from Cape Breton and St. Jean Island. Amherst decided on this policy after the killings at Fort William Henry. He felt that the French deserved such treatment after what he considered their leniency in allowing the Indians to commit such crimes against civilians.

Warfare all along the frontier was brutal. Many white settlers on both sides were taken prisoner or killed by roaming bands of allied Indians, French militia, and rangers. This type of random violence had occurred for many years since the mid-1600s, but the onset of the French-Indian War provided a new impetus to spread fear along the frontier. The British forces, especially the rangers, were able to launch waterborne attacks into the heartland of New France and against Indian settlements along the St. Lawrence. Major General Amherst cited the abuses of the French and their Indian allies when he drew up the conditions of surrender at Montreal in 1760.

French regular soldiers generally did not come into immediate contact with the civilian population of the Thirteen Colonies. Some were involved in small-scale raids along the frontier or in clearing lands of British settlers. The major British towns did not have to contend with foreign occupation. The civilian population of New France, on the other hand, had to accommodate the presence not only of British-allied Indians and rangers, but from

1758–60 had to contend with British Army regular soldiers as well.

The major evidence of French civilians suffering at the hands of British regulars occurred during the Quebec Campaign in 1759. Major General Wolfe apparently issued orders for the destruction of the countryside. His reasoning for this was twofold: first, to deny supplies to the French garrison on the north bank of the St. Lawrence River; and second, to attempt to force Montcalm to battle. Two journal entries by British soldiers give insight into the actions of some of the British regulars at Quebec. A Sergeant-Major from a grenadier company described the actions outside Quebec:

on the 20th [August] the Louisbourg Grenadiers began their march down the main land of Quebec, in order to burn and destroy all the houses on that side … [On] the 25th began to destroy the country, burning houses, cutting down corn and the like (Sergeant-Major, p. 16).

An officer with the 15th Foot also described his experiences on a march through the countryside outside Quebec. His action, like the Sergeant-Major's, took place in August 1759. He recalled:

our light infantry and rangers marched off to the Parish of St. Nicola but a little after we passed the church of St. Antonia our advanced guard was fired upon by a party of the enemy that lay in ambush in the wood … [W]e marched to the far end of the parish when we began to burn all before us (Add Mss 45662).

The British were not always given orders to ravage the countryside; in fact it appears that sometimes the opposite happened. During the 1760 campaign, some units were ordered not to abuse the population as they marched towards Montreal. A Massachusetts provincial soldier named Sergeant David Holden noted that, when his regiment marched from Chambly to Montreal, the French population was generally very civil. He commented that

the French treat us on our march with the utmost civility more over our army was very cautious in not abusing any of them or their subsistance … General Amherst returns the troops under his command abundance of thanks for their so strictly observing his orders (Holden, p. 21).

The severity of the fighting along the frontier during the early years of the conflict created ugly situations. The attacks by the French and their allied Indians spread fear and hatred among the colonists. The killing of British civilians after the surrender of Fort William Henry provided the impetus for British reprisals when troops entered civilian areas of New France.

Jean Lowry and Titus King

Capture of colonists by Indian troops was a common feature of the French-Indian War. Two contemporary accounts of English citizens who were captives of the French-allied Indians describe very different types of treatment. One of the accounts was written by a woman and the other by a man. The first described here is a harrowing account by a woman who was seized, along with her children.

Jean Lowry was living on the frontier region of Pennsylvania when, in April 1755, a band of Indians arrived outside her homestead. They immediately killed her husband, and then, as she states: '[there] being no man in the house at that time the barbarians rushed into the house, plundered the house and did what they pleased ... [T]hey set fire to the house' (1 April 1755). Mrs Lowry and her five children were seized and forced to march overland.

After traveling for four days, a group of 50 white settlers caught up with the Indian party and fired upon them. The white settlers were able to release Mrs Lowry and her children, but their ordeal was not yet over. That evening, a larger Indian party returned and attacked the camp of the white settlers. Mrs Lowry recalled that

the savages returned and surrounded our people this gave them great advantage ... [O]ur people did the best they could for two hours. A great many of our people were killed and wounded ... [O]ne wounded man was tortured and the ladies had to watch (5 April 1755).

The whites from the party who were left alive and could still march were taken as prisoners.

Mrs Lowry and her family were ordered to march on after the man being tortured had finally died. When the Indian party reached a hunting camp, Mrs Lowry began a period of intense hardship. She described the Indians

laying upon me with their [hot] rods I being so weak and spent with fatigue could not run ... so they had their leisure to exercise their barbarous customs upon my feeble body, this left many wounds on me (8 April 1755).

It was also at this point that her eight-year-old son was taken away from her.

The Indian party marched the white prisoners into an Indian village a few days later. As they entered both Mrs Lowry and her eldest daughter were given 'an awful beating' (10 April 1755). Many of the other white prisoners were 'adopted' by Indian households, and here Mrs Lowry lost her eldest daughter who was 10, and another daughter who was six, to Indian families. As she continued marching up the Allegheny River with the two children still with her, she came across the son that she had lost, but was not allowed to collect him. Mrs Lowry was a religious person, and believed that her condition and losses over the past weeks must be 'for our sins that god has delivered us into the hands of the Indians' (17 April 1755).

It appears that one important reason for the treatment that Mrs Lowry particularly received was her resolve not to be seen to cooperate with the Indians in any way – either by accepting adoption by Indians or by doing any work for them. On 23 April, the Indian party entered another village, where Mrs Lowry was beaten by several Indian women for the loss of their husbands. In this village, her two remaining children were also taken from her, although one was returned to her later in the day (24 April 1755).

Man reasoning with an Indian about to burn a captive.
(Library of Congress)

At this point, Mrs Lowry admitted that she began to moderate her behavior and to try to accept her predicament. One reason for this change of heart was that 'the Indians had threatened to sell me to the French and what cruel usage I would meet with from them' (5 May 1755). She left the Indian village for Fort Venango under the ownership of another Indian warrior. While in Fort Venango, she gave birth to another little girl, who died the same day (4 July 1755). This event makes clear that Mrs Lowry was in fact pregnant throughout the time she was marching overland. The beatings and generally poor treatment she received must have played a role in the death of the child.

The journal's pace quickens after Mrs Lowry arrived at Fort Venango, where she remained as a servant of the French commanding officer from 15 May 1755 until 27 July 1757. The French commander's wife took Mrs Lowry when she traveled from Fort Venango to Fort Niagara, and then to Montreal. In Montreal, she heard that white prisoners were being exchanged for French prisoners, and she continued to serve as a servant in Montreal until she received word of a possible exchange. In September 1758, she was allowed to proceed to Quebec City, where she was exchanged for French captives. On 16 March 1759, she returned to New York after being shipped to Great Britain. The journal records no mention of seeing any of her children ever again.

It is interesting to note how the journal of a male captive named Titus King differs from Mrs Lowry; he appears to have avoided most of the brutality that she suffered. King was a provincial soldier in Colonel Israel Williams' Regiment, Massachusetts. He and a small party of soldiers were stationed at Charlemont, 40 km (25 miles) northwest of Northampton, Massachusetts, to protect the local farming community from Indian and French irregulars. On 11 June 1755 his small band of men was attacked by a larger group of Indian warriors, and King was captured along with a small boy soldier. He noted that 'we marched 20 or 25 miles on the first day'. It is interesting to note that King's Indian captors seemed to value their prisoners rather highly. He commented that when 'the boy was not able to go any more the Indians carried him on their backs and put me to carry a pack and a gun' (12 June 1755).

The food for the trip was meager for the prisoners, and King commented on 17 June that

since we have had nothing to eat except a pigeon and an owl they killed on the way roots green barks of the tree and the like ... we was very faint and hungry ... [T]he Indians filled a large littal of this pounded corn and boiled it ... eat very heartily but I could not eat so much as I thought I should (17 June 1755).

The Indian party was marching towards Crown Point.

King and his Indian captors reached their destination in early July. King commented on the good behavior of the French officers and men: 'the French treated me pretty well with the wine and brandy and good manners'. The next day, 18 July, King left with his Indian captors, traveling by canoe up Lake Champlain towards St. Jean. One evening the Indians got very drunk and the next day, due to their hangovers, King was forced to be one of the oarsmen on one of the canoes for some of the day. It was while the Indian party was traveling on Lake Champlain that King was told that he was not going to Montreal to be exchanged, but was to become an Indian and go with the warriors to their village. One of the warriors commented, 'Frenchmen no good, Englishmen no good, Indian very good' (21 July 1755).

It appears that King accepted his new role. He was stripped of his shirt and had his hair cut and his face painted. The party arrived at

St. Jean on 22 July, where once again King was treated well. He noted, perhaps a bit regretfully, that 'the French treated me pretty well ... [but] I must live with them [Indians] in their wigwams' instead of accepting the French offer to stay with them (22 July 1755). King, repainted, and the Indians moved out on 23 July for the Indian village. On 25 July they arrived at the Indian village, where they were greeted by 200 Indians on the shore of the river. King described how the 'young Indians had sticks to whip us' (25 June 1755). He was ordered to run about 30 rods up a hill, with a crowd on both sides. He expected to be beaten, but the crowd dispersed as he ran up the hill and he was not. He had apparently been accepted as part of the village.

As he noted, however, he was still a captive of one of the Indian warriors. He remained part of the village for the rest of 1755, all of 1756, and most of 1757. As many Indian warriors left the village to fight, King became an important male figure. He was adopted as a grandfather by one of the families after their grandfather failed to return. It was expected that King would have an Indian woman and have children to help populate the village. He was formally put in Indian dress and accepted as an Indian. During the campaign season of 1757, he left with a band of warriors for Fort William Henry. However, he was sold to the French for 120 livres and sent to Montreal. He was then exchanged by the French, and by the summer of 1758, he had returned to Northampton via Great Britain.

Titus King had not endured the incredible suffering that Mrs. Lowry had lived through. This may have been partly due to the value the Indians placed on a male captive over a female captive. It may also have been due to the fact that King seemed resigned to his fate and did what he was told, whereas Mrs. Lowry had put up considerable resistance.

Treaty of Paris and the Indian uprising

The capture of Montreal more or less brought the war in North America to an end, but the larger conflict, the Seven Years' War, dragged on outside North America for another two years. Prussia, in alliance with Great Britain, continued a defensive war against Russia and Austria, and war with France continued on the continent as well. The British also provided ongoing funding and men to His Britannic Majesty's Army campaign against the French in Hanover. France and Great Britain also continued to wage war in the colonies of the Caribbean and India. Spain entered the conflict on France's side in 1761. The British had become very proficient in amphibious operations by 1760, and the Royal Navy was dominant on the seas. Campaigns against the Spanish and French colonies in the Caribbean, India, and the Philippines were all great successes for Britain. The war finally came to an end more as a product of exhaustion on the part of all parties involved than any definitive victory. For more detail, see Essential Histories *The Seven Years' War*.

Two peace treaties formally concluded the Seven Years' War. The first, signed by France, Great Britain, and Spain, was agreed on 10 February 1763 and known as the Treaty of Paris. The second, known as the Treaty of Hubertusburg, was concluded between Austria and Prussia on 15 February 1763. Only the Treaty of Paris will be examined here, since it had ramifications for the conflict in North America.

Great Britain's portion of the treaty has been characterized as swapping snow for sugar cane and sun. All of the French lands east of the Mississippi River were awarded to Britain, including the Ohio River valley, which had been one of the principal causes of the conflict. Quebec and Cape Breton were also ceded to Great Britain. Of all her North

American possessions, France was allowed to retain control of only two small islands off the coast of Newfoundland, St. Pierre and Miquelon. In exchange, France received the islands of Guadeloupe and Martinique, which she had lost during the conflict. Britain also took possession of Florida from Spain, in exchange for the Philippines and Cuba. Great Britain was now the only major European power on the Atlantic Seaboard of North America, controlling the entire coastline from Newfoundland in the north to Florida in the south.

Even with Great Britain in undisputed control of the area, problems arose almost immediately in the newly acquired territories of the Ohio River valley and the lands west of the Appalachians. The French had maintained forts and a small settler presence in the region, but had infringed little upon the local Indian population. With the British in control, some of the British colonists wished to push west from the Atlantic seaboard and open up the interior for settlement. Naturally, the Indians who were already living in the area objected to this plan, and the determination of the white settlers to carry on regardless led to a large-scale Indian uprising, known as Pontiac's Rebellion, in 1763–64.

When fighting ended in 1760 after the seizure of Montreal, Rogers' Rangers and the 60th Regiment were sent to occupy the French forts in the west, at Detroit and along the Great Lakes. The troops were given orders to accept the surrender of the French forces in the region, meet with various Indian chiefs, and explain that Great Britain had taken control of the area. Soldiers and officers were also instructed not to give the Indians gifts, ammunition, or guns, a policy which offended the Indians in the region who had recently been waging war against the British and expected to be rewarded for promising loyalty to the new government. The soldiers were warned not to give offense to any one group; peace was to be maintained at all costs.

Not only did the British disappoint the Indians who had been allied with the French; they also alienated the Senecas, one of the tribes of the Six Nations, who considered that the British had failed to keep promises made during the war. To persuade Indian tribes to side with them, the British had signed agreements promising that lands west of the Alleghenies would only be used by Indians for hunting. Trading of European goods in these areas would be cheaper and fur and skins would sell at higher prices.

As early as 1761, Indian representatives, including members of the Six Nations, demanded a meeting with the governor of Pennsylvania. The Indians contended that the British were not keeping to their promises. White settlers were moving into the region west of the Alleghenies, goods were still being sold at high prices, and furs and skins were not appreciating in value. The Indian representatives also stated a further concern, that 'there are forts all round us and therefore we are apprehensive that death is coming upon us' (Bouquet, Mss 21655). Indians who had sided with the British were also not allowed to move west into territory formerly belonging to the French. This proscription irked many Indians, who felt they had scores to settle with the French-allied tribes, and who wanted access to the hunting grounds in the Ohio River valley.

The white settlers, for their part, felt they had a perfect right to settle where they chose. Colonel Bouquet of the 60th soon became an unpopular figure, since he did what he could to arrest whites operating illegally in the region. To make matters worse, a set of orders was then handed down that Indians could be given small gifts for capturing illegal white settlers and bringing them to outposts of the 60th along the frontier (Bouquet, MSS21653). White settlers found in the area had to demonstrate their purpose for being there and present proper paperwork. Failing to do so meant that they would be arrested, and under the circumstances they were subject to military, not civilian law. White settlers were furious at what they perceived as the army's favoring the Indians over them, and the soldiers' performance of their duty progressively soured relations between settlers and regulars.

Given the size of the area that the soldiers had to patrol, white settlers were able to elude them without great difficulty, slip into the prohibited areas, and carry out large-scale hunting west of the Appalachians. The Indians in the region grew increasingly restless about these incursions, and clashes between Indians and settlers began to occur. By 1761, the Senecas, a formerly British-allied tribe, were holding meetings with members of the Delawares and Miamis to discuss attacks on the frontier region forts. They did agree that they were not ready for an all-out rebellion. At the same time as the war raged in Europe and the rest of the world, French settlers in the area began to fan the flames by meeting with various Indian chiefs and discussing a possible return of the French to the region.

By 1762, the British troops on the frontier were in a difficult position, caught between white settlers and Indian tribes. Bouquet recognized the potential for even greater trouble and attempted to reinforce the various forts, preparing them for a possible outbreak of violence. Bouquet also advised General Amherst, commander-in-chief North America, of the rising tension on the frontier and asked for further reinforcements. Most of the troops from North America were involved in the amphibious campaign in the Caribbean, however, so sufficient reinforcement was not possible.

The Indian uprising began in late 1762 when Seneca warriors killed two white settlers. War belts were sent by the Senecas to the western tribes as the signal to begin hostilities. While extremely dangerous to those in the frontier region, the uprising was not a completely unanimous effort. Members of the Senecas, Ottawas, Hurons, Delawares, and Miamis participated, but no tribe involved all of its warriors. Additionally, none of the western tribes, such as the Sauks, Puans, and Foxes, raised the war belt.

The purpose of the Indian uprising is still unclear. Its principal objective seems to have been the seizure of all British forts and posts, but then even this strategy was not implemented with any consistency. Particularly at first, the Indian effort was not a coordinated onslaught, but seemingly unrelated attacks on various forts by groups of warriors.

One indication of the fact that the Indian uprising was not as widespread or organized as it could have been was the conduct of one Indian chief, Pontiac. He was an Ottawa chief who only commanded a local village near Fort Detroit. He agreed with other Indian chiefs about the state of affairs under British governance, but instead of acting in conjunction with others, he set up a campaign against Fort Detroit by himself. Pontiac did not participate in any other actions, but Fort Detroit was such an important outpost that the British hailed him as the leading war chief and the entire uprising became known as Pontiac's Rebellion.

In early April 1763, Pontiac gathered various Indian warriors near Fort Detroit and called for action against the British fort. On 1 May Pontiac himself arrived at Fort Detroit with a small reconnaissance party to assess the British defenses and troops. He was greeted and entertained by the British commander, Major Gladwin, after which the Indian party left, promising to return at a later date. The British, although they were aware of the possibility of attack, still did not want to aggravate the situation by not being amicable. Pontiac met with another party of Indian warriors on 5 May and called for the extermination of the British at Fort Detroit. Other Indian warriors decided to join as word reached Pontiac that other forts were also going to be attacked. On 7 May, a select group of warriors marched towards Fort Detroit with weapons hidden and a plan to storm the fort.

Gladwin had received information that an attack was imminent, and had 100 men under his command. He decided to close the gates and put white traders in the area under arms to boost defensive numbers. Pontiac acted surprised when he came upon the Fort and was not received with open gates. On 8 May, other chiefs attempted to meet with Gladwin to promise that the Indians had no intention of seizing the fort. Gladwin dismissed these claims and prepared for an armed encounter. On 9 May, an armed flotilla of Indian canoes arrived. Gladwin continued to refuse to speak with the Indians, and on 10 May the siege of Fort Detroit formally began. A relief force of 95 soldiers marching toward the fort was surrounded and overwhelmed on 29 May.

Other forts along the Great Lakes and in the Ohio River valley were subsequently attacked by other Indian tribes. Some forts were seized by a surprise attack; others were able to repel the Indian attacks and then the garrison slip away during the evening. The Seneca attack at Fort Venango destroyed relations between the British and their former allies; a Seneca war party was received into the fort as allies, only to turn and massacre the garrison. By the end of June, all of the British forts along the frontier and in the newly claimed territories had been seized except for Forts Pitt, Detroit, and Niagara. Indian war parties also headed east toward Fort Bedford but were unsuccessful in capturing it. Fort Pitt was surrounded in late June, but not attacked until late July. The British managed to repulse the Indian attack, when it came, knowing that it was critical to hold Fort Pitt, as well as Niagara and Detroit, as jumping-off positions for the re-conquest of the Ohio River valley and Great Lakes Region. Colonel Bouquet and his headquarters received word of the attacks by late May.

On 28 July a relief column arrived at Fort Detroit. This force numbered 200 men drawn from regular and ranger units, but was carrying few supplies or provisions for the fort. On 31 July, the column, commanded by Captain James Dalyell, marched to destroy the Indian camp and lift the siege. They were ambushed and all but destroyed at a creek named Bloody Run, with more than 20 men killed, 30 wounded, and 100 captured. Captain Dalyell was killed in the battle, and the siege of Detroit continued.

All available troops were sent to Philadelphia to stage an expedition to relieve Fort Pitt. At this point, not only had several regiments been transported to the Caribbean to fight in the campaigns there, but the war in North America had also officially ended and many more men had been shipped home or discharged from service. Bouquet gathered a force of men from the 42nd, 77th, and 60th Regiments of Foot, as well as rangers, to open the road to Fort Pitt. He had only about 500 men with him.

Bouquet's force marched overland to Carlisle and moved out toward Fort Pitt on 18 July. They had been delayed, as previously, while the local colonial governments took their time gathering supplies for the force. The Indians besieging

Fort Pitt received word of Bouquet's movement and moved east to ambush his force. The two groups met at a place named Bushy Run, 40 km (25 miles) from Fort Pitt. On the morning of 5 August, Bouquet's forward units skirmished with Indian warriors. Bouquet, realizing that his force was in a potential ambush situation, deployed his troops in a circular defensive position and awaited the Indian attack. It came at 1.00 pm and lasted throughout the afternoon and into the evening. Bouquet's circle held out, despite many casualties. On the morning of 6 August, the Indians attacked again, undertaking coordinated attacks immediately. When Bouquet recognized that he was in danger of being breached, he decided to shorten his lines, and two light companies were ordered to fall back. The Indians saw this, mistook it for a retreat, and launched a disorganized attack.

Battle of Bushy Run, 1763

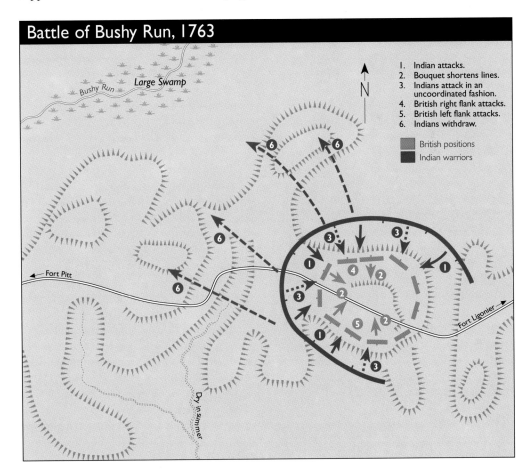

1. Indian attacks.
2. Bouquet shortens lines.
3. Indians attack in an uncoordinated fashion.
4. British right flank attacks.
5. British left flank attacks.
6. Indians withdraw.

British positions

Indian warriors

Unbeknownst to the Indians, the British had already pulled back four other companies, and the right flank of the British circle began to pour heavy fire into the attacking Indian mass, then rushed them with bayonets. The British left flank attacked the Indian mass next; the Indians attempted to withdraw, but were cut down. Bouquet related that 'two other companies were so posted as to catch them [Indians] in their retreat and entirely dispersed them, and the whole fled' (Jeffrey Amherst, p. 318). The remainder of the Indian force managed to withdraw from the field of battle. It is debatable whether Bouquet calculated the whole maneuver; what is certain, however, is that he wished to shorten his lines, recognized the tactical advantage given to him, and pushed home his attack. The battle cost both sides some 50 killed and 50 wounded.

Fort Pitt was relieved by 10 August, after which Bouquet decided that his force needed rest and decided to postpone further advances into the Ohio River valley. Small detachments were sent out to Forts Bedford and Ligionier, and provincial troops arrived at Fort Pitt in early September. Bouquet then marched towards Fort Detroit while a second column of regulars retook Presque Isle. Colonel Johnson had been meeting with members of the Six Nations concerning the Senecas who had turned on the British. The Six Nations were still officially on the side of the British throughout the crisis, and vowed to deal with the traitors. Meanwhile, the Senecas kept fighting, ambushing a relief column heading out from Fort Niagara to Fort Detroit. Another column of 90 British regulars sent out to attack the Indians was also ambushed and destroyed by the Senecas. The garrisons at Fort Pitt and Detroit readied themselves for the coming winter. Fort Detroit's siege had been lifted on 15 October, but this had happened largely because the Indians had lost interest in continuing the siege. Detroit was still in dire need of supplies.

The tension in the region which provoked the Indian uprising eventually forced the British government to proclaim a policy concerning the newly conquered territories. The Royal Proclamation of 1763 was an attempt to resolve several outstanding issues in the region conclusively, but it was still somewhat ambiguous. The principal conditions of the proclamation were: that the French settlements north of New York and New England were to become known as the new colony of Quebec; that Florida was to be divided into two new colonies, East and West Florida; that all three new colonies were to operate under English law; and that all other land not encompassed by the three new colonies was to belong to the Indians. Colonial governments that claimed land in the region, such as Pennsylvania and Virginia, were no longer allowed to grant lands in the area. Only Crown representatives could negotiate with Indians over the sale of land. No whites were to settle the region, and any whites already present in the region were ordered to withdraw to east of the Appalachian mountains. White traders were allowed to cross into Indian territory, but were required to carry a license from the commander-in-chief. The proclamation was vague about what French inhabitants of the Indian territory should do. Were they required to move to Quebec? The document was unclear on this issue.

The proclamation succeeded in achieving its objective, which was to end the Indian uprising. At the same time, it established a whole new set of problems with colonists from the Thirteen Colonies who wished to settle in the region, which would contribute to tension already developing.

General Amherst was replaced on 17 November 1763 by Major General Thomas Gage. Amherst had developed the strategy for 1764 before he left; provincials and regulars would be raised in New York to lift the siege of Fort Niagara, and under the command of Colonel Bradstreet, would be sent to subdue the Indians on the Great Lakes. Bouquet and his troops would march into the Ohio River valley and subdue the Indian tribes there. Colonel Johnson, assuming these campaigns were successful, would negotiate a treaty with the Indians and settle the uprising. Intelligence reports indicated that the Indians were growing tired of the situation. The siege of Detroit, in particular, had carried on longer than they had expected, and the British success at the battle of Bushy Run had broken the Indians' resolve. Johnson and Bradstreet arrived at Fort Niagara in early July to meet with a number of tribal chiefs who wished to discuss peace terms. Johnson managed to reach agreement with all but three of them. The terms of the treaty were not as harsh as might have been expected under the circumstances; the Indians were given several concessions, including the right to lodge complaints at Fort Detroit and a schedule for setting values on goods and skins.

Following the peace conference, Bradstreet left with his force to subdue the three tribes still in rebellion, and to spread the word that hostilities with the other tribes were at an end. Bouquet, as planned, moved into the Ohio River valley to subdue any remaining Indian hostility and receive any white captives. The campaign was over by the end of the year, and the frontier was peaceful once again.

Ramifications for the future

Since the French-Indian War was fought chiefly between France and Great Britain and their Indian allies, the conclusions and ramifications discussed are only relevant to North America. The principal outcome of the French-Indian War, from the British point of view, was that France had been nullified as an adversary in North America. To the casual observer of 1763, the situation at the end of the war presented Great Britain in undisputed control of North America east of the Mississippi River.

The situation quickly proved to be more complicated than first impressions indicated. Within a few months of the signing of the Treaty of Paris, a large-scale Indian insurrection had broken out. The British succeeded in quelling the revolt after a lengthy campaign, but the revolt raised several issues, relevant not only to relations with the Indians but also to ensure the security of new British territories. Great Britain's methods for dealing with both of these considerations only served to further alienate her subjects in the original Thirteen Colonies. Already aggrieved by numerous tensions that had arisen during the conduct of the war itself, the colonists were incensed by the government's use of armed troops to prevent their movements toward westward expansion and settlement.

The Thirteen Colonies did not feel it was their responsibility to help pay the costs of the war, and they had no intention of contributing funds for the upkeep of security along the frontier, which was widely considered to be there solely to obstruct the westward movement of settlers. The British government sought various ways of compelling the colonial governments to pay to support the Army's presence in North America, and debate on this and related issues raged between London and North America from 1764 until 1775. The colonists found

the Quebec Act of 1774 to be particularly galling. In addition to making liberal provisions accommodating the language, religion, and laws of the French Canadian population, this act also gave the colony of Quebec administrative rights over the newly conquered territories of the Ohio River valley and extensive areas east of the Mississippi. Settlers in the Pennsylvania and Virginia regions were particularly incensed by this decision, as they had always claimed these regions as their own. (For more background on these issues, see Part II)

The numerous grievances fermenting in the populations of the Thirteen Colonies had, by 1775, developed into open rebellion against the British Crown. The British Army had gained significant tactical expertise in fighting in North America during the French and Indian War, but by the time war broke out in 1775, many of the reforms instituted had been forgotten. The majority of senior officers in the British Army of this period had not waged war in North America; most of them had fought in Germany in the Seven Years' War. Those who had fought in North America were mostly contemptuous of the American soldiers' fighting capabilities, citing their experiences with provincial soldiers in the French-Indian War. In fact, the British officers disparaged the Americans' ability to wage a war as a unified entity, remembering, again, occasions during the French-War when colonial assemblies bickered and reneged on promises of supplies and men. In underestimating their colonial opponents, British leaders made a serious mistake, forgetting that the Americans had at their disposal a large group of veterans who had served in both the provincial and regular ranks. They were able to tap into a fund of knowledge and experience when the

Fort Detroit (Detroit Public Library)

fledgling United States set out to create a professional army in 1775.

France, to its credit, did not ignore the issues that had been responsible for her defeat in both the French-Indian and the larger Seven Years' War. The army implemented numerous tactical reforms. In fact, the army in North America had performed remarkably well, given the circumstances and constraints under which it was forced to operate. Many of the reforms were instituted in response to the French Army's poor performance in Germany. These reforms became the cornerstone of a movement that would lead eventually to successes for the French Army in the American Revolution (1778–83) and during the revolutionary and Napoleonic period. France was only too happy in 1778 to join the Thirteen Colonies in an open treaty, hoping to gain back some of the territories lost in the Seven Years' War. This strategy paid off to a certain extent; France did not

regain New France in 1783, but she did regain some of her lost colonies in the Caribbean, and helped to inflict a defeat upon the British. Both of these achievements helped to restore morale within the French military establishment.

The expenses incurred in both the French-Indian War and the larger Seven Years' War put France in a difficult financial position. Her attempts at financial reform were not as extensive as her military reforms had been, and the construction of a new fleet, along with other military needs, strained the budget to breaking point in the 1760s. Successful involvement in the American Revolution brought more financial burdens but no new ways of releiving them. The French crown's mounting debt and attempts to get it under control are often cited as being among the principal causes of the French Revolution. In the end, a seemingly insignificant frontier campaign in a thinly settled colonial outpost was to have enormous long-term ramifications for two of Europe's greatest powers.

The Boston Tea Party of 1773. (Topfoto)

Part II
The American Revolution
1774–1783

Introduction

The American Revolution is rooted in a fundamental disagreement about the nature of the relationship between Great Britain and her colonial holdings in North America. At the end of the Seven Years' War, Britain, still feeling threatened by French and Spanish interests in North America, reconsidered her policies towards the Thirteen Colonies. Indifference was to give way to a more streamlined administrative policy and a greater military presence. Britain considered this necessary to safeguard both her own interests and those of her colonists, and expected that the colonies would contribute towards defraying the expenses for their own protection. Some of the colonists took a decidedly different view of the matter, considering the threat from European powers minimal and resenting an increase in military and financial focus that they viewed as intrusive and autocratic.

European powers with interests in North America were monitoring the situation closely, particularly France, Spain, and the Dutch Republic. Their interest and involvement fanned the flames of a local insurrection into a world war. When tensions flared into open insurrection, the French were quick to provide first covert and later formal military and financial aid to the American rebels. In doing so, they intended to destabilize Britain's position and advance their own interests in the area, hoping eventually to redress their recent territorial

King George III of England. (René Chartrand)

losses. Spain chose not to become directly involved, not wanting to appear as an advocate of liberty for colonial possessions in the Americas, and chose instead to ally herself with France, providing aid indirectly, also in the hope of regaining lost territory. The Dutch Republic was neutral, but benefited from the conflict by engaging in direct trade with the Thirteen Colonies, and eventually became directly involved when Great Britain declared war late in the conflict.

Colonial agitation

The end of the Seven Years' War in North America sparked a dispute that would eventually lead to a rebellion among the Thirteen Colonies of New Hampshire, Massachusetts, Rhode Island, Connecticut, New York, Pennsylvania, New Jersey, Delaware, Maryland, Virginia, North Carolina, South Carolina, and Georgia. The principal disagreement concerned the placement of British regulars in North America and how the British government sought to pay for their upkeep.

Britain had emerged victorious from the Seven Years' War, but in so doing had amassed a considerable debt. Before the war, the British government had undertaken minimal contact with or interference in the internal affairs of the North American colonies, aside from passing Navigation Acts which required that exports from the colonies be transported in British ships. Tensions with the French increased as the 18th century progressed, prompting the British to consider the North American colonies from a more "imperial" perspective. The government began to examine ways that the colonies could be tied into a more efficient trading system with British colonies in the Caribbean and India.

The North American theater of the Seven Years' War (more commonly known as the French-Indian War) had provided the British government with some very negative impressions. Officials had encountered considerable difficulty in gathering supplies for the war effort, and problems with locally raised colonial militia had resulted in the deployment of British regulars to the area. There has been debate over the importance of provincial militia in the French-Indian War, but there is no doubt that colonial troops could not have won the war without the support of British regulars. Some provincial

units fought well as irregular units, but others lacked the training and discipline necessary to wage a linear-style war. The discipline of the British regular was required in this theater as in all the others, and following the war's end, the British government decided that a large contingent of British regulars should be stationed permanently in North America to offset French, Spanish, and Indian ambitions in the area.

The British government settled upon a series of new taxes on the colonies as the best way to fund establishing troops in North America. The first of these was the Sugar Act of 1764. The second, the Stamp Act of 1765, charged a duty on newspapers and other official documents. This initiative provoked a negative reaction from the American colonists. Their principal grievance was that the taxes had been levied by the British Parliament, rather than by the local colonial assemblies. Popular opinion held that it was appropriate for taxation to be levied only by locally elected officials. Groups of men formed organizations known as the "Sons of Liberty" to protest the Acts. Serious rioting erupted in the colonies, to which the local British government officials felt powerless to respond, and resulted in the repeal of the Act in 1766 following a change of government in Great Britain.

The British government's next move was the Quartering Act of 1765. This was principally devised to address the supply problems that had been common during the French-Indian War, and its requirements included the provision of wagons and drivers to supply the army in the field. It was, however, the clause concerning the housing of soldiers that created problems. This provision stipulated that British regulars were to be lodged in public houses, inns, even empty homes, if barracks were overcrowded or unavailable. Furthermore, this lodging was to be at the expense of the local colonial authorities. The reaction of the Reverend John Tucker of Boston in 1768 was fairly typical: "I think we are very afflicted and in a distressed state having the Ensigns of war at our doors . . . a tax laid on us to pay the exorbitant charge of providing barracks and for those undesired troops" (Doc. 973.38).

Initially this did not seem a very odious imposition, as most of the troops were to be stationed on the frontier or in territory

War in the Thirteen Colonies

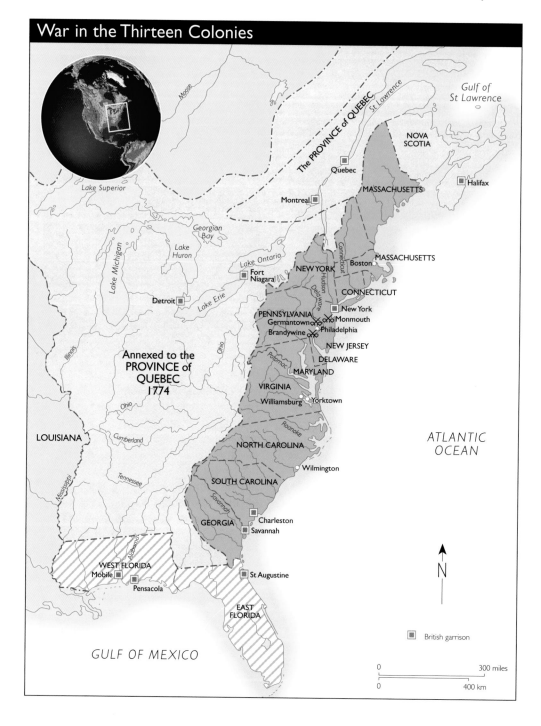

recently gained from France and Spain, such as Niagara, Crown Point, St Augustine, Mobile, and Detroit. In practice, however, the movement of troops *en route* to their final postings was extremely disruptive. Further protest ensued, and in 1769 the colonial assemblies and the British government met to work out agreements concerning particulars of the Act, in an attempt to appease both sides. The transfer of British regulars to the Atlantic seaboard in 1770, however, strained the arrangement still further.

The Townshend Revenue Act, proposed by Chancellor of the Exchequer, Charles Townshend, was to create still more problems. This Act, passed in 1767, imposed customs duties on tea, paper, paint, glass, and lead. It sparked the ire of the colonists afresh, and assemblies from New England to the middle Atlantic expressed anger at its provisions. A Virginia militia colonel, George Washington, spoke in the Virginia House of Burgesses (Assembly) in 1769, contending that only Virginians could tax Virginians, and local merchants in most ports swore not to sell British goods or to order items from Great Britain.

Tensions rose in Boston when customs commissioners were attacked by a mob. The British government responded by dispatching 4,000 British regulars to Boston to impose control. This was a role for which regulars were not trained, and their incapability only served to incite the local population to complain of a "standing army" imposing order on a "just" civilian society. Stories of robberies and assaults by soldiers were circulated, further alienating the civilian population. Events reached a crisis on 5 March 1770, when a small contingent of British regulars, attacked by an angry mob, opened fire, killing three man and wounding five. The incident, dubbed the "Boston Massacre", was exaggerated and used as propaganda against the British. The regulars were pulled out of Boston after this episode, but tension remained.

The British government changed again in 1770, and the new Parliament, led by Frederick North, First Lord of the Treasury, repealed all duties of the Townshend Act,

John Hancock, President of the Second Continental Congress. (Ann Ronan Picture Library)

except for the duty on tea. The new government, in agreement with its predecessor, believed in its right to levy taxes upon the colonies, although Lord North did feel that this stance only hurt British merchants in the end, when their goods were boycotted in the colonies.

The next crisis arose in 1773, when Lord North imposed the Tea Act, a second tax on tea. This initiative was an attempt to boost revenue for the British East India Company. The plan was to undercut the Dutch tea supply and shift the surplus of tea to the Thirteen Colonies. Americans, however, interpreted this as a further attempt to subvert their liberty. In December 1773 a small flotilla of Company ships arrived in Boston. While docked in Boston Harbor, they were boarded in the middle of the night by a group of men, led by Samuel Adams (a political agitator) dressed as Indians. The interlopers dumped the tea into the harbor, in an act of defiance that came to be known as the Boston Tea Party.

The British government, alarmed by the situation, passed the Coercive Acts in 1774

The Boston Massacre. (Ann Ronan Picture
Library)

in an attempt to restore order, especially in
Boston. Lord North felt that this would be
sufficient to contain the small fringe element
of rebellious individuals, failing to recognize
the broad base of support for some of the
actions being taken. John Hancock, a
prominent Boston merchant, and Samuel
Adams, were identified as the main
troublemakers in Massachusetts. The port of
Boston was closed and notice given that
provincial government officials implicated in
any wrongdoing could be tried in Great
Britain. Lieutenant-General Thomas Gage
returned to Boston with 3,500 regulars and
with powers to assume the role of governor
of Massachusetts. The Acts achieved the

opposite effect, provoking a negative
reaction throughout the colonies.

The Quebec Act of 1774 also played a role
in fomenting discontent among rebellious
colonists. In an attempt to resolve the future
of the French settlements of Quebec, the
British government passed an Act that has
had repercussions up to the present day. The
colony of Quebec was allowed to keep its
French language, laws, customs, and Roman
Catholic religion intact, with no interference
from London. Furthermore, the boundaries
of the colony were extended as far west as
the Mississippi, encompassing land treaties
made between the British government and
Indian tribes following the end of the Seven
Years' War. The understanding was that the
laws described in the Act would apply to this
area, in recognition of the fact that many of

the Indian tribes west of the mountains had been allied with France, and had thus been influenced by French customs and converted to the Catholic Church.

The Thirteen Colonies reacted strongly against the Quebec Act. Long-standing prejudice made them deeply distrustful of French Catholics, and many of the colonies resented this incursion into land west of the Appalachian Mountains, which they believed was theirs by right. They protested at being hemmed in by a Catholic colony and denied access to the rich lands to the west.

Many leading figures throughout the colonies felt that their liberties were gradually being worn away. Their dissatisfaction led to the First Continental Congress, formed in Philadelphia to discuss the Coercive Acts, the Quebec Act, and issues in Massachusetts. The First Continental Congress was convened by colonial leaders, including John Adams, George Washington, Samuel Adams, Benjamin Franklin, and Patrick Henry, with the aim of organizing

Lord Frederick North. (Bodleian Library)

General Thomas Gage.
(Anne SK Brown Collection)

It was not until 4 July 1776 – after the bloodletting of 1775 and early 1776 – that the Second Continental Congress, led by John Hancock, decided to declare independence from Great Britain. From this point, the Thirteen Colonies referred to themselves as "the United States of America", but as this title was not officially recognized until after the Treaty of Paris in 1783, they will continue to be referred to throughout this work as the Thirteen Colonies.

It is significant that the British government failed to recognize that the formation of the Congress indicated not just a local Massachusetts or New England rebellion, but the beginnings of a large-scale insurrection. The military situation in North America began to worsen as 1774 drew to a close. British regulars were stationed in Boston. The Quartering Act came into effect once again, increasing tension between civilians and soldiers. The delegates of the First Congress, although they considered military action a last resort, did not help the situation by calling on colonial militia to strengthen and drill more frequently. Weapons of various sizes were seized by colonists and stored away. Royal government representatives were slowly being replaced by committees who supported the conclusions of the First Continental Congress. The colonies and the British government were moving towards all-out conflict.

formal, legally recognized opposition to Parliament's actions. The Congress issued a declaration condemning the Coercive Acts as unjust and unconstitutional, and rejected the appointment of General Gage as governor. The Congress additionally addressed issues of parliamentary control over the colonies, especially with regard to taxation. At this point the Congress was not interested in independence, merely the redress of perceived injustices.

Linear and irregular warfare

Tactics

Popular images of the American Revolution
feature American "minutemen" (militia)
hidden behind stone walls and trees, firing
into Continental-style linear formations of
British Redcoats. While this type of warfare
occurred occasionally, a more accurate image
would show Americans assembling for battle
in linear formations opposite British forces
similarly arrayed and supported by their
German allies. The American Revolution had
more in common with the linear warfare
used in the European theaters of the Seven
Years' War than with the irregular skirmishes
fought on the frontiers of North America in
the same conflict.

Battle of Bunker Hill. (Anne SK Brown Collection)

The flintlock musket of the Seven Years'
War was still the chief weapon for all sides.
The ability of an army to deploy in linear
formation and maintain fire discipline was of
considerable importance in training.
Formations were required to march in step
over open terrain, maintaining cohesion, and
then deploy effectively from columns to linear
formations. The British ability to accomplish
this at the Battle of Monmouth saved the
army from destruction, as will be described
later. Following deployment in linear
formation, the men were required to deliver a
devastating volley against the enemy.
Consistent fire discipline was crucial to the
success of this maneuver.

Tactics used in the Seven Years' War also
continued to be employed, particularly
generals attempting to outflank their enemy

View of The ATTACK on BUNKER'S HILL, with the
Burning of CHARLES TOWN, June 17. 1775.

(oblique order) when the ground permitted. The British attack at the battle of Long Island is a clear example of this tactic. Prussia's success during the Seven Years' War had inspired many armies, including the newly created American forces, the Continental Army, to emulate its firing techniques and discipline, with some success – by 1777, many Continental regiments were capable of holding their line against British and German regulars.

The American Revolution was chiefly an infantry war. The British and Continental formations deployed in ranks of men two or three deep, with artillery deployed on the flanks of battalions or regiments to mark unit boundaries. The use of only a small amount of cavalry was mainly due to practical considerations. The British encountered difficulty in transporting mounts or purchasing them in North America, and the Americans felt that the upkeep of dragoon regiments was too costly. As a result, only a few dragoon regiments were formed in the Continental Army or deployed by the British Army.

Although use of traditional methods remained constant, there were innovations in irregular warfare, following on from developments of the Seven Years' War. The British army re-employed light infantry companies in 1770–71, and by 1775–76 had begun to form these into independent battalions. The Continental Army also formed light infantry companies, and they too tended to use these in independent formations. Rifles were reintroduced for use by a small number of dedicated units. The British employed German

Jäger (riflemen) and the American forces used riflemen occasionally. The numbers were small on both sides, however, and their ability to defend themselves was compromised by the amount of time it took to reload the rifle and its lack of a bayonet.

The use of combined mounted infantry/cavalry units for raiding and reconnaissance was another innovation of this period. The British began to develop this tactic in 1777 with the raising of the loyalist British Legion and Queen's Rangers corps in the New York area. These troops made a name for themselves in the later southern campaigns, with vast expanses of territory to cover. Other regiments of *Jäger* were occasionally formed into *ad hoc* mounted infantry units or attached to the Legion or Rangers, and the Americans followed suit with the mounting and use of irregular units made up of militiamen who preferred to fight in a less traditional role. The French also used mixed mounted units, the Lauzon Legion being the most famous.

Siege warfare, a significant component of the Seven Years' War, remained so in the American Revolution. Numerous battles and skirmishes were fought around fixed positions, which were dug in and defended from besieging opponents in the traditional European manner. The sieges of Savannah, Charleston, and Yorktown are classic examples.

1779 American drill book showing formation of a company and regiment and wheeling by platoons. (Anne SK Brown Collection)

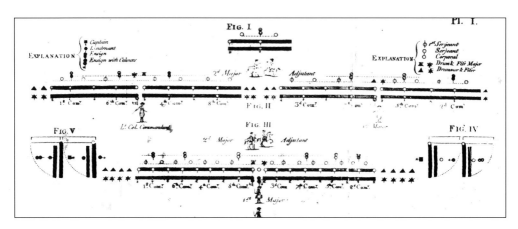

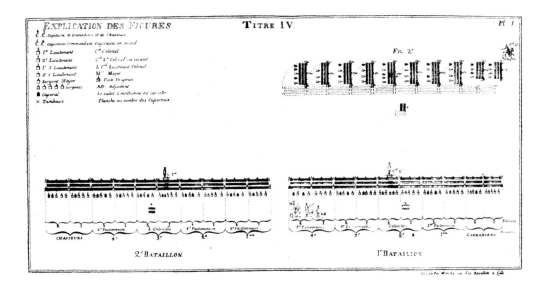

The British forces

On the eve of war in 1775, the British army stood at about 48,000 officers and men, distributed throughout the garrisons of North America, Ireland, Great Britain, Minorca, Gibraltar, Africa, and the West Indies. Eight thousand of these were stationed in North America. The numbers of the overall British establishment did not increase significantly between 1775 and 1778, when only one line regiment was raised. Only the entry of the French into the war in 1778 prompted the British government to raise more regiments – nearly 30 from 1778 to 1783. This increased establishment totals to 110,000 officers and men, plus additional numbers of militia and volunteers raised to defend Great Britain.

The British Army had been successful in the Seven Years' War, but the American Revolution presented a different set of challenges. The British faced the prospect of fighting a war in hostile territory thousands of miles from their home base. Strategic planning that focused on how to end the uprising seemed to be lacking, especially during the early years of the war. British generals were unable to capitalize on tactical advantages gained after the battles of Bunker Hill and Long Island, which could potentially have crippled the military capabilities of the Americans early in the war. Infighting among British commanders on land and sea created more problems, compounded by the arrogance of a number of British officers and government officials who considered the American forces a rabble, easily dealt with by a small force. Even if they had been capable of defeating the Americans militarily, it is questionable whether the British would have grasped how to deal with the political implications of the conflict. It is likely that they would have found themselves in the position of a garrison force attempting to contain an obstreperous political element – an unsavory prospect for any army.

The British Army consistently lacked sufficient troops to contain the insurrection, a situation made considerably worse from 1778 by the entry of first France and later Spain into the hostilities, forcing the British to disperse their forces throughout the world. The percentage of the British Army stationed in North America dropped from 65 percent in 1778 to only 29 percent in 1780 (Mackesy, pp. 524–25).

Despite these obstacles, the British Army itself was a formidable machine of war, a fact that was especially apparent during the conflict's early years. Its discipline and firepower generally outstripped those of the surrounding marches or positions, behavior that galvanized support for the independence cause from previously neutral colonists. A French officer who was present in North America as an observer noted the following causes for British defeats up to 1777:

the present military success of the Americans can be ascribed to certain handicaps the English generals have faced: their unfamiliarity with the area of hostilities; their difficulties in obtaining reinforcements and supplies once the armies have advanced inland (Recicourt, p. 206).

The British raised a series of Loyalist Provincial Corps over the course of the war. Most of these units were trained and used as regular line infantry, with light infantry and grenadier companies. Some were used as garrison troops in outposts as remote as Charleston, in the south, or Quebec and Halifax, in Canada. Selected units were used in a more irregular role, among them Butler's Rangers, who fought alongside Indian tribes in the upstate New York and middle Atlantic regions; the majority fought in traditional Continental style.

Relatively early in the war, the British attempted to establish a centralized system for recruiting, training, and equipping the corps with the establishment of a dedicated Inspector-General, Lieutenant-Colonel Alexander Innes, in January 1777. Despite this, the British authorities demonstrated little faith in the capability of the provincial corps, and did not actively promote their raising and employment until the defeats of 1777 and the entry of the French into the conflict made the need for them apparent.

The fighting qualities of the corps ranged from excellent to poor. The British Army regulars initially disdained provincial units, but revised their opinions when reports from the field indicated competence, and in some cases excellence. An American Establishment, not including all loyalist formations, was formed in 1779 (and formally listed in 1782), in an attempt to recognize the more successful units of loyalists and to repair damage caused by British regulars in their

British Light Infantryman. Artwork by Gerry Embleton. (Osprey Publishing)

American forces, and its junior officers were reliably capable under fire. These strengths were undermined, however, by the considerable problems of supply. Troops could not expect to receive adequate supplies from the local populations, which dictated dependence upon a 4,800 km (3,000-mile) supply line vulnerable to the effects of weather, privateering and, eventually, the attentions of the French and Spanish navies.

Supply shortages meant that the British Army and its German allies engaged in frequent plunder and theft in the countryside

evaluation of loyalists as second-rate. The
American Establishment compromised five
regiments, volunteers of Ireland, King's
American Regiment, the Queen's Rangers, New
York Volunteers, and British Legion. The major
areas of operation for the provincial corps
were in New York in 1778–79 and the
southern campaigns of 1780–81. It is
estimated that about 19,000 men served in the
various provincial corps throughout the war.

The British authorities also utilized the
services of some 10,000 Indians, chiefly from
the Iroquois and Algonquin nations. They
were principally employed as scouts and
raiders, in recognition of their formidable
knowledge of forest warfare. Their
deployment sparked controversy in both
America and Great Britain, and created further
support for the independence movement
among neutral colonists. Indians operated
along the frontier regions of New York,
Pennsylvania, and Virginia.

The British East India Company
continued to expand and train its native
forces (sepoys) in the use of traditional linear
tactics following the end of the Seven Years'
War. By 1775, there were about 100,000
troops in the three presidency armies of
Bombay, Bengal, and Madras. Between 1778
and 1782, two Hanoverian and eight British
regiments were sent to India to reinforce the
East India Company forces.

The fighting qualities of the sepoys were
considered to be superior. A lieutenant of the
71st Regiment of Foot noted, upon his
arrival in Madras in 1780,

*the Company's officers have acquired much
praise by their steady adherence to the duties of
their profession, which the excellent order of the
sepoys clearly confirms and which strikes every
stranger with surprise ... the frequent
opportunities of seeing service gives them
[Company troops] [a] great fund of professional
knowledge (Munro, pp. 26–28).*

The British and Company forces, however,
lacked sufficient numbers of cavalry to
contend with Haidar Ali's armies for most of
this period.

Hesse-Hanau Grenadier. Artwork by Gerry Embleton.
(Osprey Publishing)

German auxiliaries

The shortfall in British regular forces
compelled the British to seek a loan of
troops from Russia. The Russians refused to
loan troops for service in North America,
and Britain was forced to look elsewhere.
Having used troops from the German
princely states before, she made use of this
resource again, and troops from Hanover
were sent to Minorca and Gibraltar to release
British troops for North American service.

(Troops from Hanover were not considered mercenaries, since one of George III's titles was Elector of Hanover.) By early 1776, the British had negotiated treaties with Brunswick, Hesse-Cassel, Hesse-Hanu, Anspach, Waldeck, and Anhalt for troops for the war in America. Since the largest contingent came from Hesse-Cassel, all German auxiliaries were commonly referred to as Hessians.

Over the course of the war 29,166 German auxiliaries served in North America (Fletcher, p. 63). Most of the German troops were organized in traditional Continental style. The grenadier companies were often formed into independent units, and there was also a *Jäger* corps, which was in great demand after the battle of Long Island. The *Jäger* corps averaged 700 men throughout the war.

The German auxiliaries caused considerable problems for the British, principally with discipline and public relations. The German troops became known for pillaging and destroying farms and houses in 1776. While all factions were guilty of this, the Americans used the German abuses as propaganda, and the French officer von Closen noted "the ravages of the Hessians who made themselves hated by their lack of discipline and inconsideration for the peaceful inhabitants during the winter quarters in New Jersey" (Closen, p. 115).

The fighting qualities of the German contingents, like those of the provincial corps, ranged from excellent to poor. A French officer commented that 'the English, Hessian, and Anspach troops, [were] the elite of those who had been in Carolina' (Rice and Brown, Vol. I, p. 151). The Hessian troops were considered the equal of the Prussian Army, and the *Jäger* corps was held in high esteem by the American and French forces arrayed against it. The Brunswick contingent, on the other hand, which served in Burgoyne's campaign of 1777, was not so highly regarded; although well-disciplined, their fighting abilities were considered mediocre. Troops from Hesse-Hanau were criticized by Lieutenant-General Frederick Haldimand, the British commander in

Canada in 1778, as being unfit for the American war.

The fact that German troops were used as part of the British Army in North America caused great consternation amongst the American colonial population and like-minded individuals in Great Britain. Their presence has historically been given as a reason why the American people dislike and distrust mercenaries. This is a simplistic and somewhat hypocritical argument, especially considering that the American commanders apparently had no qualms about accepting the services of various soldiers of fortune from Europe.

The numbers of European troops serving with the American forces did not reach the levels of the German auxiliaries. Some of the officers, however, notably Frederick William Augustus, Baron von Steuben and Gilbert Mottier, Marquis de Lafayette, played instrumental roles in the development of the Continental Army and were accordingly awarded high-ranking positions. There were small "foreign" corps in the American forces, including Pulaski's Legion, Von Heer's Provost Corps and Brigadier-General Charles Tuffin Armand's Independent Chasseurs.

Additionally, once the French officially entered the war as allies of the Americans, the French forces employed considerable numbers of mercenary troops within their ranks. Nearly one-fifth of the French Army in France and overseas was made up of foreign troops; the famous Lauzon Legion, which served with distinction in the American colonies, was made up of foreigners whose word of command was German.

The American forces

The Americans began the war without a proper army. The troops arrayed against the British in the spring of 1775 consisted of partially trained militia. The Militia Law of 1775 designated all free men between the ages of 16 and 50 as liable for duty, and each colony formed its own militia into companies and regiments.

Private, 4th Massachusetts Regiment Artwork by Bill Younghusband. (Osprey Publishing)

countrymen. As General George Washington pointed out:

> men just dragged from the tender scene of domestic life; unaccustomed to the din of arms; totally unaccustomed with any kind of military skill . . . when opposed to troops regularly trained and disciplined and appointed supreme in arms makes them timid and ready to fly from their shadows (Weigley, p. 5).

The militia had some successes during the war against regular troops, but on the whole lacked sufficient discipline or training to undertake combat on a European-style battlefield.

There were also benefits to the colonists' ability to muster a pro-independence militia. Militia could be used to offset any loyalist attempts to provide support for the British effort; and, when used in a more irregular role, especially in raids and defense, the militia often exceeded expectations. Following the Battle of King's Mountain, 1780, an American Major-General noted:

> this battle as well as many others under Generals Sumter, Marion and others, proves that militia are brave men, and will fight if you let them come to action in their own way. There are very few actions when they are drawn up in line of battle, that they could be brought to stand and reserve their fire until the enemy came near enough. (Moultrie, Vol. II, p. 244)

A French officer, Sublieutenant Jean Baptiste Antoine de Verger, observed that "they [the militia] give occasional examples of bravery when they are superior in numbers or when in possession of some defile the enemy must pass through, into which they can fire from ambush" (Rice and Brown, Vol. I, p. 152).

The need for properly trained professional soldiers prompted the Continental Congress to sanction the formation of the Continental Army, despite widespread American bias against a standing army dating back to the English Civil Wars. The proposed structure divided American forces between the militia

The greatest problem with the militia organization was that there was no regular training schedule. When training was organized, the men were called to arms for a specific period of time, usually only 30–60 days, and then returned to their families. The militia was not considered fit to take on British regulars, even by their own

General George Washington. (Anne SK Brown Collection)

of the colonies and the regular Continental Army. Shortages of men available for the Continentals necessitated the use of militia in a supporting role to Continental operations, and as drafts for the Continental Army. The drill master, Prussian Captain (later American Major-General) Frederick Augustus, Baron von Steuben, described the plans for militia in 1779 thus: "our business is now to find out the means of rendering that militia capable to supply the want of a well regulated standing army at least as much as lies in our power" (Boston Public Library, Ch.F.7.78).

The first attempts at organizing a professional army were undertaken in the summer of 1775. The "Separate Army" was formed in upstate New York in June. The Continental Congress in Philadelphia also sanctioned the formation of troops outside Boston to be listed as a Continental Force or the "New England Army". On 2 July 1775, George Washington was named Commander-in-Chief of all Continental and militia forces serving under the auspices of the Army of the United Colonies, both existing and to be raised. He inherited a force of some 17,000 men, mostly from the New England colonies. All of the units had different establishments, making standardization difficult. Most of the army was relieved of duty by the end of 1775, leaving Washington to muster another round of troops for the 1776 campaign. This army, again, was disbanded at the end of 1776 when its enlistment contracts ended.

Eventually the Continental Congress called for the formation of the Continental Army on 26 September 1776. The American defeats of 1776 had made Congress realize that a well-trained body of men was needed, and that one-year contracts were not sufficient to prepare troops to face the British in battle. As a Hessian General noted: "General Washington and Putnam are praised by friend and foe alike but all their mastery in war will be of no avail with a mob of conscripted undisciplined troops" (*Revolution in America*, p. 40).

The new army was to have 88 regiments (battalions) formed from each of the Thirteen Colonies. The great difference between this force and previous musters was that the new army was to be raised for three years, or for the duration of the war, whichever was shorter. The three-year limitation on enlistment was imposed in response to recruits' unwillingness to join for an unknown duration. The Continental Army's authorized strength was 75,000 men, which it never attained. The highest level of recruitment ever reached was 18,000, in October 1778.

The Continental Army was divided among three major armies, the Northern (Separate), Main, and Southern armies, each of which took on different numbers of battalions over the course of the war. The Continental Army consistently encountered problems in providing enough men and supplies. It was forced to compete against recruiters for the colonial militia to assemble sufficient troops, and conscription was periodically employed in an attempt to fill the army's ranks. During 1777, many commanders had difficulty clothing and arming the men in their regiments, and even in friendly territory it was difficult to supply enough food. Pay was also a considerable problem, as the paper money used to pay troops and officers dropped steadily in value during the course of the war. Even facing severe shortages of supplies, men, and officers, however, the Continental Army was still able to form for battle year after year. The British were unable to completely destroy it, and on more than one occasion were defeated by the combined force of Continental and militia troops.

There is a debate among historians as to whether the Continental Army represented a levy of supporters of the independence movement, or its members had more in common with their European counterparts – men who joined the army only for payment and signing bonuses. Some contend that the militia of the time represented a more politicized element of the American forces. One historian noted that "there was little commitment among the American rank and file to the constitutional cause of Independence and very few of our patriots chose to re-enlist for a second or third time" (Duffy, p. 285).

It is still debatable whether the Continentals were a "republican" army or a purely professional force with no concern for political issues, but ultimately they performed well in the field and proved themselves to their European allies. A French officer commented:

I admire the American troops tremendously! It is indescribable that soldiers composed of men of every age, even of children of fifteen, of whites and blacks, almost naked, unpaid and rather poorly fed, can march so well and withstand fire so steadfastly (Closen, p. 102).

In developing tactical training, the Continental Army had several sources of information available. Some of the senior generals appointed had seen service in British units during the Seven Years' War. Their experience was bolstered by input from a series of foreign officers who had come to advise the army and to seek adventure. They came from Prussia, Poland, France, and other European states. This infusion of officers caused confusion in the American chain of command but also provided significant expertise in organization and tactics.

The Continental Army drew up its own tactical manuals, which were largely based upon contemporary British documents. Major-General von Steuben spent the winter of 1777–78 drilling the Continental Army along Prussian military lines. He also regulated the size of battalions and standardized a specific drill to be followed by all units of the Continental Army.

In 1781, there was further organizational streamlining, partially because a number of regiments were being disbanded due to lack of manpower. The fighting capabilities of the American forces remained fairly strong despite this; members of the French contingent commented on the American forces upon arrival in Newport, Rhode Island, in 1780. Sublieutentant de Verger noted that:

the American Continental troops are very war-wise and quite well disciplined. They are thoroughly inured to hardship, which they endure with little complaint so long as their officers set them an example, but it is imperative the officers equal their troops in firmness and resolution (Rice and Brown, Vol. I, p. 152).

Another significant asset for the Continental Army was its understanding of the need for small reforms within the organization. A French officer, Lieutenant-Colonel Jean Baptiste Tennant of Pulaski's Legion, wrote an important paper examining army structure. It appears to originate after 1779, when the original commander of Pulaski's Legion was killed and succeeded by Lieutenant-Colonel Tennant. The paper, called "Uniformity Among American Troops" outlined "a scheme for establishing uniformity in the services, discipline, manoeuvre of formations of troops in the armies of the United States" (Boston Public Library, Ch.F.8.55a).

Tennant proposed innovations designed to accommodate the specific needs of the Continental Army. Pointing out that the army, unlike its European counterparts, did not have the benefit of large cadres of men and officers with years of military experience, he stressed that to compensate:

the manoeuvres to be introduced must be as simple as possible. The chief objectives are for the officers to know how to lead their platoons and keep their men together and for the soldiers to keep rank and file … that all manoeuvres be performed … in greatest silence (Boston Public Library, Ch.F.8.55a).

He also recommended the appointment of an Inspector General to formulate training throughout the army, but stipulated that:

before introducing any new thing the Inspector General is to propose it to the Commander-in-Chief in the field … neither the Inspector General nor inspectors of any other detached army shall be authorized to give a general order without previously communicating it with the Commander-in-Chief for his approbility (Boston Public Library, Ch.F.8.55a).

The French forces

The French Army had emerged from the Seven Years' War at a low point, having been defeated in North America, Europe, and India. Evaluation of its performance had brought about a number of reforms from 1763 to 1775. Artillery units were revamped and standardized into seven large regiments, and infantry regiments were regularized as well. By 1776 all regiments comprised two battalions, with each battalion composed of one grenadier, one chasseur (light infantry), and four fusilier companies.

The training of the infantry and cavalry was standardized and revamped to include summer training camps. The Crown undertook to supply the regiments directly with clothing and muskets to counteract the officers' practice of profiting on military supply contracts. Military enlistment was fixed at eight years, to provide a large corps of properly trained soldiers. By 1778 there were more than 200,000 men in the French Army. The French Army had no continental commitments during the war, as it had in the Seven Years' War, and was therefore able to direct most of its energies against British interests throughout the world.

The performances of the French Army at Yorktown and in the West Indies demonstrated the successes of the reforms and presented a different army from the one that the British had fought in the Seven Years' War. A French expeditionary force arrived at Newport in 1780, under the command of Lieutenant-General Jean de Vimeur, Comte de Rochambeau. Thomas McKean of the Continental Congress reviewed the troops in Philadelphia and afterwards wrote to Rochambeau: the brilliant appearance and exact discipline of the several Corps do the highest honor to

French officer of the Armagnac Regiment. (Canadian Parks Services)

their officers, and to afford a happy presage of the most distinguished services in a cause which they have so zealously espoused (Rice and Brown, Vol. I, p. 46 footnote 72).

Shot heard round the world

The year 1775 marked the formal outbreak of hostilities between the British and Americans. A small skirmish in Lexington led to a larger confrontation in Concord, and the British withdrawal from Concord sparked a savage fight for survival and the beginning of outright conflict. The battle of Breed's Hill (Bunker Hill), in June, was the first pitched battle of the war. This was followed by a bold American attempt, in December 1775, to seize and conquer Canada. After these events there could be no turning back. It was war.

The armed struggle for America began on 19 April 1775 in the towns of Lexington and Concord, Massachusetts. It could easily have been sooner. By late 1774, the British government was growing tired of its contentious North American colonists. General Gage, Commander-in-Chief in North America, received orders in December to arrest the instigators, but he considered the number of British troops available locally too small to be effective. Most of the British forces in North America were gathered and sent to Boston, nearly 13 battalions of infantry by the spring of 1775. Gage still considered this inadequate to deal with a possible insurrection.

In early April, Gage received reports that a large cache of weapons and gunpowder was being stored at Concord, 26 km (16 miles) northwest of Boston. The local militia was aware that the British knew about the stores, but not when the British might move against it. Senior members of the Continental Congress, such as John Adams and John Hancock, were in Lexington, and there was fear that the British would move to arrest them.

On 18 April at 8:00 pm the commanding officers of the British regiments in Boston were ordered to send their light and grenadier companies to the beach near the Magazine Guard by 10:00 pm. These troops numbered between 600 and 700 men and were commanded by Lieutenant-Colonel Francis Smith of the 10th Foot and Major John Pitcairn of the Marines. The troops were ferried across the Charles river towards Cambridge. All of the troops landed on Cambridge Marsh by midnight, but had to wait till 2:00 am before moving, in order to allow the shipping and unloading of provisions to be completed. Lieutenant Barker noted, "few but the commanding officers knew what expedition we were going upon" (Barker, p. 31). Paul Revere and William Dawes secretly left Boston and rode towards Lexington and Concord to raise the alarm that the British were marching on the stores.

As the British troops marched towards Lexington, they began to receive intelligence that a large group of armed men was forming near the common at Lexington. Lieutenant-Colonel Smith sent a messenger back to Boston for reinforcements. A reinforcement brigade was ordered ready to move from Boston overland to Lexington. Due to orders not being conveyed correctly and time wasted to correct the mistake, the brigade was delayed and did not march until 8:45 am (Mackenzie, p. 19). The Lexington militia formed a company of 70 men on Lexington Green, under the command of Captain John Parker, a veteran of the Seven Years' War.

Major Pitcairn and his companies arrived at Lexington Green just as the militia was forming up at around 6:00 am. Major Pitcairn called upon the militia to lay down their arms and return to their homes. The American commander, Parker, told his men not to fire; the British moved forward and a shot was fired. There has been extensive debate about who actually fired the first shot. Lieutenant Barker contends that "on our coming near them they [the American

Tarring and feathering a British official. (Ann Ronan Picture Library)

militia] fired one or two shots" (Barker, p. 32). The situation was confusing for both sides, and Barker mentions that, after the initial shots, "our men without any orders rushed in upon them, fired and put them to flight" (Barker, p. 32). The firing lasted for 15–20 minutes, when Pitcairn managed to restore order. Eight militiamen lay dead and 10 more were wounded. The British had suffered one wounded man.

Following this engagement, Pitcairn and the light infantry moved on to Concord to destroy the cache of weapons. The militia surrounding Concord was mobilized and moved to intercept the British column. The British seized Concord, and the light infantry was sent to secure bridges north and south of town, while the grenadiers dealt with destroying the weapons and gunpowder in the area. A fight broke out at the North Bridge after the British had occupied both sides. As the militia moved forward, the British withdrew from one side and fired a volley into the militia. An American stated that 'we were all ordered to load [muskets] and had strick orders not to fire till they fired first then to fire as fast as we could … the British … fired three guns one after another … we then was all ordered to fire … and not to kill our own men' (Barrett, p. 10). The Concord militia opened fire and according to a British officer, "the weight of their fire was such that we were obliged to give way" (Lister, p. 27).

The British suffered one killed and 11 wounded, including four officers. They withdrew towards Concord, and orders were received at around midday for all units to fall back towards Boston, the military stores having been destroyed. As the troops left Concord, sniping began from houses along the road to Boston. About 2 km (one mile) outside of Concord, the British column crossed at Meriam's Corner, where it became bunched up. Militiamen opened up on the large column, inflicting heavy casualties on the flanks and rear.

The relieving brigade from Boston met up with the remainder of the British column at Lexington, bringing the numbers of British troops close to 1,500 men. The combined force marched out towards Boston. As a British officer noted: "we were attacked on all sides from woods, and orchards and from stone walls and from every house on the road side" (Evelyn, p. 54). The British reaction to this sort of attack was described as follows: "the soldiers were so enraged at suffering from an unseen enemy, that they forced open many a house from which the fire proceeded, and put to death all those found in them" (Mackenzie, pp. 20–21). Militiamen poured in from all the surrounding towns to fight against the withdrawing British column, but the British were able to keep them at a distance with the use of flanking parties and a very good rearguard formation.

When they arrived in Cambridge, the British column decided to head towards Charlestown, as the bridge from Cambridge to Boston had either been destroyed or was heavily defended. The column arrived at Charlestown at 7:00 pm and occupied the area until boats were sent to ferry the troops back over to Boston. The militia did not pursue the British into Charlestown because the area was open terrain. As Barker noted: "the rebels did not chuse [sic] to follow us to the Hill as they must have fought us on open ground and that they did not like" (Barker, p. 36).

The British lost about 70 killed and 170 wounded during the day's fighting, while the Americans are estimated to have lost 100 men killed and wounded. The British had been successful in extricating themselves from the area and had applied good lightinfantry tactics in clearing the militia from the stone walls and houses that lined the road to Boston.

Bunker Hill

Following this first skirmish, the surrounding colonies sent militia reinforcements to Boston during the remainder of April and May. By the end of May, militia numbers had swelled to about 17,000 men. The British received reinforcements in the shape of

Major-Generals (later Lieutenant-Generals) Sir William Howe, Sir Henry Clinton, and Sir John Burgoyne as well as the 35th, 49th, and 63rd Regiments of Foot over the course of May and June. Gage finally felt equipped to occupy the two dominant heights commanding Boston, Dorchester Heights and Charlestown (Breed's Hill). The rebels received word of this and began to dig a redoubt on Breed's Hill on the evening of 16 June 1775.

The British decided to attack the American positions on Breed's Hill, in an episode that has come down the years of history as the battle of Bunker Hill. Colonel William Prescott was in charge of the American forces on the hill; these were estimated at a few thousand men. Defensive positions had been dug from the redoubt down to the Mystic River in an attempt to rebuff any flanking attack from the British.

The British sent a force of 2,000 men over to Charlestown in the early afternoon of 17 June, under the command of General Howe. Howe, a veteran of the French-Indian War, understood the needs of light infantry and the difficulties of assailing a fixed position frontally, so it is even more surprising that his main attack was a frontal assault. This can perhaps be attributed to the arrogant belief that the rebels would flee once they saw the British regulars advancing.

The British left, under the command of Brigadier Robert Pigott, had marched to within yards of the American lines when a heavy volley was fired into their midst. A second volley followed, forcing the left wing to fall back. The British troops were supported by artillery, but this had no impact on the first attack. One American observer described "the balls flying almost as thick as hailstones from the ships and floating batteries . . . our people stood the fire some time" (Haskell, p. 273). Howe's troops on the right flank were similarly unable to breach the American defenses. Pigott launched a second frontal attack with no more success. A British officer said, "the oldest soldiers here [Boston] say that it was the hottest fire they ever saw not even the

Battle of Minden [1759] . . . was equal to it" (Balderston and Syrett, p. 33). Howe's second attempt on the right wing failed as well.

Reinforcements arrived as the decision was made to attempt a third and final attack. The American defenders, meanwhile, were running low on ammunition, and Prescott ordered his men to hold their fire until the last possible moment. The British line advanced, and when they were within 30–60 feet (9–18 m), the Americans fired their last rounds. The British pushed forward with bayonets fixed, driving the Americans from their positions. The Americans managed to retreat over the Charlestown Neck without much opposition, however, as Gage failed to translate the victory into a decisive rout.

The British had seized the hill, but it was a Pyhrric victory. Of the 2,500 British troops involved, 228 had been killed and 800 wounded. The Americans, on the other hand, had lost only 100 killed and 270 wounded. These casualties were the worst the British suffered during the war. As Gage noted in a letter that was published in the *London Gazette*, "the tryals [sic] we have shew that the Rebels are not the despicable Rabble too many have supposed them to be" (22–25 July 1775). This battle also made clear to the Americans that, though they might be successful in defense, they would require a professional Continental-style army to challenge the British in the open fields of America.

After the casualties suffered at Breed's Hill, the British decided not to attack Dorchester Heights. While Charlestown was occupied, the British remained holed up in Boston for the rest of the year. General Gage was replaced by General Sir William Howe as Commander-in-Chief of America in October 1775.

Battle of Quebec

The final military campaign of 1775 took place in upstate New York and Canada. American forces had seized the British posts at Fort Ticonderoga and Crown Point in May

1775. In June, the Continental Congress created the Separate Army, giving the command to Major-General Philip Schuyler, along with orders to attack Canada. Schuyler's deputy, Brigadier Richard Montgomery, a former British regular, was given field command of the army. He was ordered to attack towards Montreal and rendezvous with a New England force under the command of Brigadier Benedict Arnold. Arnold's force followed the Penobscot river (in present-day Maine), intending to arrive outside Quebec City, the principal British garrison in Canada.

Battle of Lexington. (The National Army Museum)

and arrived fatigued and hungry outside Quebec in mid-November. Montgomery arrived in early December. The British commander and governor at Quebec, Lieutenant-General Sir Guy Carleton, had only 1,800 troops, nearly all of whom were newly raised militia or recruits. Most of the regulars had been sent to Boston.

The Americans fielded about 1,000 men. They attacked the city on 31 December, one day before many of Arnold's New England troops' terms of enlistment ended. A snowstorm began as the attack was launched; an American soldier described the scene:

this morning about 4 AM the time appointed to storm the city our army divided into different parts to attack the city ... we got near the walls when a heavy fire of cannon and small arms began from the enemy, they being prepared and expecting us that night ... came to the wall cannon roaring like thunder and musket balls flying like hail (Haskell, 1/1776).

Brigadier Montgomery was killed and General Arnold wounded. The Americans suffered heavy losses, and, though they remained outside the city, the threat to Quebec had passed.

The British strategy of 1775 had been to apply overt military action to try to resolve a problem that was essentially political in origin. Their aim in doing so was to quell the growing dissatisfaction of the colonists and in this they failed. The concentration of British regulars in Boston had not frightened the local population into submission. On the contrary, the population had become more openly hostile in the presence of troops. The attempt to seize and destroy the weapon caches in Concord, while technically successful, had sparked an all-out rebellion. Lack of strategic planning found the bulk of the British North American forces hemmed into Boston, surrounded by a hostile citizenry. The victory at Breed's Hill, won at such great cost, had left the senior commanders in Boston hesitant to

Montgomery's advance went according to plan, but the British and Canadian militiamen at St John's, Quebec, unexpectedly held out for five weeks. Montreal fell on 13 November 1775, with cold weather setting in. Arnold's force had underestimated crossing the Maine frontier,

Lieutenant General Sir William Howe.
(Anne SK Brown Collection)

destroy the local American forces
surrounding them.

Finally, the Americans had almost
succeeded in capturing Canada. While an
American victory would almost certainly
have provoked a more definitive response
from the British, the reality remained that
the Americans had successfully invaded as
far as Quebec, conclusively demonstrating
just how vulnerable the British were in

dealing with the insurrection. Senior
members of the British government called
for a naval blockade of the colonies, but the
ultimate decision was to concentrate
resources in a land war.

The Americans had been able to achieve
great things in 1775. They had forced the
British into Boston and kept them trapped
there. Some members of the Continental
Congress recognized, however, that the
British were not going to give in easily and
stressed the need for proper military training
and force to counter the British regulars.

Colonial and world war

This chapter will deal with the two distinct theaters of the American Revolution: the land war and the sea war. First, an overall history of the war at sea will cover 1775–83 and the chief engagements of the various navies. Naval engagements that directly affect land operations will be dealt with alongside the relevant land campaign.

The land war in North America encompassed a large area, involving the interests of numerous colonial powers, and the incursions of France, Spain, and the Dutch Republic in 1778, 1779, and 1780 respectively, gave the war a more global character. For this reason, the account of the land war will be divided into subheadings covering years and areas of operation. The war in North America will be divided into the northern campaign, encompassing New England, upstate New York, and Canada. The middle Atlantic campaign will focus on operations in lower New York, New Jersey, and Pennsylvania. The southern campaign will cover the operations from Virginia to Georgia. From 1778 onwards, an additional subheading entitled "Outside the Thirteen Colonies" will be included. This section will consider the British, French, Spanish, and later Dutch engagements in Florida, the West Indies, Europe (Minorca, Gibraltar, and the English Channel), and India. There was also some fighting on the West African coast, but this was relatively minor and will not be discussed due to space considerations.

The naval war: 1775–83

The main naval engagements of the American Revolution were between France and Great Britain, although the Spanish fleet entered the fray in 1779, tipping the balance in France's favor. The Royal Navy spent most of the war period on the defensive, and the French Navy, though able to grapple with the Royal Navy, was unable to decisively cripple the opposition and bring the naval conflict to a close. The naval war was characterized by local victories, undermined by the failure of the commanders to capitalize on their successes. Only a few engagements influenced the land campaigns in any way, although the naval forces were instrumental in transporting and landing ground forces in North America, the West Indies, and India.

The most important component of each navy was its ships of the line. The naval term "ship of the line" refers to three-masted, square-rigged vessels carrying 60 or more cannon on board (the minimum firepower to be able to stand in the 'line' of battle against an enemy). Ships with fewer than 60 cannon were referred to as cruisers and frigates. First-rate ships carried 90–100 guns; second-rate usually fielded 80–90 guns; third-rate ships had 64–74 guns. Fourth-rate ships (frigates) usually carried 50 guns, and fifth- and sixth-rate ships (cruisers) carried 24–40 guns.

The Royal Navy North American Squadron, under the command of Admiral Lord Howe, spent 1775–78 concentrating on three major naval efforts: supply and reinforcement of the British Army; blockade of the American coast; and raids on strategic points along the coastline. The entry of the French into the hostilities in 1778 committed the Royal Navy to a world war destined to stretch its resources very thin. The Royal Navy did not follow the strategy successfully employed in the Seven Years' War and attempt to blockade the French Navy in its chief ports of Toulon and Brest. Instead, efforts were principally focused on protecting the West Indies and British home waters, with smaller deployments in North America and the Indian Ocean. In 1778, there were 41 ships stationed in North America, and eight ships in the West Indies. By 1780, the numbers had been effectively reversed, with 13 ships in North America and 41 in the West Indies (Conway, p. 158).

As with the British Army, the Royal Navy was not committed to a serious building program until the threat of French opposition became a reality. As of 1 July 1778, the Royal Navy stood as follows: 66 ships of the line – 30 in European waters, 14 in North America, 13 *en route* to North America, and the rest serving in or *en route* to Minorca and India (Dull, *French Navy* p. 359). By 1782 the Royal Navy's strength had increased to 94 ships of the line, but did not outnumber the combined strength of the Spanish and French fleets, at 54 and 73 ships respectively (Dull, *French Navy* pp. 363–365).

Tactics also remained largely unchanged; Royal Navy commanders had been given "Fighting Instructions" that tied them rigidly to "line-ahead" tactics. The line-ahead was similar to linear formations of the land armies. The idea was for a squadron to form in line and attack the enemy fleet with broadside fire along a continuous line, hoping for a break in the enemy's lines of ships. Many commanders did not follow this system, however, choosing instead to attempt the "melee." The melee, or penetration of the enemy's line of ships, was intended to inflict damage by more aggressive means. Some commanders were brought before court martial for deliberate use of the melee, but most were exonerated, reflecting the opinion of the courts martial that battle tactics should be decided by the commander at sea.

The French Navy had emerged from the Seven Years' War with a poor reputation and immediately set to work to reform the service. New ships were built, naval officers considered unfit to command were relieved of duty, naval artillery was improved, and, most important, training was established as a priority. Two major naval works devised and implemented were the 'Tactique Nava' and 'Les Manoeuvres', both of which were considered to be superior to the British "Fighting Instructions". The absence of a Continental threat to France led to the decision to combat the Royal Navy on the high seas from the European theater to India and the West Indies. On 1 July 1778, the French Navy stood at 52 ships of the line; 32 ships were stationed in European waters, with 12 ships *en route* to North America and the rest in the Mediterranean and Indian oceans (Dull, *French Navy* p. 359).

The Spanish fleet also played an important role in the war on the high seas. On 1 July 1779, the Spanish fleet stood at 58 ships of the line. The vast majority of the Spanish ships were stationed in European waters and Gibraltar, with smaller squadrons in the New World (Dull, *French Navy* p. 361). The Spanish ships were very well designed and some naval historians considered them superior to both their French and British counterparts. Unfortunately, the Spanish Navy lacked a well-trained officer and ratings corps to man the ships, and neither the tactics nor the professionalism of the Spanish Navy was equivalent to those of the French and British.

In the autumn of 1775, the Continental Congress authorized the construction of a small American fleet, consisting of only five ships. The Continental Navy and the recently raised Continental marines captured the Bahamas Islands from the British in 1776, marking the first combined American naval-marine operations. The Continental Navy was successful in raiding parts of Nova Scotia and even parts of the British coast, but was never strong enough to cause real damage to the Royal Navy. The serious threat to the British came from the privateering activities of the Continental Navy and commercial fleets. Development of an American Navy ceased after the French joined the American effort.

The first significant engagement between the French and British navies took place on

27 July 1778 off the coast of Brittany. The British squadron, under the command of Admiral Lord Augustus Keppel, engaged a French squadron under the command of Admiral Comte d'Orvilliers. The French force was able to slip back to Brest. Both sides suffered damage but the battle decided nothing. The rest of the engagements recounted here were those considered locally decisive.

In January 1780, Admiral Sir George Brydges Rodney and a squadron of ships left Great Britain with provisions and stores for Gibraltar. On 16 January, his squadron fought an engagement with a Spanish squadron under the command of Don Juan de Langara. One of the Spanish ships was destroyed and another six were captured. The Spanish squadron blockading Gibraltar was easily dispersed and Rodney was able to lift the siege. Rodney and his squadron sailed for the West Indies, where they engaged a French squadron commanded by Comte de

French ships of the line. (Library of Congress)

Guichen on 17 April and 15 May 1780. The French ships were damaged, but Rodney was unable to completely destroy the squadron, only to delay its landing in the West Indies. In September 1781, squadrons under the command of Rear Admiral Thomas Graves and Comte de Grasse met off Chesapeake Bay Capes. De Grasse had sailed from the West Indies with reinforcements for the French forces in North America and 24 ships of the line. He was able to land his troops unmolested. Admiral Graves sailed with 19 ships of the line, drawing from the West Indies and North American squadrons. The two squadrons engaged for more than two hours, with both sides suffering heavy damage. For the next two days each side watched the other, but following reports of a larger French squadron on the way, the British naval high command decided to withdraw to New York. This decision meant, incidentally, that British troops at Yorktown could not be reinforced, which sealed their fate. This is discussed in more detail later.

In April 1782, the main West Indies squadrons of the British and French navies met off the coast of Dominica and Guadeloupe. The French flotilla, under the command of de Grasse, had sailed for Jamaica with an invasion force of 10,000 troops. The British combined squadrons, under the command of Rodney and Rear- Admiral Samuel Hood, chased de Grasse. During the engagement, Rodney was able to smash through the French lines with a mêlée attack. Five French ships were taken in the battle of the Saintes, but Rodney failed to pursue the remainder of the French line. Admiral Hood criticized him for this action, but it did stave off the invasion of Jamaica and so is considered a decisive engagement.

The Royal Navy was uncontested in the East Indies between 1778 and 1781. The French admiralty did not wish to engage the Royal Navy until 1782. From then the British commander, Rear-Admiral Sir Edward Hughes, engaged a French squadron under the command of Admiral Pierre-Andre Suffren de Saint-Tropez five times in two years. The French were victors in all the engagements, but like the Royal Navy they were unable to capitalize on their advantage. The British were therefore able to hold on to their gains in India and the Indian Ocean.

The land war: 1776

The spring of 1776 marked further moves towards America's political independence from Great Britain. The fighting of the previous year and the raiding and burning of towns by the Royal Navy had pushed the American colonies beyond the reach of conciliation and closer to cutting their ties conclusively. The colonial governments were authorizing the use of privateers, war against loyalists, opening of trade with European nations, and the embargo of British goods. After much wrangling over terms and conditions, the Thirteen Colonies declared political independence from Great Britain on 4 July 1776 and recreated themselves the "Thirteen United States of America".

The political and social implications of the Declaration of Independence have been debated for decades and fall outside the scope of this work, except to say that this act galvanized some elements of society and alienated others, particularly those who considered themselves neutral on the question. Citizens who wanted outright independence felt that the Declaration of Independence was the last step towards that independence. The second Continental Congress had finally and formally decided. However, some people who sympathized with the original grievances felt that the Declaration of Independence had gone too far. They did not want to sever ties with Britain.

The effect on the Continental Army appeared to be positive. An American colonel commented that:

the Declaration of Independence ... was announced to the army in general orders, and filled everyone with enthusiastic zeal, as the point was now forever settled, and there was no further hope of reconciliation and dependence on the mother country (Tallmadge, p. 9).

Such a state of affairs also made a clear distinction between loyalists and American republicans, a situation that provoked a violent civil war among the civilians of North America.

The British had a strategy in place for the 1776 campaign season. Lord George Germain was the Secretary of State for the American Colonies from November 1775 to February 1782. He was a former military officer and

his role was to coordinate military and political strategy with the British commanders in America. Its first component was the British Northern Army. This group, under the command of Major- (later Lieutenant-) General Sir John Burgoyne, was to sail for Quebec to lift the siege, then transfer command to General Carleton to clear Canada of American forces, and strike south towards the Hudson river. A second contingent, leaving from Halifax under the command of General Howe, would attack

Declaration of Independence. (The British Museum)

Lord George Germain. (René Chartrand)

the New York and Long Island region and
link up with Carleton coming from the
north. The intention was to cut off New
England from the rest of the colonies,
leaving it to "rot" under a Royal Navy
blockade. A third and smaller expedition was
to attack Charleston in the south.

Northern campaign

During the winter months of 1775–76, the
British troops in Boston were hemmed in on
three sides. General Howe refused to fight
Washington and the New England Army,
preferring to wait for reinforcements. Howe
was unaware that the New England Army
that surrounded him was at times barely
capable of offering resistance as it tried to

cope with ongoing problems of desertion and re-enlistment. General Washington had artillery captured from Fort Ticonderoga placed on Dorchester Heights, and by early March 1776 the guns were in place and firing upon the British in Boston. Howe ordered an attack to take place, but had to cancel the order on account of inclement weather. Howe then decided to evacuate Boston, and did so on 17 March 1776. The British officer Kemble recorded: "troops ordered to embark at 5 in the morning and completed by 8 and under sail by 9" (Kemble, p. 73). The British force sailed from Boston for Halifax, Howe considering that his troops needed rest and refitting before heading towards their next battle in New York.

In Canada, the British relieving force arrived outside Quebec on 6 May. The Americans lifted the siege and fell back towards Montreal, while the British pushed towards Trois-Rivières. The American Army had suffered from smallpox and low morale over the course of winter 1775–76, but upon receiving reinforcements attacked the British camp near Trois-Rivières on 8 June. The attack failed, and the American Army began to retreat towards Lake Champlain. By the end of June, the Americans had withdrawn from Montreal, Fort Chambly, and St John's. The British halted their pursuit when they reached Lake Champlain, as Carleton wished to build a flotilla to launch an attack towards Crown Point in the south. This delay allowed the American forces to regroup and fortify the southern areas of Lake Champlain.

On 11 October, Carleton sailed with his flotilla and captured Crown Point. His force then moved towards Fort Ticonderoga, where the American garrison refused to surrender. With winter coming on, Carleton decided that a blockade of Ticonderoga was not feasible; wintering in that region without adequate shelter would cause casualties, so he withdrew to winter quarters on the frontier of Canada. The Americans had been driven from Canada, but the objectives of the campaign had not been achieved. Fort Ticonderoga and the southern area of Lake

Champlain were still in American hands. As a result, Carleton was branded as being too hesitant, and when the campaign resumed in 1777, the invasion force was under the command of General Burgoyne, who had to finish the job of clearing the southern areas of Lake Champlain.

Southern campaign

A combined force was organized for British operations in the American south. One contingent, under the command of Major- (later Lieutenant-) General Sir Henry Clinton, originated in Boston, while a second was organized to sail from Ireland. Their objectives were to coordinate the raising and support of loyalist corps in the southern colonies. Both contingents encountered problems in reaching their destinations; Clinton arrived at Cape Fear on 12 March, after the loyalists of North Carolina had been embodied and soundly defeated at Moore's Creek Bridge on 27 February 1776. Following the arrival of the second contingent, Clinton decided to set sail for South Carolina and capture Sullivan's Island, which protected the estuary leading to Charleston.

The attack on the island highlighted the problems of coordinating an amphibious operation. The naval commander, Admiral Sir Peter Parker, and Clinton communicated poorly, failing to coordinate plans and intelligence. The fort protecting the island, commanded by Colonel William Moultrie, was well fortified, with capable gunners manning the defenses. The British attack began on 28 June. The fort not only withstood the attack, but also inflicted heavy damage on the Royal Navy ships. Commanders on land could not launch their attack because the Royal Navy could not get close enough to provide support. The British withdrew and the force sailed for New York to link up with Howe's troops, arriving on 2 August.

Middle Atlantic campaign

General Washington sent Major-General Charles Lee, a former British regular, to assess the defenses of the New York City region. Lee understood that defending the region would be too problematic, as the British would certainly have a numerical as well as a naval advantage, permitting them to land troops at will. General Lee decided to fortify areas where the Americans might at least hold up the British regulars and inflict heavy casualties. He was then directed to head south to shore up defenses in South Carolina.

In April, General Washington moved to New York to make preparations for the defense of the region with the remainder of the New England Army. Forts were constructed along the Hudson and designated Forts Lee and Washington. Washington also needed men to defend the area, and summoned some 20,000 soldiers, many of them militia, from the colonies around New York. As Colonel Tallmadge noted: "the American Army [was] composed principally of levies, or troops raised for short periods, and militia" (Tallmadge, p. 8). Washington sent most of his troops to Long Island and constructed fortifications along the heights of Brooklyn and the hills south of the heights. The troops on Long Island were placed under the command of Major-General Israel Putnam, whose defensive lines were poorly organized – too long and too lightly held. Washington, however, approved the plans, and they proceeded accordingly.

Unlike South Carolina, the amphibious operations carried out in New York Harbor were an excellent example of coordinated army/navy planning. Howe and his troops reached New York from Halifax in late June. On 2 July, light infantry units seized control of Staten Island. The rest of the British Army was disembarked to camp there for the remainder of July, while Howe awaited reinforcements from Europe and Clinton in the south. The bulk of the reinforcements arrived from Europe in early August, mainly Guards regiments and German auxiliaries.

On 22 August, the first British units landed on Long Island. The British officer Kemble wrote: "landed about 9 in the morning . . . without the smallest opposition . . . the whole on the shore by 12 o'clock making fourteen thousand seven hundred

men" (Kemble, p. 85). A force of light infantry, grenadiers, and other regiments proceeded east to reconnoiter the American fortified positions in the hills south of Brooklyn Heights. The British commanders realized that a direct assault would be difficult, while forward units under the command of General Clinton noted that the American left flank was weakly defended. The British decided on a flanking attack to roll the Americans up from behind.

By 25 August, all of the British troops, nearly 20,000 men, had been assembled on Long Island. The battle of Long Island was to be the largest battle of the war in terms of total numbers of men involved. General Howe sent a large force, commanded by General Clinton, to attack the American left flank. Two brigades, under the command of Major-General James Grant, were under orders to attack the American right flank while Clinton's units dealt with the left, creating a diversion. The Hessian Division, under the command of Lieutenant-General Leopold von Heister, was to attack the American center, commanded by Major-General John Sullivan.

Clinton's force moved into position overnight on 26–27 August, and General Grant's brigades began to move towards the American lines. A British captain described how "we got through the pass at daybreak without any opposition . . . we fired two pieces of cannon to let him [General Grant] know we were at hand" (Scheer and Rankin, p. 166). The battle began at 9:00 am with General Grant's troops and the Hessian division attacking.

The American Colonel Tallmadge commented, "before such an overwhelming force of disciplined troops, our small band could not maintain their ground, and the main body retired within their lines" (Tallmadge, p. 9). The British and Hessians smashed into the American center, which began to collapse. The fighting in the trenches and redoubts was quite bloody. A British officer described how "the Hessians and our brave Highlanders gave no quarter and it was a fine sight to see with what alacrity they dispatched

Battle of Long Island. (Colonial Williamsburg)

the Rebels with their bayonets after we surrounded them" (Scheer and Rankin, p. 167).

The American right flank held up better than the center line until Clinton's force began to attack from the rear. Some of the fiercest fighting took place as the American right flank attempted to pull back. The troops of the Maryland regiments acquitted themselves well in attempting to force a hole in the British lines. After a series of heavy fights in the marshes behind their positions, the American right wing broke up into small parties and attempted to reach the fortified lines at Brooklyn Heights.

Colonel Tallmadge recorded the bitterness of the fighting on Long Island: "this was the first time in my life that I had witnessed the awful scene of a battle . . . I well remember my sensations on the occasion, for they were solemn beyond description" (Tallmadge, pp. 9–10). An American private soldier recalled how, when his unit was shipped over to Long Island to support the defenses at Brooklyn Heights, "[they] now began to meet the wounded men, another sight I was unacquainted with, some with broken arms, some with broken legs, and some with broken heads" (Martin, p. 24).

The British were outside the defenses of Brooklyn Heights by midday, but Howe decided not to attack right away. He feared that the defenses were too strong, although he was mistaken in this assumption and they might have been easily breached. By 10:00 pm on 29 August the Americans had begun to withdraw 9,000 men from Long Island and retreat to Manhattan, over the East River. The British were not aware of the withdrawal and as one British officer noted: "in the morning to our great astonishment found they had evacuated all their works on Brookland [Brooklyn]" (Kemble, p. 86). Part of the reason for this was, as pointed out by Colonel Tallmadge, that "the troops began to retire from the lines in such a manner that no chasm was made in the lines" (Tallmadge, p. 10). It is estimated that the Americans lost nearly 3,000 men killed and wounded, plus another 1,500 captured. The British lost 300 men killed and 500 wounded.

General Howe did not move against Washington's army on Manhattan Island because peace negotiations were still a possibility. The Declaration of Independence proved a stumbling block, however, and on 15 September 4,000 British troops landed on Manhattan Island at Kip's Bay, after clearing most of the western end of Long Island. The British decided to secure the beachhead area instead of attempting to cut off the retreating American forces from lower Manhattan. This strategy allowed the Americans to retreat up the west side of Manhattan Island.

A combined force of Hessians and British light infantry was repulsed at Harlem Heights in northern Manhattan on 16 September. The Americans held fortified positions at the northern end of the island, and the British decided not to attack frontally. Instead, they embarked and landed to the north of Manhattan on 12 October. Washington recognized the danger of being cut off, and decided to pull most of his troops off the island and into Westchester County of New York, leaving a large contingent at Fort Washington while the

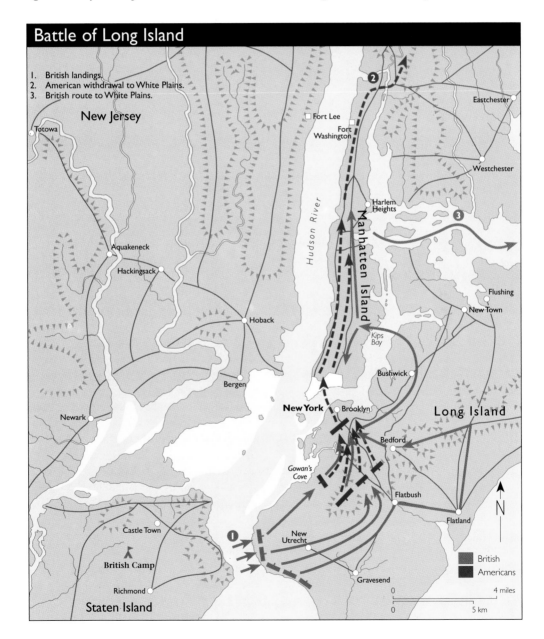

Battle of Long Island

1. British landings.
2. American withdrawal to White Plains.
3. British route to White Plains.

New Jersey

Totowa

Fort Lee

Fort Washington

Eastchester

Westchester

Aquakeneck

Hackingsack

Hudson River

Harlem Heights

Manhatten Island

Flushing

New Town

Hoback

Kips Bay

Bergen

Bushwick

New York   Brooklyn   Long Island

Newark

Bedford

Gowan's Cove

Flatbush

Flatland

N

Castle Town

British Camp

New Utrecht

British

Americans

Richmond

Gravesend

Staten Island

0   4 miles
0   5 km

British troops enter New York City.
(The British Museum)

majority withdrew to White Plains and entrenched themselves there.

The British forces attacked the American positions at White Plains on 28 October. Colonel Tallmadge reported that "at dawn of the day, the Hessian column advanced within musket shot of our troops . . . at first they fell back, but rallied again immediately" (Tallmadge, p. 14). The focus of the battle was Chadderton's Hill, which dominated the area and was held by the Americans. After two attempts, British forces took the hill, and the

rest of the day was spent with the two sides exchanging cannon and small-arms fire. After a few days, General Washington withdrew further afield with his troops. Here again, General Howe failed to press his advantage to try to capture and destroy Washington's army. Instead he returned to Manhattan Island to besiege Fort Washington.

The British Lieutenant-General Earl Hugh Percy had previously made an attempt on Fort Washington from the south but had recognized that it was well defended. By 15 November, the fort was surrounded on all sides by British troops, including Royal Navy ships on the Hudson River. George

20 November. Cornwallis was able to threaten Fort Lee, which was evacuated. He pushed hard to entrap Washington and his army. Howe followed and landed with another contingent, meeting up with Cornwallis at New Brunswick, New Jersey, in early December. Howe also dispatched a contingent of 7,000 men under the command of General Clinton to seize Newport, Rhode Island. Both the town and the island on which it was located were in British hands by 8 December, giving the British control of Narragansett Bay.

Cornwallis and Howe together chased Washington and his army across New Jersey. On 8 December, Washington and his army crossed the Delaware River as the British entered Trenton. On 14 December the British were ordered into winter quarters in New Jersey. British and Hessian troops were quartered throughout the region, and General Washington devised a bold scheme. He decided to attack the Hessian positions in Trenton on 25 December, and his plan was completely successful. The Hessians were soundly defeated, for two reasons: the Hessian Colonel Rall had failed to fortify their positions; and the date of the attack meant that many soldiers had been celebrating the holiday. The Americans lost four men wounded, compared with more than 1,000 Hessians captured.

Washington re-crossed the Delaware on the night of 25 December, only to go back again on 27 December, when he headed towards Trenton. Howe had ordered Cornwallis and 8,000 troops to find and destroy Washington's force. Cornwallis' force came into contact with Washington in Trenton on 2 January 1777. A Hessian officer noted: "the jägers and light infantry, supported by the Hessian Grenadiers, attacked the enemy at once, whereupon he withdrew through Trenton across the bridge" (Ewald, p. 49). Washington was caught at Assunpink Creek. During the evening, however, Washington, realizing his position, marched first due east then due north towards Princeton. Ewald described "this clever man [Washington] who did not doubt

Washington withdrew across the Hudson into New Jersey on 16 November, but a large group of troops remained stationed on the eastern side of the river, under the command of General Lee, to forestall any British incursion into southern New England.

On 16 November, Fort Washington was attacked from three sides. The fort fell with more than 3,000 American soldiers killed, wounded, or captured, and American control of the Hudson was compromised. Following this victory, Howe decided to divide his forces. He sent Major- (later Lieutenant-) General Earl Charles Cornwallis and 4,000 soldiers to Closter, New Jersey, on that Lord Cornwallis would realize his mistake during the night and would dispatch a corps … whereby he would be forced by circumstances to surrender" (Ewald, p. 49).

The British forces at Princeton were surprised and compelled to give ground. Washington, however, was forced to head to the mountains in Morristown when news arrived that Cornwallis was heading towards Princeton. Morristown offered Washington the option of counteracting a British move from either New York to the north along the Hudson or across New Jersey towards Philadelphia.

The British had lost more than 1,000 men in the course of one week. Howe pulled his forces back to New Brunswick, thus abandoning most of New Jersey. As with operations in Canada, the British were put on the defensive and would have to regain lost ground in the campaigns of 1777, when they aimed to seize Philadelphia. The successes of late 1776 had given the American cause a significant boost in morale. An American soldier commented that "our taking the Hessians has given our affairs quite a different turn as the militia are embodying in all parts of the Jerseys" (Shaw Papers Ms. N-49.47). The Hessian officer, Ewald, appraised public opinion of Washington and Cornwallis:

[actions at Trenton and Princeton] raised so much hubbub and sensation in the world and gave Washington the reputation of an excellent general, derived simply and solely from Lord Cornwallis' mistake of not marching in two columns to Trenton (Ewald, p. 50).

The British had lost the initiative and were clearly no longer within striking distance of Philadelphia, the perceived governmental headquarters of the Thirteen Colonies. George Washington and the remnants of his army had survived the 1776 campaigns. The foundations of the Continental Army had been laid. A French officer writing a report described the American forces thus: "men need only the experience of defeats in order

to learn how to defend themselves properly and acquire the military effectiveness necessary in order to inspire respect on the enemy" (Recicourt, p. 211).

The land war: 1777

The British strategy for 1777 provides the clearest example of poor strategic planning by generals in North America. General Burgoyne and his army were ordered to push south from Canada and take Albany and the Hudson River. Burgoyne was expected to wait in Albany to link up with General Howe. General Howe did not see that

Burgoyne required his support, and, holed up in New York with his troops, decided that they would not link up with Burgoyne as planned. Leaving only a secondary group in New York to push north, Howe took the major part of the British army in New York and set out to seize Philadelphia by amphibious assault. Howe felt that, since Philadelphia represented the independence movement, the seizure of the Continental Congress might force an end to the conflict.

Historians have debated the "what ifs" of this decision-making process thoroughly, but it is indisputably clear that both Howe and Burgoyne underestimated the American forces and paid a high price for their

miscalculation. The war became global partly due to the incompetent performance of 1777. After the campaigns of 1777, Great Britain would be forced to strip her army in North America to fight a global war against France and later Spain and the Dutch Republic.

The "Main" Continental Army, under the command of General Washington, was deployed to counter the British attacks in Pennsylvania. It suffered defeats in this undertaking but survived, never being completely destroyed. The "Separate Army",

British amphibious attack on Newport, Rhode Island. (National Maritime Museum)

now referred to as the "Northern Army", under the command of General Philip Schuyler with Major-General Horatio Gates as his subordinate, formed to fight Burgoyne's army. The majority of troops used to defend New York from the British were made up of militia from New England and New York, with Continentals representing a small corps of the total numbers.

Northern campaign

The principal northern campaign began in Canada. Lieutenant-General Burgoyne advanced from St John's, Quebec, towards Lake Champlain with 10,000 men in June 1777. A secondary drive of 1,600 troops, regulars, provincials, and Indians was sent from Fort Oswego in the west under the command of Lieutenant-Colonel Barry St Leger. St Leger was to march due east along the Mohawk river and link up with Burgoyne at Albany.

Burgoyne's force reached Fort Ticonderoga on 1 July. The American commander at Ticonderoga, Brigadier Arthur St Clair, expected the attack to come from the front, but General Burgoyne placed cannon on a hill opposite. St Clair, recognizing the danger, withdrew his force of 3,000 militia and Continentals to the south on 5 July. Leaving a small detachment at Ticonderoga to maintain communications with Canada, Burgoyne pushed south to harry St Clair's rearguards, reaching Skenesboro by 10 July.

At Skenesboro, Burgoyne decided to march overland to Forts Ann and Edward instead of returning north to travel down Lake George. The Americans anticipated Burgoyne's plan, and set out to block his path. A British officer, Lieutenant William Digby, noted on 24 July:

the enemy have felled large trees over the roads which were turned so narrow as not to allow more than one man ... we were obliged to cut around the wood which was attended by much fatigue and labour (Add. Mss. 32413).

Supplies became a problem early in the campaign; Burgoyne commented on 9 and 10 July, "the army much fatigued, many parts of it having wanted their provisions for two days" (7204-6-4). He also described the effect of the terrain: "the toil of the march was great ... forty bridges to construct and others to repair" (7204-6-4).

The British reached Fort Edward on the Hudson River on 30 July, and occupied Fort George on the same day. The Americans were still falling back to the south and across the river in the Saratoga region, but the ever-present need for supplies forced the British to stop and rest at Fort Edward. On 11 August, a detachment of 600 men, comprising German auxiliaries, provincial troops, and Indians, under the command of Lieutenant-Colonel Frederick Baum, was instructed to march southeast towards Bennington, "to obtain large supplies of cattle, horses and carriages" (7204-6-4). Brigadier John Stark and 2,000 New England militiamen met Baum's column outside Bennington on 16 August, where they surrounded and destroyed them. A second German column, which had been sent in aid of Baum's efforts on 14 August, closed in on Bennington as the militia pillaged Baum's camp. The militia re-formed to destroy the second column as well. Burgoyne shortly received word of the defeat and loss of almost 1,000 men.

Lieutenant Digby wrote on 20 August that "the German detachment at Bennington was destroyed and ... St Leger was forced to retire to Oswego" (Add. Mss. 32413). On 19 August, Major-General Gates took over command of the Northern Army from General Schuyler. Recruits were on the rise as word of the successes at Bennington spread and raised spirits in the area. On 13–14 September, Burgoyne's army crossed the Hudson River near Saratoga. Supplies were still at a premium for the British, and an officer in the Royal Artillery described a general order that warned troops to "be cautious of expending their ammunition in case of action ... the impossibility of a fresh supply ... avoid firing on a retreating army" (Hadden, p. 150).

Upon taking command, General Gates marched north towards Bemis Heights, which controlled the main Saratoga–Albany road. General Schuyler had fortified Bemis Heights in August. The first firefight between the two armies occurred on 18 September, when British soldiers foraging for food were ambushed by American forces. On 19 September, Burgoyne set out to deal with Bemis Heights, only to be intercepted by Major-General Benedict Arnold, who smashed into the British column with 3,000 troops at Freeman's Farm. The fighting was heavy; Lieutenant Digby related that "the clash of cannon and musketry never ceased till darkness … when they [Americans] retired to their camp leaving us the master of the field but it was a dear bought victory" (Add. Mss. 32413). The British suffered more than 600 men killed and wounded in this incident, while the Americans lost just over 300 men killed and wounded. Burgoyne decided to stay in the area and build a defensive position for the army after he received word from

Lieutenant-General Clinton in New York, promising a push up the Hudson River.

Clinton marched north with 3,000 troops on 3 October, and his force moved quickly, seizing Verplanck's Point, as well as forts Montgomery, Constitution, and Clinton by 7 October. Clinton sent a detachment of 2,000 men and supplies towards Albany to meet Burgoyne, whose situation was rapidly deteriorating. The Americans had all but cut off communications between Burgoyne and Canada, seized Fort George, and threatened Fort Ticonderoga.

Burgoyne decided to attack the American positions at Bemis Heights once again on 7 October, instead of falling back towards the Hudson. He sent a strong force to engage the American left flank; this was repulsed and fell back to the British lines. An American soldier noted, "a body of the enemy [was] advancing towards our lines … at about 4 o'clock the

Shooting of British Brigadier Simon Fraser by American Sharpshooters, 7 October 1777. (National Archives of Canada)

Northern campaigns

battle began ... the rifles and light infantry fell upon the enemy's right flank and rear ... they then retreated with great precipitation and confusion" (Dearborn, p. 108). British morale was very low, and sank further when Clinton's detachment was forced to return after the pilots refused to proceed any further up the Hudson, leaving Burgoyne's troops stranded and outnumbered two to one.

On 8 October, Burgoyne decided to pull back, only to discover that Gates had already cut off his retreat. Burgoyne created a defended camp north of Saratoga and the Americans began to close in. Lieutenant Digby observed: "their cannon and ours began to play on each other. They took many of our batteaus on the river as our artillery could not protect them" (Add. Mss. 32413).

Another British officer noted: "we are now become so habituated to fire that the soldiers seem to be indifferent to it" (Anburey, p. 181).

On 14 October, Burgoyne began to negotiate the surrender of his forces, and on 17 October the remains of his force marched out of camp. The British surrendered almost 6,000 men, shattering British prestige the world over. The surrender effectively removed any threat to the Hudson River region and New England from the north. The American forces had distinguished themselves, but the British commanders had forgotten the rules they had learned in the French-Indian War about waging war in the hilly, wooded countryside of the American frontier. The American generals, especially Arnold, had demonstrated themselves equal to the task required of them. The militia had fought well when they had the advantage of terrain, as at Bennington, while the Continentals had fought well at Freeman's Farm.

Middle Atlantic campaign

Howe's campaign in the Middle Atlantic centered around the engagements at Brandywine and Germantown. He moved troops into New Jersey in an attempt to draw Washington and the "Main Army" out for battle. This maneuver produced a series of skirmishes, but was a failure overall, prompting Howe to return to Staten Island. Over the course of July, troops embarked onto Royal Navy ships and transports, and on 23 July the fleet sailed. On 25 August, the fleet landed its cargo on the northern reaches of Chesapeake Bay at the Head of Elk. Washington received word of the landing and marched south with the Main Army, 18,000 strong, to confront the British (Tallmadge, p. 20). Washington placed his army at Brandywine Creek and built up the area into a defensive position.

Though strong generally, the American position had left its flanks unprotected. Howe, approaching with his troops, realized

The Carribbean

the potential for another successful flank attack. An American soldier described how, "at 8 o'clock in the morning on the 11th [September] a considerable body of the enemy appeared opposite to us" (Shaw Ms. N-49.47).

The battle commenced at 10:00 am. A sizeable column of Hessian and British units were sent in opposite the center and left flank of the American lines, under the command of Lieutenant-General Wilhelm von Knyphausen. A large formation of light infantry, plus Guards and Grenadiers units, under the command of General Cornwallis, moved without being detected against the American right flank, in a march 30 km (18 miles) long, intending to create havoc in the American lines. The other British lines were successful in pushing the American lines back, and the British left flank finally joined the battle at about 4:00 pm. As Major John Andre noted: "the rebels were driven back by the superior fire of the troops, but these troops were too much exhausted to be able to charge or pursue" (Andre, p. 46).

The Americans reacted but did not panic. When the British left flank finally smashed through the American lines, the Americans began to retreat, but in fairly good order, not as a rabble. A French officer serving with the American forces declared: "if the English had followed up their advantages that day, Washington's Army would have been spoken of no more" (5701-9).

The battle at Brandywine Creek cost the Americans more than 1,000 men killed, wounded, and captured. The British lost half that number. The British had won but were not in a position to follow up their victory aggressively; they were simply too tired after marching 30 km (18 miles). The two armies fell back towards Philadelphia over the next few weeks and a series of small skirmishes took place. On 26 September, the British marched into Philadelphia. This was an important achievement psychologically, but not as important strategically as Howe's continued failure to completely destroy Washington's Main Army as it withdrew to the west of the city. The Continental Congress had already been evacuated to Lancaster and later moved to Yorktown. Howe moved to the north of the city and encamped his army at Germantown.

Following the defeat and occupation of Philadelphia, Washington set out to destroy the British camp at Germantown. He deployed four columns, two militia and two Continental, intended to converge on the

Battle of Germantown. (Anne SK Brown Collection)

British lines simultaneously. An American private soldier recorded that at:

about daybreak [4 October] our advanced guard and the British outposts came in contact … they soon fell back and we advanced, when the action became general. The enemy [was] driven quite through their camp. They left their kettles … affairs went on well for some time (Martin, pp. 72–73).

The American advance became bogged down in trying to take a position held by the 40th Regiment at Chew House. As Major Andre noted, "these [soldiers of the 40th Regiment] not only maintained themselves a great while but drove the rebels off repeatedly" (Andre, p. 55). By the time the Americans moved on, the rest of the British forces had rallied. Colonel Tallmadge stated, "during this transaction [Chew House] time elapsed, the situation of our troops was uncomfortable, their ardor abated and the enemy obtained time to rally. In less than thirty minutes, our troops began to retire, and from the ardor of the pursuit, were in full retreat" (Tallmadge, pp. 22–23).

Not all of Washington's troops took part in the battle due to the weather, but again the British were unable to follow up their victory to encircle and destroy the Main Army. The losses for the Americans were some 1,000 killed, wounded, and captured, while the British lost 500 men.

Howe pulled back his defensive lines around the city of Philadelphia, and once again the British found themselves on the defensive with the Americans, although weakened, still able to inflict damage upon their troops. The British cleared defenses on the Delaware River to allow seaborne supplies to reach the city. Washington was having difficulty keeping his army together, as enlistment contracts expired for many men. This depletion convinced Washington not to attack, but Howe was left once again at the end of 1777 without a decisive victory to his credit. Washington withdrew his army into winter quarters at Valley Forge, Pennsylvania in mid-December, where the

troops were retrained under the drill instructor eyes of Major-General von Steuben.

The campaign of 1777 finally ended in November. The British had been soundly defeated at Saratoga, and the war seemed likely to become a global conflict with the entrance of France. Howe had defeated the Main Army, but had been unable to conclusively destroy it. The American "capitol" had been taken but even this decisive action did not signify the end of the war. The year 1778 marked the true beginning of the end of the British presence in the Thirteen Colonies. Both the British Army and the Royal Navy were redirected to other parts of the world to deal with French and, later, Spanish antagonism. The years 1775–77, in retrospect, were the closest the British came to ending the uprising with military force. It is debatable whether the political rebellion would have continued if the American forces had been decisively defeated in a land war.

The land war: 1778

The British forces in North America were centered around New York, Philadelphia, Newport, Florida, Halifax, Quebec, and Montreal. A formal alliance, signed on 6 February 1778 between the American and French governments, forced a change of strategy. Over the first few months of the year, Benjamin Franklin was instrumental in lobbying the French court to support the American cause. British commanders were reassigned. General Clinton was ordered to take command of the forces in the Thirteen Colonies, replacing General Howe. In Canada General Carleton was replaced by Lieutenant-General Frederick Haldimand.

Senior commanders in North America and Great Britain realized that the focus of war had shifted fundamentally, and that France had become the primary threat. In March, Clinton received his orders for the whole of 1778. He was to withdraw British forces from Philadelphia, and send troops to New York and then to the West Indies to fight the French. The British were to hold New York, Newport, and Canada. Naval raids were scheduled along the New England coast, and a southern campaign was planned. The overarching strategy was that the British Army would control major towns along the coast, and the navy would allow it to raid at will. Peace negotiations were to be opened between the Continental Congress and the British government.

Middle Atlantic campaign

General Washington and his Main Army had a difficult winter at Valley Forge, 30 km (18 miles) north of Philadelphia. Many men were released from duty when their enlistment contracts expired, but a corps of men and officers remained who were properly trained for linear warfare, thanks to the training program created by Major-General von Steuben and battle experience gained. Colonel Tallmadge noted on the eve of the 1778 campaign that the Main Army began 'feeling somewhat like veteran troops' (Tallmadge, p. 27). Washington used the winter to develop a plan for militia to be used to guard specific areas, releasing Continental troops and extra militia units for mobile operations. In spite of this, personnel shortfalls continued. The number of men enlisted was still well below the army's authorized strengths, which limited Washington's ability to attack Philadelphia. Many historians consider the Continental Army that marched out of Valley Forge against Clinton's army the most highly trained and disciplined American force of the entire conflict.

On 8 May, General Clinton arrived in Philadelphia to take over command from General Howe. Clinton was ordered to withdraw from Philadelphia, and decided to march overland to Sandy Hook, New Jersey. Three thousand loyalists who feared for their safety were shipped by sea to New York, and on 18 June Clinton set off with nearly 10,000 troops and more loyalist refugees towards New York. An American soldier remembered: "we heard the British army had left Philadelphia ... we marched

immediately in pursuit" (Martin, p. 122). The American force shadowed the withdrawing British Army, monitoring the train of supplies and men, which stretched for 19 km (12 miles). Very high temperatures made for very slow going.

Major-General Charles Lee was sent with 5,000 men to harass the British rearguard, while the rest of the Main Army stayed further back. On 28 June, Washington ordered Lee to attack the rearguards, although he was not certain of their size. Lee sent in the attack near Monmouth Court House. The fighting quickly became confused; as British officer Kemble noted: "Lee then advanced to begin the attack, but falling in with our two Grenadiers Battalions, and a Battalion of Guards, who facing about charged and pushed them above two miles" (Kemble, p. 154). This account was confirmed by an American soldier: "our division under the command of General Lee advanced towards the enemy. They formed in a solid column then fired a volley at us they being so much superior to our numbers we retreated" (Greenman, p. 122).

Lee had smashed into the British Second Division, led by General Cornwallis. Washington deployed the remainder of his army to face the British counterattack, the brunt of which was borne by New England regiments. A heated verbal exchange occurred between Lee and Washington following Lee's retreat. Lee was relieved of command and would later face court martial for not obeying orders. Lee was also suspected of being a British sympathizer. An American soldier, describing the scene, said: "a sharp conflict ensued; these troops [New Englanders] maintained their ground until the whole force of the enemy that could be brought to bear had charged upon them" (Scheer and Rankin, p. 331). Major Andre described how "this column [American] appeared to our left and rear marching very rapidly and in good order" (Andre, pp. 78–79). The British, while successful at points along the line, launched attacks without proper orders and were unable to maintain consistent pressure.

Lieutenant General Sir Henry Clinton.
(Anne SK Brown Collection)

The battle was the longest of the war,
beginning in early morning and lasting all
day. Small pieces of land were exchanged, as
were artillery duels. General Washington was
able to push the British back to their original
positions by the early evening. The American
forces succeeded in holding the line against a
British assault in the open field and retaking
lost territory. The heat of the day had taken
a toll, however, and neither side attempted
another assault as night approached. Clinton
withdrew his force when evening fell,
unmolested by the Americans. He was
running short of supplies, and needed to
reach Sandy Hook and meet the Royal Navy.
The British had lost nearly 1,000 men killed,
wounded, and captured, while the American
forces had lost just half that.

The outcome of the Battle of Monmouth
was indecisive. The Americans claimed
victory, but Clinton disputed "the manifest
misapplication of that term [victory] to an
army whose principle is retreat and which
accomplishes it without affront or loss"
(Clinton, p. 97). Clinton was able to withdraw
to Sandy Hook and was evacuated to New
York by 6 July, before the French fleet arrived,
so he had fulfilled his orders. The British had
failed to destroy or even force the Americans
from the battlefield, which provided another
morale boost for the Americans. More
important, the Americans successfully counter-
attacked and seized ground in the open. As a
Hessian officer commented:

*today the Americans showed much boldness
and resolution on all sides during their attacks.
Had Generals Washington and Lee not attacked
so early, but waited longer, until our army had
pushed deeper into the very difficult defiles in
this area, it is quite possible we would have been
routed* (Ewald, p. 136).

Northern campaign
On 11 July a French fleet, carrying
4,000 soldiers, arrived off Sandy Hook under

the command of Admiral Charles Hector
Comte d'Estaing. Clinton's successful
withdrawal and redeployment meant that
New York was no longer a feasible target, and
the fleet shortly sailed for Newport, Rhode
Island, arriving off the coast on 29 July. On
9 August a second force, this one American
and commanded by Major-General John
Sullivan, arrived with 10,000 Continental
and militia troops, to invest the British
position from the north. The British had
3,000 troops at Newport under the
command of General Sir Robert Pigot.

The French fleet was followed closely by
British Admiral Lord Howe, who arrived off
the coast in August to lift the siege. Evaluating
the opposition, Major John Bowater noted:
"the French fleet is heavier than ours, but we
outnumber them" (Balderston and Syrett,
p. 167). The French fleet set out to engage the
British, only to run into a storm on 11 August
which damaged both. The weather forced the
French to withdraw to Boston, which in turn
caused problems for the American land forces,
as the British continued to be resupplied,
reinforced, and supported by the Royal Navy.

General Sullivan was irate with d'Estaing's withdrawal, which forced the Americans to lift the siege by 27 August. This episode soured relations between the French and American commanders, as each side accused the other of lack of effort. A British relieving force under the command of Major-General Charles Grey arrived at Newport after the French withdrawal. Supported by the Royal Navy, a series of raids began along the New England coast, destroying supplies and ships and gathering stores from remote places such as Martha's Vineyard.

Coastal raiding was not all; during the summer and autumn months, a series of raids led by British provincial corps, including Butler's Rangers and allied Indian tribes, struck from Fort Niagara along the frontiers of New York and Virginia. Fighting along the frontier had been increasing steadily throughout 1778, and raids had struck settlements as far east as Cherry Valley, 80 km (50 miles) west of Albany. American efforts to counterattack were unsuccessful, and by the end of 1778 Washington and his senior officers were drawing up campaign plans for 1779.

Southern campaign

In November, Clinton released 5,000 troops for operations in Florida and the West Indies. Meanwhile, Lieutenant-Colonel Archibald Campbell was sent with 3,000 troops, both regulars and provincials, to seize Savannah, Georgia. The Americans at Savannah, under the command of Major-General Robert Howe, were a small detachment, and were easily defeated on 29 December. Savannah fell, as did the surrounding area. Campbell continued northwest and his force reached and captured Augusta, Georgia, near the end of January 1779.

Outside the Thirteen Colonies

The French were the first to move in the materially important West Indies, seizing the British island of Dominica on 7 September 1778. The British went on the offensive in December; they landed on St Lucia on

13 December, after reinforcements had arrived from New York, occupying the northern side of the island. Admiral d'Estaing landed 7,000 reinforcements on the opposite end of the island, and on 18 December the French attempted to destroy the British fortifications. Their efforts were unsuccessful and they suffered heavy casualties, forcing them to

withdraw on 29 December and surrender the island to the British force.

In British East India Company was embroiled in a war with the Maratha Confederacy. Word reached Bombay and Madras of the French intervention on the American side, prompting British East India Company forces to move against French posts in India. All of these had been seized by the end of 1778, except for Mahe. In taking this action, however, the British sparked a war (also known as the Second Mysore War) with the local ruler,

Battle of Monmouth Court House.
(The National Army Museum)

Haidar Ali of Mysore, who had been partially allied with the French. The war in India largely pitched the British East India Company and regular forces against the Indian princes' armies until at least 1782, when a strong French force came to the aid of Haidar Ali.

The campaigns of 1778 clearly illustrate the shift of British focus from North America to the colonial interests throughout the world threatened by the French. The Americans took advantage of the situation and proved themselves in battle at Monmouth. The Continental Army continued to have difficulties but remained in good order as it went into winter quarters for 1778–79. The British were hemmed in at New York and Newport, and it was apparent that the focus of the war was going to shift to land campaigns in the south. Monmouth, the longest battle of the war, was also the last major battle in the north. From 1779, the war in northern New York and the southern colonies was to become even more bitter as loyalists, Indians, and rebels fought fiercely for control of the interior.

The land war: 1779

The campaigns of 1779 in North America were relatively small compared to previous years. There were minor operations at Stony Point on the Hudson River and along the Penobscot River in Massachusetts (present-day Maine). There was a successful American campaign against Indian and loyalist raiders on the frontier. The remainder of North American operations occurred in the south. The principal reason for both the smaller-scale battles and geographical shift was that Spain entered the war against Britain in 1779, putting British interests around the world in still greater danger. The British also believed that the colonies in the south might be more loyal to the British cause.

Northern campaign

On 16 June 1779, British Brigadier Francis McLean landed at Castine, Massachusetts, on Penobscot Bay with 600 regulars. The town was strategically located to offset New England privateering efforts against British shipping. A Massachusetts militia force of 1,000 men, under the command of Brigadier Solomon Lovell, was dispatched to remove the British, landing on 28 July. The Americans decided to lay siege to the fort instead of undertaking an immediate assault. A Royal Navy force arrived to lift the siege on 13 August, compelling the Massachusetts militia to withdraw into the woods and the American ships in the bay to be scuttled.

Washington ordered Major-General Sullivan, along with 2,500 Continentals and militia, to march from Eaton, Pennsylvania, towards Fort Niagara, New York, in May. A second force of 1,500 New York militia, commanded by Brigadier James Clinton, was to meet up with Sullivan and lay waste to the Indian lands from Pennsylvania into New York. Sullivan understood how to operate in the woods, and deployed small units of skirmishers to protect the flanks of his force. John Butler, the commander of the loyalist Butler's Rangers, set out to fortify the local tribes for the onslaught.

The two American forces met on 22 August, and set to work burning the harvests and villages of the Indians. On 27 August, Butler, with 250 Rangers, joined by 600 Indians commanded by Joseph Brant, prepared to meet the 4,000 Americans. The two forces met at Newtown on 29–30 August. The Americans successfully avoided an ambush, and the Indians and Rangers were pushed out. They headed towards Fort Niagara, opening the Genesee and Mohawk valleys to the American forces. The Americans destroyed 40 villages and nearly 160,000 bushels of corn. The Indian population flooded towards Fort Niagara. The operation was successful for the Americans, but it did not signal the end of the raids along the frontier. Joseph Brant, along with his Indian warriors and Butler's Rangers, would return.

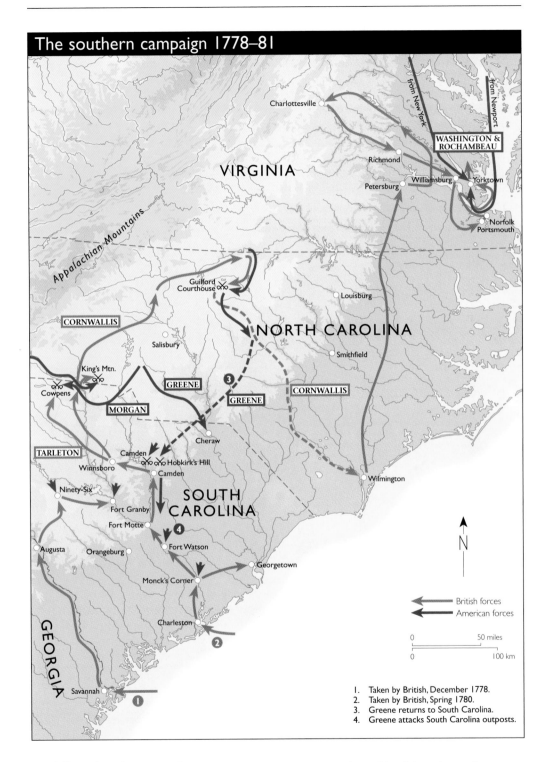

The southern campaign 1778–81

1. Taken by British, December 1778.
2. Taken by British, Spring 1780.
3. Greene returns to South Carolina.
4. Greene attacks South Carolina outposts.

British forces
American forces

0   50 miles
0   100 km

Middle Atlantic campaign

Clinton advanced north from New York in late May, and seized Stony Point and Verplanck's Point on the Hudson River on 1 June. He hoped by this action to force Washington to leave the defended regions of West Point and seek battle in the open, but Washington did not fall into his trap.

Clinton next arranged for a series of raids along the Connecticut coast, trying to make Washington move east into New England. Washington not only failed to take the bait, but retook Stony Point on 15 July instead. As Colonel Tallmadge noted, "such was the ardour and impetuosity of the Americans, that they surmounted all difficulties ... and captured the whole garrison in a short time with bayonet alone" (Tallmadge, p. 31).

Verplanck's Point remained in British hands. The British recalled all troops from the Connecticut coastal raids and moved towards Stony Point. The Americans withdrew, destroying defenses as they went. From this point, the fighting in the Hudson River and New York City areas deteriorated into an ongoing series of skirmishes between units foraging and undertaking reconnaissance.

Southern campaign

Lieutenant-Colonel Campbell had succeeded in taking Savannah and Augusta in 1778, but not all of Georgia had been subdued. Brigadier-General Augustine Prevost arrived in late January 1779 with a second British contingent from Florida, also taking over as the senior British commander. Major-General Benjamin Lincoln, meanwhile, replaced General Howe as commander of the American forces in the south.

The British abandoned Augusta in March, following reports of a large Carolina militia marching south, leaving loyalists in the interior exposed to pro-independence factions. Brigadier Prevost marched to Charleston, South Carolina, and laid siege to the town. Lincoln received news of Prevost's move and turned towards Charleston in pursuit. Prevost was outnumbered, and was forced to lift the siege on 12 May. Lincoln followed Prevost's force as it withdrew and the two forces skirmished at Stono Ferry in late June. Prevost then moved his troops back towards Georgia, while the Americans requested support from the French Admiral d'Estaing.

D'Estaing arrived off Savannah on 1 September with 3,500 French troops, who landed on 12 September, as Lincoln and his force were moving in from the north. Prevost was able to delay the impending French attack by asking for a few days to decide whether to surrender, although in fact he was using this time to wait for reinforcements to arrive to strengthen the defenses. By 5 October, the French siege batteries were in place and American forces ringed the town. A French officer noted on 6 October that this course of action was a mistake: "we should not have constructed works. In doing so we afforded the English time to strengthen theirs. We regret that we did not attack on the first day" (Jones, p. 26).

The French command was anxious to end the siege, and on 9 October the combined French and American forces attacked. Prevost had foreknowledge of the attack from a deserter in his camp. The attack began in the early hours of the morning, described by a French officer as "a very lively fire of musketry and of cannon upon our troops from the trenches" (Jones, p. 30). Men from the South Carolina Continentals and French forces were able to seize a few ramparts, but were ultimately forced back with "disorder in the columns" (Jones, p. 36). The American and French forces lacked a coordinated attack plan, and within three hours the attack was called off.

The British forces lost 16 men, and the Americans and French more than 1,000 killed and wounded (Jones, p. 37). On 18 October, d'Estaing left, taking the French fleet with him. Lincoln, as Sullivan in Newport had been before him, was angered by this decision. So far, American–French cooperation had not proved a decisive factor in the North American campaign.

The British decided to stage a combined naval/land raid to relieve pressure on Prevost and the British regulars and loyalists in Georgia. On 5 May 1779, a fleet of 1,800 men departed from New York, landing at Hampton Roads, Virginia on 11 May. The army set out to destroy all the tobacco stockpiles and shipping in the area. The

Major General Charles Lee. (Anne SK Brown Collection)

ABOVE Siege of Savannah: French and American lines in the foreground. (Library of Congress)

RIGHT British camp in southern England. (The National Army Museum)

operation was successful, claiming the destruction and capture of more than 140 vessels and £2 million worth of goods and property, and the fleet returned triumphantly to New York on 24 May.

Outside the Thirteen Colonies

The principal problem facing the British in 1779 was Spain's decision to enter the war. As described in the section on naval war (pp. 34–37), the naval balance shifted towards France and Spain as a result of this decision. Spain entered the war as an ally of the French, rather than of the Americans, on 8 May; her main aim in doing so was to regain territory lost in the Seven Years' War. The British garrisons in western Florida were not aware of the Spanish entry, and so the British garrison at Baton Rouge was later seized in September 1779, an excellent

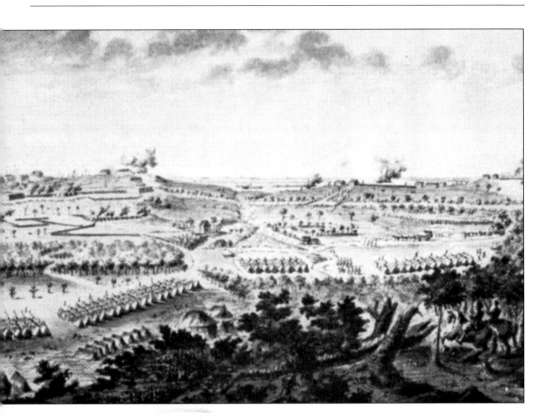

ABOVE Siege of Gibraltar. (Anne SK Brown Collection)

RIGHT The French capture of Grenada.
(The National Army Museum)

performance by the Spanich regulars and Louisiana militia.

The combined forces of the Spanish and French fleets gave the British Isles a fright during the summer of 1779. A combined force of 66 ships planned to assemble and invade Great Britain. The Royal Navy was aware of the potential threat, but had two possible invasion sites to protect, southern England and Ireland. On 30 July, the combined force, under the command of Admiral d'Orvilliers, sailed from Brest, picking up troops at Le Havre and St Malo. It appeared off Plymouth on 16 August. The British fleet, under the command of Admiral Sir Charles Hardy, was out of commission, stationed off Ireland. Local militiamen were sent immediately to repel any attempted

landings by the estimated 30,000 enemy soldiers.

Despite its superiority in numbers, the Franco-Spanish fleet was apparently wary of attempting a landing, even before Hardy returned. A decisive British naval victory after the troops had been landed would potentially have left 30,000 troops stranded on the coast of England. The British fleet arrived with 39 ships in early September; Hardy refused to attack, preferring to await a move by the Franco-Spanish force. The invasion force decided to withdraw by mid-September; their ships were battered, the men growing tired and ill, and relations between the French and Spanish commanders had soured. Battle had been avoided, and the threat of invasion averted.

The first significant Spanish action upon entering the war was to lay siege to Gibraltar. Reinforcements were sent from Britain to support the British governor, George Augustus Elliott, although the first relief did not arrive until the beginning of 1780, under the command of Admiral Rodney. Gibraltar was under siege for the remainder of the war,

with relieving fleets entering to help the garrison stay alive.

The entry of Spain and France into the war threatened British interests in the West Indies and Central America. Before d'Estaing sailed for the ill-fated siege of Savannah, he had had several successes in the West Indies, capturing St Vincent in mid-June and Grenada a month later. The British badly needed troops in the area, fearing an attack on Jamaica next. Luckily for them, nothing happened for the rest of the year, for they were unprepared to face it.

In India, the French post at Mahe fell in March 1779. Of more critical importance to the British, however, was the enmity that their actions provoked in Haidar Ali and his large army. His armies directly engaged the British, and continued to do so for the rest of the war.

By the end of 1779, the British military effort in North America had decidedly shifted towards the south. Prevost's defense of Savannah had sparked renewed interest in a southern campaign. General Clinton had been frustrated in his attempts to bring the Main Army to battle. The requirements of other theaters had made it clear that Clinton would not be able to rely on London for additional reinforcements. He therefore decided to abandon Newport, Rhode Island, and withdrew his force to New York. He assembled a large army in New York, and on 26 December embarked with more than 7,000 men for a campaign in South Carolina, with Charleston as his first objective. A large contingent of British troops remained in New York to protect the city, but the British post at Verplanck's Point was withdrawn. Washington had been having difficulty keeping his various armies together during the stalemate in the north. The campaign in the south over the course of 1780–81 would be decisive for the future of North America.

The land war: 1780–81

The land war in North America shifted to the southern colonies during the last phase of the war. The British generals, Clinton and Cornwallis, sought a decisive campaign in the south, believing that a large percentage of the population were loyalists. While maintaining a presence in New York, the British shifted their principal focus southward.

General Washington was having problems with his troops. The Main Army remained in the New York area to counteract British attempts to push into the Hudson River valley or across New Jersey. The army's ability to wage war was limited by periodic mutinies, and the Southern Army bore the brunt of the fighting. The arrival of a large French contingent in 1780 enabled Washington to send the Main Army, bolstered by French reinforcements, south to Virginia. A classic siege at Yorktown followed, an incident that few foresaw might be the last major engagement of the war.

Southern campaign
In December 1779, General Henry Clinton left New York with more than 17,000 British troops, landing south of Charleston on 11 February 1780. The American commander, General Lincoln, received word that the British were accompanied by a large contingent of Carolina loyalist refugees. He thought that the British had another motive for their movements besides military conquest, "that of settling the country as they conquer" (Boston Public Library, G.380.38.207 b). The British, upon reaching Charleston, attempted to surround the town. Lincoln had 1,800 Continentals and about 2,000 militia to combat the British advance, and it was up to him to decide whether to engage in battle, withdraw, or hold out in the town. Ultimately, however, it was General Clinton who decided Charleston's fate.

By early April, British troops had crossed the northern routes of the town. A reinforcement of 700 Continentals arrived just after the town had been completely surrounded on 14 April. The British began to dig siege lines and prepare artillery positions to bombard the defenders. Heavy fire was

Battle of Camden

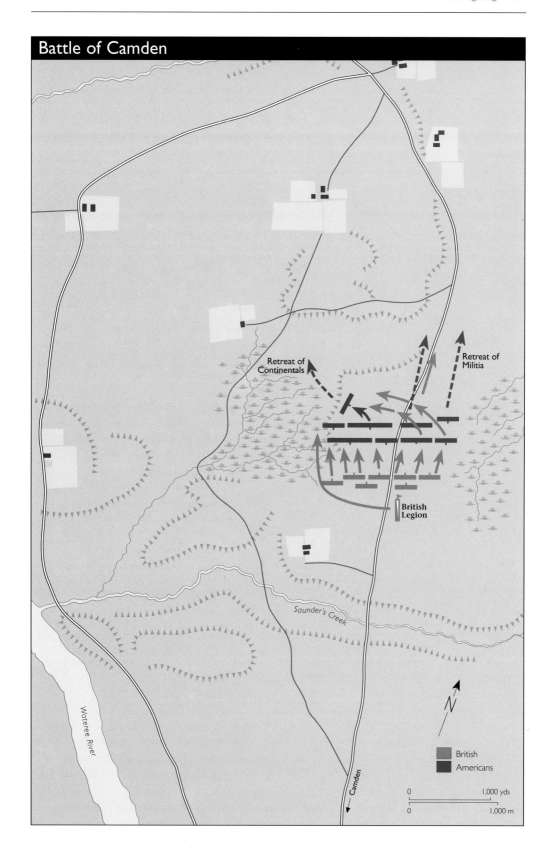

Retreat of
Continentals

Retreat of
Militia

British
Legion

Saunder's Creek

Wateree River

Camden

N

British
Americans

0   1,000 yds
0   1,000 m

Lieutenant General Earl Charles Cornwallis.
(Anne SK Brown Collection)

than 2,000 Continental soldiers were captured, as well as 1,000 militia troops.

On 29 May, the mixed loyalist force known as the British Legion and commanded by Lieutenant-Colonel Benastre Tarleton, having moved north from Charleston, destroyed a Virginia Continental force at Waxhaws. The American force was almost wiped out, and there is still debate about what happened when the Americans attempted to surrender, and whether Tarleton ordered the killing of prisoners. Either way, the Legion and Tarleton became synonymous with brutal fighting methods.

This incident, which occurred in the interior, sparked a command decision to move inland to suppress any subsequent civilian rebellion. On 8 June, Clinton left Charleston with 4,000 troops to head to New York. He had received word that the French fleet and expeditionary force had arrived, and feared that New York was a potential target. General Cornwallis took over command of the rest of the British forces in the south following his departure.

The British presence in South Carolina further inflamed the civil conflict already smoldering there. As the American General Moultrie noted, 'large armed parties of Whigs and Tories were continually moving about and frequently falling in with each other and fighting severe battles ... the animosities between the two parties were carried to great lengths ... to enumerate the cruelties which were exercised upon each other would fill a volume' (Moultrie, Vol. II, p. 219). Part of the reason for the increased hostility was a proclamation issued by Clinton before he left, demanding that all colonists must decide once and for all on whose side they were; no neutrality would be tolerated.

As the British marched into the interior, supply shortages created discipline problems, and the behavior of the British regulars won them few supporters. Cornwallis issued another proclamation, this one to the troops, regarding theft of cattle and provisions: "I do by this proclamation most strictly prohibit and forbid the same; and I do

exchanged, but the British were able to dig a second line and position themselves within yards of the American lines. A Hessian officer, Captain Johaun Hinrichs reported that "the enemy stood our fire well and returned it till about noon ... but since our fire was so violent that we did not see them coming they were compelled to withdraw. At two o'clock in the afternoon the enemy hoisted a large white flag" (*Siege of Charleston*, p. 289). An American observer recorded that, on 12 May, "the Continental troops march out and pile their arms and the British take possession of the town" (G.380.20). This was the worst single defeat for the American forces during the war. More hereby give notice, that if any person offend herein … [he] shall be further punished in a manner … [that he] doth deserve" (Tarleton, pp. 121– 122).

General Lincoln was captured at Charleston and the hero of Saratoga, Major-General Horatio Gates, assumed command of the American forces in the south. He was able to rebuild the Southern Army with Continental soldiers from Maryland and Delaware and southern militiamen. His force consisted of only 1,500 Continentals and almost 1,000 militiamen. Gates arrived outside Camden, South Carolina, in early August. This was the main supply depot for the British forces in the interior, and Cornwallis, hearing of Gates' advance, had arrived with reinforcements from Charleston.

On the morning of 16 August, the two armies clashed. The American left flank was composed of untrained militia units, with the Continentals on the right flank and in the rear of the first line. The British force moved forward and attacked the left flank first. Gates recorded that "at daylight the enemy attacked and drove in our light party in front, when I ordered the left to advance and attack the enemy; but to my astonishment, the left wing [Virginia militia] and North Carolina militia gave way" (Tarleton, p. 146). The Continentals fought hard. As Tarleton noted, "[Continental commander Baron de Kalbe] made a vigorous charge with a regiment of continental infantry through the left division of the British . . . after this last effort of the continentals, rout and slaughter ensued in every quarter" (Tarleton, p. 107). A second Southern Army had been badly defeated. Baron de Kalbe was killed and Gates fell from grace in the American command structure.

Following this victory, Cornwallis decided to push into North Carolina. He had failed to properly subdue South Carolina, however, and his communications and outposts were vulnerable to attack from militia forces as he advanced. Cornwallis marched into North

Carolina in early September, with a second column of provincial troops under the command of Major Patrick Ferguson on his left flank. Cornwallis and the main corps reached Charlotte, North Carolina, in late September. Ferguson moved further north with his corps but was unable to convince many loyalists in the area to join up; his destructive actions against rebels had aroused too much hatred.

On 7 October, Ferguson's force of 800 men was surrounded at King's Mountain by a militia force of 2,000 expert forest-fighting men. Ferguson's force was 48 km (30 miles) from Cornwallis' column, and could expect no support. A loyalist described how:

at about two o'clock in the afternoon twenty five hundred rebels … attacked us … the action continued an hour and five minutes; but their numbers enabled them to surround us … we had to surrender to save lives of the brave men who were left (Allaire, p. 31).

Baron de Kalbe. (New York Public Library)

A North American militiaman, James Collins, commented, 'after the fight was over, the situation of the poor Tories appeared to be really pitiable; the dead lay in heaps on all sides while the groans of the wounded were heard in every direction' (*Fire of Liberty*, p. 200). The British force was completely destroyed, forcing Cornwallis to withdraw to South Carolina for winter quarters, and lowering the morale of southern loyalists.

The American Southern Army was re-formed while Cornwallis spent the winter south of Camden, South Carolina. He was to be reinforced by a contingent under Major-General Alexander Leslie, who had been undertaking raids in Virginia. Command of the American Southern Army was given to Major-General Nathaniel Greene on 2 December 1780. He had another force of 1,000 Continental troops and various militia forces at his disposal. The fighting in the backcountry between rebels and loyalists continued unabated throughout the winter months.

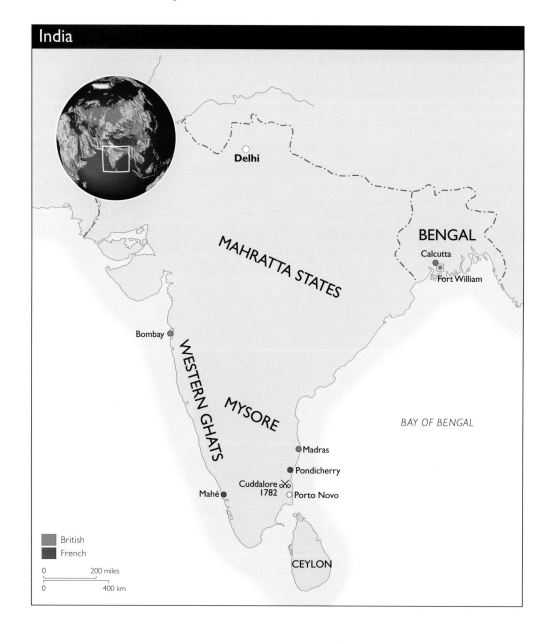

India

Delhi

MAHRATTA STATES

BENGAL

Calcutta

Fort William

Bombay

WESTERN GHATS

MYSORE

BAY OF BENGAL

Madras

Pondicherry

Cuddalore 1782

Mahé

Porto Novo

CEYLON

British
French

| 0 | 200 miles |
| 0 | 400 km |

In January 1781, Cornwallis decided to march back into North Carolina. General Green dispatched Brigadier Daniel Morgan and a small Continental corps to disrupt the British lines of communication and fight in the backcountry. Cornwallis dispatched a force of the British Legion and other troops, under the command of Lieutenant-Colonel Tarleton, in a mobile force to protect the left flank of the British forces and counteract Morgan's corps.

Morgan's and Tarleton's forces clashed north of Cowpens, on the border between North and South Carolina, on 17 January. Morgan deployed his riflemen at the front of his force, with the militia and Continentals forming the second and third lines. The riflemen were to shoot once, then withdraw through the ranks of the other lines. The battle began at daylight, with Tarleton sending his tired troops immediately into battle. The American riflemen created holes in the British line as it advanced. The British pushed forward and the Americans, militia and riflemen, began to pull back. The British surged forward and the Americans turned and delivered a heavy volley. The British attack fell apart as the Continental troops moved forward. Tarleton and a few hundred men were able to escape, but the force had lost more than 700 men killed and captured.

The reasons for Tarleton's defeat were twofold. First, Morgan had deployed well and was able to shift his forces without much disruption. Second, as loyalist officer Alescambe Chesney noted: "we suffered a dreadful defeat by some dreadful bad management ... the rout was almost total" (Add. Mss. 32627). The Legion was an important asset for the British forces and, in one battle, Cornwallis had lost nearly all of it.

Cornwallis continued his advance into North Carolina after reinforcements arrived from General Leslie, and the American and British forces met again on 15 March at Guilford Court House in North Carolina. Cornwallis had only 2,000 troops; the Southern Army outnumbered him two to one. General Greene, however, elected to

Brigadier Nathaniel Greene.
(Anne SK Brown Collection)

take the defensive. The Americans were drawn up as "three lines: the front line was composed of North Carolina militia ... second line of the Virginia militia ... third line, consisting of two brigades, one of Virginia, and one of Maryland continentals troops" (Tarleton, p. 314).

The battle lasted for three hours. The first line of North Carolina militia fired once before breaking. The Virginia militia stood longer, delivering strong volleys. The British dealt with the first two lines of militia and turned towards the Continental troops. The British continued to press and, though suffering heavily, began to break the Maryland Continentals, causing the American right flank to falter, after British artillery fired into the confusing mass. As Greene reported: "the engagement was long and severe, and the enemy only gained their point by superior discipline" (Tarleton, p. 316).

The British lost some 100 men killed and more than 400 wounded. The American forces lost only 78 killed and nearly 200 wounded. It was a Pyrrhic victory for

Cornwallis, and afterwards he headed south to Wilmington to rendezvous with the Royal Navy and receive much-needed supplies and reinforcements. Greene turned towards South Carolina.

While in Wilmington, Cornwallis had to decide whether to move into Virginia or to return by sea to Charleston. Brigadier Greene had moved into South Carolina, while General Lord Rawdon and his troops attempted to hold parts of the interior centered around Camden and Fort Ninety-Six. Greene attacked Lord Rawdon outside Camden, at Hobkirk's Hill, on 25 April; the British were able to defeat the American force. On the same day, Cornwallis and his force marched towards Virginia.

The remainder of the campaign in the Carolinas was one of gradual withdrawal for the British forces. On 10 May, the British pulled out of Camden, and by June, the only post in the interior still in British hands was Fort Ninety-Six. Greene laid siege to it, but was forced by a British relief column to lift the siege. The British, however, recognizing the distance from Charleston to Fort Ninety-Six, subsequently withdrew from the area, and by mid-summer they controlled only the coastal strip from Savannah to Charleston. Greene had lost many of the battles, but in the end he won the campaign in the Carolinas.

Virginia and Yorktown

Cornwallis countermanded orders from London that his troops were to remain in the Carolinas. British troops had already been stationed in Virginia to stage raids in the area and relieve pressure on the British forces in the Carolinas. Virginia was intended to be a secondary campaign, but Cornwallis turned it into a primary operation without receiving approval from London or Clinton in New York. Cornwallis' actions clearly demonstrate the friction that had arisen among senior generals in North America. As a result of his decision, the operation in Virginia became the decisive campaign.

In January 1781, a British force of 1,500 troops was dispatched by Clinton to Virginia, commanded by Benedict Arnold, the former American general. Arnold had switched sides in 1780 because he felt that he was being sidelined by Congress and the Continental Army. He had been commander of an important American post, West Point, on the Hudson River. General Clinton had negotiated with him to turn over plans of the strategic fort to the British, but the plot was uncovered before it could be implemented. Arnold escaped to New York and was given command of a British force in the rank of major-general.

In March 1781, a second British force of 2,000 men, under the command of Major-General William Phillips, arrived in

Major General Benedict Arnold.
(Anne SK Brown Collection)

Virginia. General Phillips assumed command of all British troops in Virginia upon his arrival, and continued the raids in Virginia. Cornwallis arrived in mid-May and met with Phillips at Petersburg, Virginia. The combined British force now totaled more than 7,000 men and was under the overall command of Cornwallis, who took over after Philips died of typhoid fever. The American commanders in the region, Major-Generals de Lafayette and von Steuben, had been focusing on trying to increase the numbers of Continental troops while contending with two earlier campaigns staged by Arnold and Phillips.

As Cornwallis arrived, the American forces withdrew from the southern areas of Virginia. The two armies met and skirmished. The mixed-force British irregular units, the British Legion and Queen's Rangers, ranged far and wide, carrying out raids throughout the southern area of the colony. Cornwallis set out to trap and destroy the American forces through a series of maneuvers, but was unsuccessful, and the British withdrew towards Williamsburg in late June. Cornwallis received orders to embark 3,000 troops for New York. He withdrew towards the James River at Greenspring Farm. Lafayette followed up his withdrawal, and Cornwallis defeated a small American corps that reached Greenspring Farm on 6 July. Cornwallis then withdrew towards Portsmouth, where he received word that his troops were to remain in Virginia.

By early July, Cornwallis had received orders to establish a fortified winter base for the Royal Navy. Yorktown was chosen as a suitable site, and by the beginning of August, the British had begun the work of fortifying the area and the adjoining Gloucester Point. In doing so, the British had committed themselves to a defensive position, and the American forces stationed in Virginia began to close in on Yorktown.

The year 1780 and winter of 1781 was a difficult time for General Washington and the Main Army. In the spring of 1780, the Main Army stood at 4,000 men and was suffering from lack of supplies. Discipline was an increasing problem as the war in the north became ever more hopelessly stalemated. In May, troops from the Connecticut regiments threatened to march into New Jersey and seize stores. They were restrained from doing so by other troops, principally the Pennsylvania regiments. Ironically, in January 1781, elements of the Pennsylvania regiments themselves mutinied, this time over supplies and timely pay. The issue of delayed pay was exacerbated by the fact that the money issued by the Continental Congress was rapidly being devalued. At the end of January, elements of the New Jersey regiments also mutinied. All three revolts collapsed, and the ringleaders were found and punished, but it was clear that the Main Army was in need of a campaign.

Washington benefited at this stage from the arrival of a French expeditionary force of 5,000 troops that landed in Newport in 1780, under the command of Lieutenant-General Rochambeau. They were subsequently reinforced in Virginia with an additional 3,000 men. With Cornwallis heading towards Yorktown, the Main Army and the French expeditionary force on 14 August decided to wage a campaign against Cornwallis. Proposed attacks against New York had to be rejected due to the lack of French naval support so far north, as the French Admiral de Grasse had agreed to go only as far north as the Chesapeake River.

The joint American and French force, numbering more than 8,000 French and 2,000 Continentals in the summer, marched south, but in a deceptive manner. More than 4,000 Continentals and 2,000 militia remained in New York, intending to keep the pressure on Clinton while concealing from Cornwallis that Yorktown was their eventual destination. The French troops provided an important dimension to the American contingent; they were regular troops, trained and disciplined to deal with the likes of the British Redcoats. With the addition of more than 5,000 Continental troops and a large artillery train, the British forces faced a solid opponent. The naval engagement at the Capes, entrance to Chesapeake Bay, in early September, although not significant in terms

French troops landing at Newport. (New York Public Library)

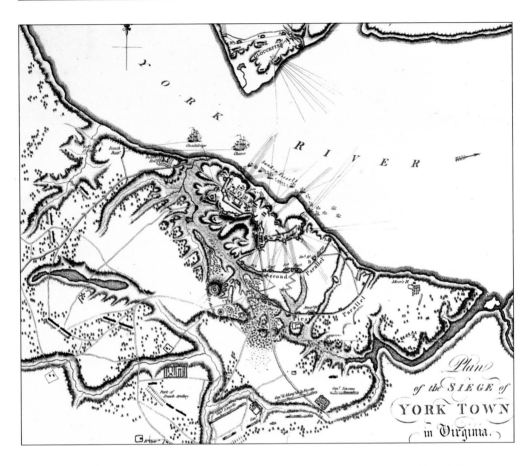

ABOVE Siege of Yorktown: the American and French positions are to the south and west of Yorktown. Redoubts 9 and 10 are listed as A and B to the southeast of Yorktown. (Bodleian Library)

BELOW Surrender of Yorktown. (Anne SK Brown Collection)

of ships damaged, became decisive when the British Admiral Thomas Graves withdrew to New York, isolating Cornwallis.

The main American and French forces gathered in Williamsburg on 26 September. The American forces numbered over 8,000 men while the French numbered over 8,000 men. The Continental Army marched towards Yorktown in three columns of troops, two French and one American. As a French officer noted, "we arrived about six o'clock that evening [28 September] before the town of Yorktown and immediately began to invest it" (Rice and Brown, p. 57). The siege of Yorktown followed the practices of any European-style siege: both sides embarked on raids, and fired artillery at redoubts and trenches. A French officer commented that "the day was spent in cannonading and firing bombs at each other in such profusion that we did one another much damage" (Rice and Brown, p. 59).

The French and American engineers dug their trenches, progressing closer to the British positions, and the siege increasingly centered on the taking of two British redoubts, nos. 9 and 10. On the evening of 14 October, the French and American troops launched an attack on the redoubts. The French commander, William Count de Deux- Ponts, detailed the attack and, although uncommunicative to a degree, noted that firing took place during the French attack. He stated that

the first fifty les chausseurs [light infantry] carried fascines, of the other fifty there were only eight who carried ladders, after them came the grenadiers ... [They] advanced with the greatest silence .... [and] opened fire ... we lost not a

moment in reaching the abbatis ... [It] was cleared away with brave determination ... I gave the order to fire ... the enemy kept up a sharp fire ... our fire increasing and making terrible havoc among the enemy (Deux-Ponts, pp. 145–146)

On 16 October a sortie of 300 men was launched from the British lines to destroy and spike the guns in two allied artillery batteries. The undertaking was considered a success, yet the guns were firing again within six hours of the attack. As Cornwallis noted, 'the action, though extremely honourable to the officers and soldiers who executed it, proved of little public advantage' (Tarleton, p. 429).

On 19 October, Cornwallis surrendered the garrison at Yorktown. The British garrison troops marched out and laid down their arms, flanked by the American army on one side and the French Army on the other. Clinton had intended to send a relieving force of 7,000 men, but news arrived that Cornwallis had already surrendered before he could do so.

The battle for Yorktown was the last major engagement of the land war in North America, but the war was not yet over. The British were still fighting a war outside the North American theater, and had not intended Yorktown to be the last major engagement on American soil. The Americans, for their part, had plans to drive the British garrisons out of both Charleston and New York. Other considerations for the French prevented the launch of attacks on British forces stationed on the coast of the Carolinas, or Georgia, or in New York. After Yorktown, the war shifted almost completely to the West Indies, India, Florida, and Europe.

Massachusetts professional

The soldier discussed in this section was called Benjamin Gould. There are no dates for his age or for the year that he died. His story originates from a manuscript written in his own hand at the end of the war. It provides an interesting account of an American soldier of the period who served during the siege of Boston, as well as in operations in New York City and near Saratoga.

Gould begins his story with his enlistment in Captain John Beecher's company, which was part of Colonel Moses Little's regiment. Little's regiment is listed as a Continental infantry regiment. No date is provided, but Gould's regiment was part of the army that occupied Boston following the British withdrawal on 17 March 1776. Gould claims that he joined the army as a sergeant. If this is true, then he must have had previous military experience as a private soldier, although he does not provide any background information.

Gould's regiment was ordered to New York City as the threat to that area increased. He describes how his regiment arrived in the New York area just as battle began on Long Island: "in the morning we heard a heavy cannonading … it was the enemy, taking Long Island and New York and our army retreating from it." Following the defeat on Long Island, his regiment was ordered to proceed to Fort Washington, on Manhattan Island. His regiment was ordered to make carriages and to supply the fort with additional material in preparation for a possible siege. The regiment arrived as the artillery began preparations for the British arrival.

Gould comments that supplies ran low during the regiment's tenure at Fort Washington. He reports when Royal Navy ships appeared off the west side of the fort on the Hudson, and records that a detachment of British troops was reported to

be only 5 km (3 miles) from the fort. He states that "[we] could not spare a man to draw provisions and [were] obliged to live upon potatoes and cloves for several days". Instead of attacking right away, however, the main British force headed north to White Plains in an attempt to catch the Main Continental Army.

It is at this point that the manuscript becomes somewhat confusing. Up to now, Gould described his regiment as if it were an infantry unit. His parent regiment, Little's, Massachusetts Battalion, is listed as an infantry formation in 1775 under the command of Brigadier Nathaniel Greene's brigade. The manuscript, however, raises the possibility that Gould had been transferred to an artillery unit. He describes orders "to make the best grape [shot] I could". Also, his regiment was ordered to proceed to White Plains to support the Main Army. His subsequent description of the battle of White Plains supports the theory that he fought with an artillery unit, especially when he describes how "when our army retreated I struck the left tent and took the last cannon from our lines."

This description ends the narrative of the 1776 campaign. Gould mentions the ongoing problem of keeping the numbers of men in the Continental service constant for a long period of time. At the end of 1776, his own Continental service comes to an end, and he is offered service with the Massachusetts Militia, with the proviso that he could "leave at anytime for service with the Continentals if he wished." He notes, "taken from the Continental Service and placed in the militia in the summer of 1777." His new militia unit was sent to fight against the British advance down Lake Champlain and along the Hudson, but he does not make it clear in which of the

British caricature of American soldiers at Boston – not an accurate depiction. (The British Museum)

several Massachusetts militia regiments involved in this campaign he served.

Gould's unit most likely arrived during the month of September when, as described earlier, American units were operating behind Burgoyne's line of advance to disrupt his supply networks. His unit was given four days' supplies and ordered to operate on Lake George. American forces had seized Fort George on 18 September, and from there they had pushed north to Fort Ticonderoga. Gould's unit operated in the area around Lake George "for 17 days." His narrative is unclear, but it appears that his unit marched south towards Bemis Heights, since he next describes a major action on the 7th (presumably of October, when an engagement took place at that location). Although he was with a unit of Massachusetts militia, they are not specifically mentioned in accounts of the battle. Massachusetts Continental regiments and various New England militia units were present, however, and his unit may have been attached to one of these groups for the battle.

Gould describes how, on "the seventh [October] at about one o'clock we were laid by

the cannon of the enemy who were marching to attack us." He appears to be describing the last British attack against Bemis Heights on 7 October. He goes on to record that:

we returned to our places and was immediately ordered to march … it was but a few minutes before the enemy fired upon us … a second shot our men seemed terrified at this but soon received and stood their ground nobley [sic] … the enemy made no refrain but retreated precipitately. He also describes coming across an abandoned British camp and his actions: "I took nothing out of it but a bottle of beer which was very exceptible [sic] as we were very dry".

Gould's unit was given its discharge on 1 November 1777, but he stayed in the area to settle accounts. He next refers to 1780, when he notes receiving command of a militia company. This implies that he received a commission, either after the Battle of Bemis Heights or when he was called up for the militia in 1780. Gould and his company were ordered to West Point; they arrived there on 20 June 1780, and he spent the remainder of his service on garrison duty at West Point. He was discharged at the end of the conflict.

War on the homefront

Impact on local populations

Although the war was economically costly for all sides, it differed significantly from the Seven Years' War in that the impact on the local populations was relatively minimal. The home populations of France, Great Britain, and Spain did not suffer under foreign occupation. Large numbers of troops were raised in each country and inevitably created tension and damage by the fact of their presence, but they were not occupying forces. The large number of troops even proved an unintended boon to the British government when the Gordon Riots of 1780 broke out, and the armed forces were used to restore law and order.

The fighting in the West Indies and India undoubtedly created problems between the local populations and the various armies. The numerous and powerful cavalry of Haidar Ali set out to destroy the communications and supplies of the East India Company armies, which left civilians caught between two armies. As with all campaigns in the region, soldiers deserted from one side to the other as economic conditions dictated.

The Thirteen American colonies suffered the most when measuring impact on the civilian populations. Both sides, including the French Army, were guilty of abuses and maltreatment of the civilian population. The behavior of the French Army in 1780–81 was exemplary in its restraint from plundering and looting, but the French force that invested Savannah in 1779 was not so commendable. The Americans and French eventually formed a special mixed unit of French and American dragoons to police both armies (see Boston Public Library, G.380.38.1.60b, 30/9/1779).

The British and their German auxiliaries were consistently accused of pillaging, raping, and general disorder by the colonists. The British advance across New Jersey in 1776 was considered a particularly brutal episode. An American observer described how:

familys ... escape[d] from the Regular Army and left a Great Part of their goods behind them in their Houses for want of carriages to take them away, Great part of which fell into the Regular hands and they not only burnt up all the fire wood ... [but] stript shops, out houses and some dwelling houses (Collins, p. 4).

Many British regulars considered the conflict as a rebellion, and consequently had minimal sympathy for the civilians.

The German auxiliaries' attitude was similarly contemptuous. Lieutenant-Colonel Kemble of the 60th Foot noted on 3 October 1776 that "ravages committed by the Hessians, and all the Ranks of the Army, on the poor inhabitants of the country make their case deplorable" (Kemble, p. 91). Kemble also succinctly described the effects of these actions: "the country all this time unmercifully Pillaged by our troops, Hessians in particular, no wonder if the Country people refuse to join us" (Kemble, p. 96).

Senior British commanders attempted to confront this issue, but it was never conclusively resolved. As previously described, a series of proclamations was written and distributed amongst the troops at the onset of the 1780–81 southern campaign, in an attempt to forestall some of the problems. The British Army's supply problems complicated the situation and more or less condoned this sort of behavior; units were sent out on foraging parties to round up cattle and other supplies. They were supposed to pay for the items, but of course abuse was common. Naval landings were carried out specifically to steal and

The burning of New York. British soldiers apprehend and deal roughly with suspected rebels who were blamed for starting the fires. (The British Museum)

destroy stores that could be destined for the Continental Army, with inevitable repercussions for civilians. The civilian populations of New Jersey and southern New York and New England were at the mercy of the British raiding parties.

The regions around New York and southern New England also suffered from their proximity to encampments of the Continental Army. There were cases of outright robbery and abuse by troops on the civilian population. As the various armies marched across New Jersey in 1776 and 1777, the countryside was stripped bare of food and supplies. The Continental Army and militia also carried out attacks on suspected loyalist families in the area. Their properties were looted and, depending upon the local commander, certain members of the family were killed. An American private soldier commented that in 1780 "there was a large number [of loyalists] in this place and its vicinity by the name of Hetfield who were notorious rascals", and who escaped. The soldier went on, "thus these murderous

villains escaped the punishment due to their infernal deeds" (Martin, pp. 180–181). There were critics of this policy within the American high command. Major-General Israel Putnam commented in August 1777, in response to a local assembly motion from Salem, Massachusetts, to confiscate lands of suspected loyalists: "I think such things are counter to the spirit of your resolves" (Boston Public Library, Ch.F.7.85).

The southern campaign raised the level of violence within the civilian population to outright civil war. The fighting in the backcountry lasted from the official outbreak of war until well after the siege of Yorktown. The British Army's practices and fighting tactics, as with the war in the north, turned neutrals into rebels. The American Brigadier-General William Moultrie described the march of the British regulars and "their severities against the unhappy citizens, many of whom they hung up or otherwise cruelly treated ... the war was carried with great barbarity" (Moultrie, Vol. II, p. 219). Lieutenant-Colonel Tarleton's view of the civilian population counters this: "the foraging parties were every day harassed by the inhabitants ... [They] generally fired from covert places, to annoy the British detachments" (Tarleton, p. 160). The conflict turned into an irregular war in the south, and abuses were perpetrated by both sides. A loyalist reported how "a Henry Meholm, an old man of 81 years of age, this day met us … [He] had walked upwards of an hundred miles [160 km] … his errand was to get some kind of assistance. He had been plundered by the Rebels, and stripped of everything" (Allaire, p. 19).

Trade and economy

The economic costs of the war were heavy for Great Britain. The average yearly cost of the war was £12 million. The Royal Navy was not able to control the seas as she had done in the Seven Years' War. Taxes on the general population increased as the war dragged on, and duties on items not already being taxed were imposed to increase revenue further. The average land tax during the war was established at four shillings for every pound (Conway, p. 189), and the government borrowed heavily to make up for the shortfalls. This load of debt was added to the outstanding debts amassed during the Seven Years' War.

Trade also suffered as a result of the war. The revenue raised from trade with the Thirteen Colonies was wiped away. The merchants who traded with the American colonies felt the pinch, especially those in the tobacco trade. The export market was also hit hard. The revenue raised from the selling of woolen and metal goods dropped sharply as the markets dried up. The incursion of France and Spain into the war increased the pressure on Britain's import and export trade as more markets dried up due to naval pressure and privateering.

The need to increase shipping to get provisions and troops to North America prompted the Admiralty to lease a significant number of merchant ships. This provided additional opportunities for American privateers and Spanish and French fleet seizures, causing further disruption. It is estimated that 3,386 British merchant ships

were seized during the war (Conway, p. 191). The British were able to recoup some of these losses with their own privateering efforts on Spanish and French shipping.

The war did provide some benefit for a number of industries in Great Britain. The expansion of the navy and army meant an increased demand for the supplies needed to build ships, outfit troops, and supply forces in North America. Overall, however, the import and export trade fell drastically, creating significant revenue problems for the British government.

The American colonies also suffered economically as a result of the war. At first, the war increased prosperity; the trade of the Thirteen Colonies was no longer restricted to Great Britain, and merchants could trade throughout Europe and the West Indies without the interference of Royal Customs officials. American privateering activities infused additional wealth into the cause. As the fighting dragged on, however, American resources became strained as shipping was destroyed or seized by Royal Navy raids.

Ironically, the Americans' biggest financial problems concerned the imposition of taxes to raise currency. Individual colonies fought to keep the right to vote on tax issues, and the Continental Congress was forced to accept that they would not be given the power to raise taxes. Coin circulation had proved insufficient to keep the war going as early as 1775. The Congress turned to the establishment of paper money or bills of credit to raise funds. The expansion of the economy during the first two years of the war allowed for paper money to be infused into the economy without any problems. As the war continued and the costs rose, however, both the Congress and the colonies continued to print money, creating enormous inflation problems.

By 1780, the Congress and colonies combined had issued over $400 million in paper money, and inflation had skyrocketed. In an attempt to stop the inflation, the Congress tried to impose reforms, but these succeeded only in devaluing the Congress' dollars. The Congress also asked the colonies.

to fund, equip, and outfit their own troops in the Continental Army. The European allies also gave the Americans nearly $10 million in loans to keep the war effort afloat, but by 1780 there was widespread disaffection within the army over issues of pay and supplies. As Colonel Tallmadge noted: "the pay to the army being entirely in continental paper, we were greatly embarrassed to procure even the necessary supplies of food and clothing" (Tallmadge, p. 33). The inflation and debts produced by the war were to plague the newly formed United States for a number of years.

France, like Great Britain, piled debts from this war on those still outstanding from the Seven Years' War. French debt at the end of the war stood at 3,315.1 million *livres* (Conway, p. 242), spent in developing a sizeable army and navy, and providing material support to the American cause. This debt created significant economic problems after the war. In fact, many historians contend that the debt incurred during both the Seven Years' War and the American Revolution, compounded by the financial crisis of 1786, were among the principal causes of the French Revolution.

Spain also suffered, but not as greatly as France. Spain nearly doubled her spending from 454 million *reales* in 1778 to over 700 million *reales* in 1779 (Lynch, p. 326). Then the conflict disrupted the revenue stream from South and Central America. Spain at first sought more taxes, but when this did not solve the issue, royal bonds were issued to make up the shortfall. This did not work either, and finally in 1782 the first national Bank of Spain – the Banco San Carlos – was created to centralize financial efforts. When the war finally ended, the revenue from the colonies came into the bank to help pay off the loans and bonds during the war years, enabling Spain to pay off most of her debts relatively quickly.

Boston loyalist

A series of letters written from 1768 to 1776 by a female loyalist in Boston provide insight into the political agitation of the time in general, and the state of affairs in Boston in particular. Most of the letters were written to friends in Great Britain, and provide a different perspective on the "patriots" or "rebels" than the images commonly portrayed. Her brother, Henry Hulton, was the Commissioner of Customs for His Majesty's Government in Boston. In late 1775, Mrs Hulton left for Britain as a loyalist refugee. Her letters are then written to a friend but they incorporate information conveyed to her by her brother regarding the siege of Boston. There is no information regarding her age, but she was most likely of middle age during the 1770s. She died in Britain in 1790.

In a letter dated 31 January 1774, Mrs Hulton describes the brutal practice of "tarring and feathering". Many people who were loyalists or government officials were subjected to this treatment by radical elements of the rebel cause. This letter was written before General Gage arrived with a large contingent of troops and describes how:

the most shocking cruelty was exercised a few nights ago, upon a poor old man and tidesman one Malcolm ... [A] quarrell was picked with him, he was afterward taken and tarred and feathered ... they gave him several severe whippings at different parts of town (January 1774).

She also notes the aftermath of the attack: "the doctors say that it is impossible this poor creature can live they say his flesh comes off his back in stakes' (January 1774).

A letter from March 1774 vividly portrays the mindset within Boston, even as the British troops arrive. It is clear that the loyalists felt besieged and were awaiting the British troops to impose law and order. Mrs Hulton describes the city:

[Boston] is a very gloomy place, the streets almost empty, many families have removed from it and the inhabitants are divided into several parties at variance and quarrelling with each other. Some appear disponding others full of rage ... those who are well disposed towards government are termed tories, they daily increase and have made some effects to take power out of the hands of the patriots, but they are intimidated and overpowered by [their] numbers. (March 1774)

She also states: "I don't despair of seeing peace and tranquillity in America tho they [patriots] talk very high and furious at present. They [patriots] are preparing their arms and ammunition and say if any of the leaders are seized and they will make reprisals on the friends of the government" (March 1774).

The next letter is dated a year later, after the British advance and battles at Lexington and Concord. Mrs Hulton attempts to describe the fighting on 19 April, including one particular incident that clearly demonstrates how misinformation occurs, and subsequently provokes retaliation. Near the bridge at Concord, a young American boy hacked a wounded British soldier with an axe. It appears that the young boy overreacted with fear when the British soldier stirred. British troops, returning, saw a soldier with an axe wound to the head, and the rumor quickly circulated that the soldier had been scalped, an Indian custom considered brutal and barbaric. Hearing and believing this false information, many British soldiers retreating to Boston took vengeance on captured "patriots". Mrs Hulton told an even worse tale: "two or three of their people [British Redcoats] lying with agonies of death scalped and their noses cut off and eyes bored out … which exasperated the soldiers exceedingly" (April 1775).

Writing from Great Britain in January 1776, Mrs Hulton described the state of Boston, passing along information from her brother, who had remained with his family. He told of how "provisions and fuel were scarce and very dear, supplies once certain, temperatures weather and the winter get very severe … amidst all this alarms dangers and distresses the small pox spread universally" (January 1776).

Mrs Hulton's last letter, dated February 1776, documents the condition of Boston on the eve of the evacuation, as well as two instances of attacks on suspected loyalists. Accounts of the attacks may be slightly exaggerated, but they are not dissimilar to stories told by "patriot" forces describing the behavior of loyalists or British/German troops in North America. In Boston, "the poor soldiers endured great hardships and fatigues deluged with rain then chilled with frost whilst they are in their tents without straw".

She related one action by "patriots": the cruelties which are exercised on all those who are in their [patriots'] power is shocking, by advice from Kennebec the committee there sentenced a man to be buried alive for wishing success to the King's troops and that action had been executed upon him. Even more disturbing was a story originating in Roxbury [outside Boston]: Mr Ed Brindley's wife whilst laying in had a squad of rebels always in her room who treated her with great rudeness and indecency exposing her to view their banditti as a sight "see a Tory woman" and stripped her and her children of their linen and clothes (February 1776).

Mrs Hulton's brother was evacuated with the British contingent from Boston to Halifax. He wrote to his sister from there in June 1776. His letter sums up the fate of many of those who had sided with the British government or were suspected of loyalist sympathies: "we suffer a loss of property with many worthy persons, here [in Halifax] alas are many families who lived in ease and plenty in Boston that now have scarce a shelter or any means of substance" (June 1776).

Stalemate

As noted previously, the British Army presence in North America was drastically reduced after 1778 and received reinforcements on only a few subsequent occasions. The vast majority of the army was deployed to contend with threats elsewhere in the world. France was able to deliver a large expeditionary force to North America in 1780 that performed successfully in Virginia, but the remainder of the French forces posed an effective threat to British interests elsewhere. Most French troops earmarked for overseas duty were sent to the West Indies, but a sizeable force was also sent to aid the Spanish in the Minorca and Gibraltar campaigns. Another five regiments were sent to fight in India, and the remainder of the army stayed in France, posing a continuing threat to the British Isles. The Spanish land forces, although not as well equipped or trained as their French or British counterparts, provided an additional headache for the British outposts in the Floridas and Caribbean.

The West Indies and the Caribbean

The first major land engagements in the West Indies occurred in 1781, after a series of indecisive naval engagements during 1780. Following a declaration of war on the Dutch Republic in late December 1780, the British moved against the Dutch colony of St Eustatius and seized it on 3 February 1781. Tensions between neutral states and the British had been exacerbated by Royal Navy seizures of neutral shipping. The Dutch had carried on trade with the Thirteen Colonies throughout the war, and Russia and the Scandinavian states had begun to form a "League of Armed Neutrality" to protect

their shipping from the various belligerents. Britain feared that the powerful Dutch naval and merchant fleet would also join, and decided to attack them before they could do so. British aggression put Dutch colonies throughout the world at risk.

The defeat of Cornwallis at Yorktown freed the French Admiral de Grasse to return to the West Indies in December 1781. The French land forces were led by Marquis de Bouille, governor of Martinigue. The French moved against the British-occupied island of St Lucia. On 10 May, the French landed on the island, but upon deciding that the British defensive works were too strong, they re-embarked. The British force holding St Eustatius was defeated by a French force on 26 November, and St Martin and St Bartholomew fell in quick succession. The British island of St Kitts became the next target, and on 11 January 1782 6,000 men landed on the island and launched a siege. On 13 February, the British surrendered the island. The French also seized Monserat and Nevis in February 1782.

This success encouraged the French and Spanish to attempt an assault on Jamaica. However, their incursion was so vigorously rebuffed by the British Admiral Rodney, at the battle of the Saintes, that they decided to call off the invasion. Instead, the Spanish turned their efforts to the British islands in the Bahamas, whose small British garrisons were easily overwhelmed by 5,000 Spanish troops. Rochambeau's expeditionary force was ordered to the Caribbean in the winter of 1782–83 in preparation for another attempt on Jamaica, but the fighting in the Caribbean slowed down during 1783, when news arrived that peace negotiations had begun. The last operation was conducted by British provincial units from Florida, who seized parts of the Bahama Islands in April 1783.

Of secondary importance to the fighting in the West Indies were the campaigns in Honduras, Nicaragua, and the Floridas between British and Spanish forces. A small force of regulars, provincial troops from Jamaica, and sailors seized the Spanish base at Bacalar, on the Honduran coast, on 20 October 1779. Sickness followed, soon driving the British out of the area and back to Jamaica. In 1780, the British decided to move against the Spanish establishment in Nicaragua, and a force was sent against the San Juan river area and Lake Nicaragua. The expedition, successful at first, was soon bogged down by disease and lack of supplies. As the British commander, Lieutenant-Colonel Stephen Kemble, noted: "should the sickness continue [it would] absolutely put an end to our pushing forward" (8010-32-1). An officer in the Jamaica corps also noted: "sickness is rampant" (8010-32-3). Sickness also occured in the Spanish forces, but not to provoke a surrender sufficiently. The British were forced to withdraw most of the troops, and the remaining small British force was easily overwhelmed before the end of the year.

The Spanish, led by Bernardo de Galvez, had great success against the British garrisons in the Floridas. They set out to take the British garrisons at Mobile and Pensacola' and took Mobile on 14 March. After a year's activity, the Spanish moved towards Pensacola in early 1781. The siege of Pensacola was a joint Franco-Spanish effort of some 7,000 men, against a British garrison of only two regular regiments plus assorted provincial corps units. The Franco-Spanish force began to envelop the town in March 1781, commencing a siege that would last for close to two months. A Spanish observer, noting the supply problems, commented: "that afternoon [6 May] the general told me of the great difficulty in which he found himself ... not enough [cannonballs] to supply the batteries ... almost all the cannonballs fired by the enemy were gathered up" (Saavedra, p. 168). Nevertheless, the British surrendered on 9 May. The reason given for the surrender was that "a shell from one of our howitzers

Battle of Pensacola. (Anne SK Brown Collection)

Frederik William Augustus, Baron von Steuben. (Anne SK Brown Collection)

fell into the powder magazine ... the majority of the soldiers had perished in the explosion" (Saavedra, p. 171).

Europe

The initial threat to Britain of invasion from France had receded somewhat after the joint Franco-Spanish fleet had returned to port in France and Spain at the end of 1779, but it was still not possible for the British to release ships or soldiers for duty in other areas. The attentions of France and Spain were principally focused on Minorca and Gibraltar, but the Channel Islands were still in danger. A second French attempt to invade the islands took place in January 1781, and St Helier was seized. The British retaliated and recaptured the island.

The fight for Gibraltar centered on the ability of the British to reinforce and resupply the garrison. The Spanish and French were able to lay siege effectively, but

were unable to completely seal off the port or destroy all the relief fleets coming out from Britain. The British garrison was having a difficult time though. A Spanish officer commented, regarding a Hanoverian deserter, "scurvy makes great ravages among the men ... [They] are extremely fatigued" (5701-9). The siege continued throughout the course of the war, but the British never gave in.

During the summer of 1781, a Franco-Spanish fleet attempted to seize the British island of Minorca. On 19 August 1781, 8,000 troops landed and laid siege to the British Fort St Philip. The siege dragged on until February 1782, when the British surrendered the island and the garrison.

India

As noted previously, the British dispatched the French forces quickly in 1778, but then had to deal with the large armies of Haidar Ali. The British fought a series of four wars, called the Mysore Wars, with Haidar Ali and his son, Tipu Sultan. Haidar Ali and his army attacked the Carnatic in the summer of 1780, and were met by two British columns of company troops from Madras and British regulars. The British column of 4,000 men, under the command of Lieutenant-Colonel William Baillie, was defeated at the battle of Pollimore on 6 September 1780. General Sir Eyre Coote, hero of the battle of Wandiwash and Commander-in-Chief in India, arrived after the defeat with a significant reinforcement of troops from the Bengal Presidency. By the end of 1781, Coote had defeated Haidar Ali's army at the battles of Porto Novo on 1 July, Polilur on 27 August, and Sholinghur on 27 September. Even so, Coote had failed to completely push Haidar Ali out of the Carnatic. The British forces lacked sufficient numbers of cavalry to drive home their advantages.

The first actions of 1782 were undertaken by the French, who landed three French regular regiments at Porto Novo in aid of

Battle at St. Helier, Jersey. (Anne SK Brown Collection)

Haidar Ali on 21 February. The fighting for the year was primarily carried on by the French and British fleets off the coast of the Carnatic and Ceylon, although the British garrison on Ceylon surrendered in August.

Haidar Ali died in late 1782 and his son, Tipu Sultan, took over command of the kingdom and army. Tipu returned to the Carnatic area, along with a second French force, which arrived at Porto Novo on 16 March 1783. The British, recognizing the danger, immediately set out to destroy the French regular forces and contingent of sepoys. The two armies met outside Cuddalore in June.

The French built a defended position, which the British attacked on 13 June. The battle lasted all day, as a British observer noted: "the bloody contest continued without intermission until 5 o'clock in the evening when a cessation of firing took place … both lines were overcome with fatigue [thus they] lay upon their arms" (Munro, Narrative, p. 328). The French outer defenses

had been breached, but they withdrew safely to the town's walls. On 25 June, the French launched an unsuccessful attack on the British siege lines. Both sides withdrew upon receiving the news that peace negotiations had begun back in Europe earlier in the year.

The war with Tipu continued into the following year, but ended eventually because Tipu could gain no further French support, leaving the British free to concentrate on his army. The Mysore Wars did not end officially until 1799, when Tipu's capital, Seringapatam, was taken and Tipu himself killed.

Peace

In February 1782, Lord Germain resigned as British Secretary of State for America. Lord North and his government resigned on 20 March. The new government, led by the Marquis of Rockingham, took office. Rockingham's government wanted peace with the American colonies so that it could concentrate on the Bourbon menace, and in

June, Lieutenant-General Haldimand, Commander-in-Chief of Canada, was advised that all offensive operations against the Thirteen Colonies were to cease.

British and American negotiators began to meet during the summer of 1782. The negotiations lasted for five months, as the two sides worked out the boundaries of the new country and other relevant issues, such as fishing rights. The preliminary peace was formally established between the British and the new American government on 30 November 1782. Under its terms, the British accepted the independence of the United States; all British troops stationed in the United States would withdraw. The land between the Appalachian Mountains and the Mississippi river was given to the United States, and they also received access to George's Bank, the fishing grounds off Newfoundland. The United States agreed to honor debts accrued during the war and to treat loyalists fairly. Many loyalists, however, chose to leave the country and move to Canada, the West Indies, or Great Britain, not trusting their new government and fearful of the future. Orders arrived on 14 July 1782 for the British to evacuate Savannah; Charleston followed on 18 December 1782. New York was not formally evacuated until 25 November 1783.

The French and Spanish had made considerable progress in eradicating the humiliations of the Seven Years' War, but the war was becoming a stalemate, and all sides were weary of it. Preliminary peace talks began among the British, French, Spanish, and Dutch in late 1782. By January 1783, an armistice had been agreed and a preliminary peace treaty signed, although fighting continued in some regions too distant to hear immediately of the agreements.

The Treaty of Paris was signed on 3 September 1783. Britain handed over the Floridas (East and West) and Minorca to Spain, retaining Gibraltar and the Bahamas. France regained Senegal, St Lucia, Tobago, and her interests in India, notably Pondicherry. The paucity of decisive naval victories for either side made it difficult to claim any major territorial gains. The British were able to retain possessions in the West Indies that they had held before the war began, and lost nothing in India.

Influence of the American Revolution

The American Revolution arose out of a dispute that began with Great Britain's change in policy towards her colonies. The trend towards a cohesive worldwide British empire, commercially and strategically powerful, was not checked by the outcome of the war. Rather, it meant that Britain shifted her focus from the Thirteen Colonies as the centerpiece of this empire, and began to concentrate on the potential of India instead. The drive for empire would shape the fate of Britain, and of most of the world, throughout the 19th century and beyond.

In the wake of defeat in North America, Britain was also forced to assess once again the strengths and weaknesses of her army and navy. This evaluation led to reforms, which prepared the British Army and Royal Navy for further conflict with France, Britain's traditional enemy, during the French Revolution and the reign of Napoleon.

As described above, France suffered economically from her participation in the war, even though she fought on the winning side. The debts incurred in supporting the Americans with money and arms contributed to the steadily worsening economic situation at home, and are frequently cited as one of the root causes of the revolution that inflamed France only a few years later. There is a popular belief that the French Revolution was motivated by events in America, and it is ironic that this may be true, although not necessarily for the reasons commonly cited.

After the Treaty of Paris, the newborn United States of America was left independent and possessed of the rights for which she had fought – to trade freely, impose her own taxes, and determine her own military requirements. Possessed of a flourishing economy and boundless national resources, her opportunities appeared limitless. Indeed, the United States would succeed, with the help of liberal trade policies and the recruitment of successive waves of enthusiastic immigrants, in transforming itself into the most powerful English-speaking country on Earth in less than two centuries. The infant nation was also left in 1783 with the delicate problem of bringing together 13 distinct entities with diverse and sometimes contradictory needs and views into a cohesive unit, and of reconciling the power of the local assemblies with the creation of an effective national representative government.

United States and British North America 1783–1807

The period between the end of the American Revolution, in 1783, and 1807, marked a period of significant growth for both the newly independent United States and the emerging colony of British North America. Expansion created friction, and problems arose that ultimately resulted in armed conflict between the two in the War of 1812.

The United States

The US emerged from the Revolutionary War as an independent state, but not a fully unified one. In the postwar period, the fledgling nation struggled to develop a functional governmental structure that was acceptable to the various states, whose views on the matter were widely divergent. The issue of security for the new country, how best to ensure it, and the role of the Continental Army in doing so, was another subject for debate.

Neither of these discussions was new; both of these matters had been the subject of ongoing debate throughout the Revolution. The fundamental question behind both of these issues was: where do states' rights end and the federal government's powers begin?

In 1783, Generals Washington and Steuben argued for a standing army in the postwar period. They cited outstanding territorial disputes with Indians, as well as the fact that British regular troops were still stationed in British North America. Despite these arguments, opposition to the idea of a standing army was widespread and entrenched in the United States. The traditional Englishman's fear of a large standing army (dating back to Cromwell's exploits in the 17th century), combined with more recent experience of the British Army during the French-Indian War and Revolution, bolstered this stance. The chief practical reason against a standing army, however, was cost. After the American Revolution, the US government was in dire straits financially.

Washington and Steuben submitted separate security proposals to a Congressional committee which outlined similar plans. The standing army was to consist of 2,600 officers and men, formed into four regiments of infantry and one of artillery. A militia supporting the standing army would be able to draw from all able bodied males between the ages of 18 and 25, who would be called for training for 25 days each year. The states were generally unhappy with this proposal, as it gave control of the militia to the federal government, rather than to them.

The Congressional committee determined that these plans were too ambitious. After the final peace was signed with Great Britain in 1783, Congress called for the Continental Army to be disbanded, except for 55 men who were to be based at West Point and 35 men at Fort Pitt. Congress also decided that the militia should not be controlled by the federal government, but by each state individually. Washington resigned his position as commander-in-chief, and Henry Knox remained as the senior officer who disbanded the Continental Army.

The United States initially created its federal government under the Articles of Confederation. This lasted only a few years due to the fact that its powers were so limited, and those of the individual states so great. Deployment of the armed forces provides a good example of how this scenario played out in practice during the confederacy period. Congress had the right to declare war, but it had to rely upon the states to furnish the government with militia troops and money in order to wage that war. Congress had had the Continental Army at its disposal as well during the war, but in the postwar period it was forced to rely entirely upon the states for both troops and money.

In 1784, Congress realised that it still needed forces to deal with potential threats, not only from the Indians but also from the British along the frontiers. They called upon New Jersey, New York, Pennsylvania and Connecticut to furnish 700 men from their militias to be formed into a regiment to patrol the frontier. This caused an immediate problem, as not all the states provided the required men, and Congress was powerless to compel compliance. In 1785, Congress called for another regiment to be placed at their disposal for a three-year period, with similar results. It took until 1786 to organize an adequate number of men, and the 1st American Regiment was born. Their posting was mostly along the Ohio River, and their remit to safeguard against Indian raids and police the area to stop white settlers from entering Indian territory illegally. The irony of this was that the British Army had been stationed in the same area in the 1760s to carry out the same job – only to be accused of limiting the rights of the American settlers. The troops from the 1st American Regiment would face the same accusations.

The federal government's limited powers during the confederacy period also became glaringly apparent in their response to a rebellion that began in western Massachusetts, commonly known as Shays' Rebellion. The rebellion grew out of the major economic crises of the postwar period. The war had left many farmers in western Massachusetts in debt, with their creditors calling in loans and demanding hard currency. The farmers reacted by petitioning the Massachusetts state government to lower taxes and institute judicial reform. The rebellion broke out in August 1786, when an armed party

"The Looking Glass for 1787." A satire touching on some of the major issues in Connecticut politics on the eve of the ratification of the US Constitution. The two rival factions shown are the "Federals," who represented the trading interests and were for taxes on imports, and the "Antifederals," who represented agrarian interests and were more receptive to paper money issues. The artist here evidently sides with the Federals. Connecticut is symbolized by a wagon loaded with debts and paper money, the weight of which causes it to sink slowly into the mud. Many of the leading men of each faction are depicted proclaiming their beliefs. One of the Antifederal members shouts "Success to Shays," referring to their sympathy for Shays' rebellion. (Library of Congress)

of farmers kept the Court of Common Pleas from sitting. Courts in other parts of Massachusetts were stormed at the same time, in an attempt to stop the imprisonment of farmers for failure to repay debts.

Captain Daniel Shays, a veteran of the Revolution, became the figurehead of the rebellion. He led a large group of armed farmers and took control of the Supreme Judicial Court in Springfield, Massachusetts. In response, the Massachusetts government deployed more than 4,000 militia troops, but the rebellion had had time to gather steam and would take time to bring under control. Congress called for the establishment of a

second regiment to be sent to Massachusetts. This took more time, while the Massachusetts government attempted to resolve the problem before "federal" troops arrived. By early 1787, Shays and his men were preparing to storm the Springfield Arsenal. The government was prepared and the militia was stationed to protect the arsenal. The militia defeated the farmers in a short battle. Shays and several others were captured in the fray; 14 men were tried and found guilty of treason. The death sentence was commuted and the men were later pardoned.

Shays' Rebellion highlighted major deficiencies in both the governmental structure of the US and in the military organization's preparedness to defend the state. The constitutional convention held in Philadelphia in 1787 included a number of people who called for a more centralized and powerful federal state, citing Shays' Rebellion as a prime example of the need for reform. George Washington noted: "there could be no stronger evidence of the want of energy in our governments than these disorders." James Madison, a proponent of strong central government, noted: "the rebellion in Massachusetts is a warning." There were, however, many delegates who favoured the confederation model, fearing a powerful central government and standing military. One of these, Patrick Henry, noted: "Congress by the power of taxation, by that of raising an army, and by their control over the militia, have the sword in one hand and the purse in the other. Shall we be safe without either?"

By 1790, all 13 existing states (joined in 1791 by the new state of Vermont) had finally ratified the Constitution, and a strong central government was born. The balance of power between state and federal governments, however, remains an issue to this day. To give due credit to the delegates of the convention, they devised a complicated plan to attempt to achieve a proper balance between the states and the executive, judicial and legislative branches of the federal government. The standing of the armed forces was at the forefront of the discussion. The Constitution divides the military power of the state into a standing or professional army controlled by Congress, and militias controlled by the individual states. The militias could be called out for limited federal service "to execute the laws of the union, suppress insurrections and repel invasions." This division was further defined in the Second Amendment, which states: "A well regulated militia being necessary to the security of a free state, the right of the people to keep and bear arms shall not be infringed."

The Constitution may have called for a professional force, but the economic and political realities of the period limited its development and expansion. Only the threat of outright bloodshed prompted Congress to authorize and provide funding for expansion. Settlers had flooded into the area known as the Northwest (which today comprises Illinois, Indiana, Michigan, and Wisconsin), and their arrival had created great unrest among the Indians already settled in the area. The American troops based along the frontier were not able to properly police the area assigned to them. To make matters worse, the US government suspected that the British had colluded with the Indians in the region.

In the spring of 1790, the army was expanded to more than 1,200 men. Later in the spring, Congress authorized the further expansion of the 1st American Regiment to three battalions. This swelling of the ranks emboldened the army commanders to make a show of force against the Indians in the region. The mixed force of militia and the 1st American Regiment, poorly commanded and lacking in tactics, was badly beaten by the Indians. The show of force had the opposite effect from the one desired, as it boosted the Indians' morale and spurred them to greater efforts.

A second expedition was planned for the 1791 campaign season. The regulars were reorganized and more militias called out. This campaign was no more successful than the first, and in 1792 Congress called for the organization of two battalions of infantry and artillery to spearhead a third campaign. They also decided to reorganize the army along different lines, and created a legionary corps, Legion of the United States, similar to Pulaski's Legion or the British Legion of the Revolutionary War. Hedging their bets, they also opened negotiations with Indian leaders.

This schedule gave the new troops more time to train for war and organize themselves for a campaign. The new formation was commanded by Anthony Wayne, who is often referred to as the father of the American regular army. With reforming measures complete and negotiations breaking down, the army set out on campaign in the summer of 1794. They won a decisive battle against the Indians at Fallen Timbers, in present-day Ohio, on August 20, finally striking a definitive blow to the power of the Indian tribes in the eastern region of the Northwest.

Congress also passed the Militia Act of 1792 during this period. The Act made it mandatory for all free white male citizens between the ages of 18 and 45 to enrol in the state militia. The men were to provide their own muskets, and the federal government had the right to call out the militia for a three-month term of service once a year. Enforcement of the Act rested with the states, and training of the militia was the responsibility of officers from each district.

This standardization was to cause unforeseen problems. By 1794, the US government's ability to project military might rested with two distinct forces: the state militias, which, due to various constraints, were not uniform in quality or ability; and a regular army, which was trained and disciplined much as the old professional Continental Army had been, but was small in numbers.

Another military milestone for the US was the Naval Act of 1794. This called for the creation of a small navy to defend US interests and for forts to be built in suitable coastal locations. The Act was motivated by rising tensions in Europe, and by Congress' fear of French or British raids, rather than outright invasion. By 1812 there were 24 forts along the Atlantic coast.

Congress had hoped to expand the regular army on the strength of Wayne's success, and there had been talk of expanding the army to as many as 30,000 men. This number never materialized. By 1796, the Regular Army had abandoned the Legion organization and adopted the traditional pattern of infantry and artillery units. By 1801, there were 3,700 men in the army, divided into four infantry regiments, two regiments of artillery and two companies of light dragoons.

President Thomas Jefferson founded the United States Military Academy at West Point in 1802. Following the pattern set by military academies across Europe, the training at West Point centred on the instruction of engineers and artillery officers. West Point eventually became a respected institution, but its early years were undistinguished. A member of the directing staff, writing in 1805, described it as "a foundling, barely existing among the mountains, and nurtured at a distance out of sight, and almost unknown to its legitimate parents."

During Jefferson's tenure as president, the Regular Army remained at around 3,000 men. The state militia organizations experienced considerable difficulty in trying to train their forces. Tensions between the US and Great Britain continued to mount, and in 1808,

Jefferson called for a three-fold expansion of the Army, to 10,000 men and officers.

The United States went through a painful process of government and military organization, from the birth of the nation in 1783 up to the War of 1812. Many issues that had arisen during the Revolution concerning Congressional power and the role of a standing army remained unresolved until the Articles of Confederation had been replaced by the Constitution. The expansion of a standing army was an unavoidably slow process, for economic as well as political reasons. Nevertheless, by 1810, the US had laid the foundations of a centralized government and military structure that would be established and functioning when the young country again went to war.

British North America

British military development in North America followed a pattern similar to that just described in the period between the end of the American Revolution and the beginning of the War of 1812. British North America during this period comprised the provinces of Nova Scotia, Newfoundland, New Brunswick, Prince Edward Island (St John's Island), and, post-1791, Lower and Upper Canada (present-day Quebec and Ontario). By 1791, all the provinces had established institutions of limited representative government, except for Newfoundland.

Following the end of the American Revolution, British loyalists from the former Thirteen Colonies applied for repatriation to British North America. The loyalists were resettled throughout the British provinces. At the time of the Treaty of Paris in 1783, there were more than 2,400 British Army regulars stationed in Nova Scotia. They were shortly joined by more than 14,000 loyalists and disbanded British Army regulars from the former colonies. Many of the newly arrived loyalists went north to Cape Breton to settle, and in fact Cape Breton established a separate government in 1784.

New Brunswick was also created in 1784. Thirteen regiments of the Provincial Corps from the Revolution had been settled in the region in 1783, along with 10,000 civilian loyalists. The colonists settled the region from the Bay of Fundy up the St John River, but no militia was created until 1787. The Legislature of New Brunswick required that all fit males between the ages of 16 and 50 enrol in one of the local companies, bringing his own weapon and ammunition. Relying on militiamen to supply their own weapons caused problems, as noted in the Militia Act of 1792, which documented one instance where 3,000 militiamen had no weapons when called out for service. Many of the militiamen were from the old Provincial Corps, but they had sold their weapons for goods and equipment for their farms.

Many of the newly arrived loyalists and disbanded British regulars enrolled in the militia organization. With the Royal Navy in control of the seas, Nova Scotia was considered to be in no danger and the militia was only a paper organization. This changed in 1793, when war broke out between France and Great Britain. Most of the British regulars stationed in New Brunswick and Nova Scotia left for service in other parts of the world. The Nova Scotia provincial government called for the raising of a Provincial Corps, the Royal Nova Scotia Regiment, to help protect the region. In 1795, Newfoundland followed suit and created the Newfoundland Regiment of Fencible Infantry, as did New Brunswick with the King's New Brunswick Regiment.

In British North America, as in the United States, the issues surrounding an embodied militia were complex and ongoing. The Nova Scotia Militia Act of 1796 called out the militia for four days a year, a period wholly insufficient for training. When peace was restored to Europe with the Treaty of Amiens in 1802, Nova Scotia felt itself secure enough once more to disband the Royal Nova Scotia Regiment, and New Brunswick did the same with the King's Regiment. The Newfoundland Regiment of Fencibles remained active, since its men and officers could be called upon for service anywhere in the world.

Napoleon's ascent to power plunged Britain into war again in 1803. A new regiment was formed in Nova Scotia, the Nova Scotia Regiment of Fencible Infantry, and a battalion of British regulars was sent to reinforce the region. The militia in Halifax was activated, and initiated training at a higher level than other Nova Scotia and Cape Breton militiamen received. New Brunswick raised the New Brunswick Regiment of Fencible Infantry. Like their Nova Scotia counterparts, this unit could serve anywhere in North America. The number of men was still insufficient to defend the province, and remained so until 1807. Prince Edward Island was effectively defenceless during this period; its militia was tiny and any British regulars in the area had all but disappeared in 1793.

Upper and Lower Canada

Smaller numbers of loyalists settled in Quebec and the territory along the St Lawrence River, and the vast majority of the population remained French-speaking, dating back to the area's history as a French possession until 1763. In 1786 and 1787, Sir Guy Carleton, Lord Dorchester and Governor of Canada, decided to assess the military preparedness of the area. He had 2,000 British regulars stationed along 1,000 miles of territory, from Gaspé to Fort Detroit and the Northwest region. The Militia Ordinance of 1787 called for the embodiment of militias for two years, to force them to train properly. On paper, the French-speaking regions claimed 636 officers and 24,000 men; the English-speaking areas claimed 63 officers and 1,000 other ranks. In reality, the numbers were much lower.

There was tension in Quebec between the incoming English-speaking settlers and the established French-speaking population, commonly known as *les habitants*. In 1791, the British government decided to divide the province into two separate administrative entities, thus Quebec became Lower Canada, predominantly French-speaking and administered using French legal structures. The remaining area became known as Upper Canada (roughly comprising present-day Ontario), predominantly English-speaking and subject to English law and custom. By imposing the divide, the British government hoped to attract English-speaking settlers to Upper Canada and placate the resident French population.

When war broke out between Great Britain and France in 1793, the demand for troops elsewhere strained British regulars in Lower Canada. The British government shipped 2,000 muskets to help outfit the Lower Canada militia. Both Lower and Upper Canada raised troops for service, two battalions named the Royal Canadian Volunteers. These battalions, like all the others, were short of men and officers.

The Lower Canada Militia encountered similar problems. In 1799, Sir Robert Shore Milnes, Lieutenant-Governor of Lower Canada, reported that the militia had 28,000 French-speaking and 1,300 English-speaking rank and file, "but not one effective man." The government offered land grants to officers and men to make the militia a more attractive proposition. By 1801, this appeared to be having a positive effect on men reporting for duty, but Milnes reported following a tour of inspection that the militia was still not sufficiently trained and could not be relied upon in an emergency.

The Royal Canadian Volunteers were also disbanded after the Treaty of Amiens and the British regulars in the province further reduced. With the resumption of hostilities, the local militias, realising the potential dangers, took training and drilling more seriously. Their numbers were still low, but British regulars considered their troops good quality.

Lieutenant Governor John Simcoe, former Colonel of the Provincial Corps unit, Queen's Rangers, is considered the motivating force behind a formalized militia system in Upper Canada. He realised in 1793 that British regulars would be required in other areas and that a functional militia system was a necessity. He reformed the Queen's Rangers and set out to organize the system properly. He called upon the British government to provide weapons for the militia, and also set out to create a naval force to protect the Great Lakes and St Lawrence River area. The militia was to provide pilots and captains for the boats as well as troops.

In the mid-1790s, militia from Upper Canada became involved in the friction between American troops and Indians living in the Northwest. As the American General Wayne and his forces moved into the region to confront the Indians, the Canadian militia was called out to protect Fort Miami and observe the progression of the campaign. The United States had more than once accused the British regulars and Canadian militia of collusion with the Indian tribes, and tension was high. Some Canadian militia from Fort Detroit also took part in the campaign, but both sides managed to keep their heads and avoided direct confrontation. Jay's Treaty, which was signed in 1794 and enacted completely by 1796, surrendered British claims to some of the disputed forts in the Northwest. Many considered this a positive step towards peace with the US.

As a result of Jay's Treaty, the numbers of British regulars in the region were further reduced. The Queen's Rangers and companies from the Royal Canadian Volunteers served in the region to safeguard against any threat. As with the rest of British North America, the troops were further reduced in 1802 and the militia was excused from duty.

By 1808, the British government felt the threat to British North America from the United States was increasing, and sent a reinforcement of British Army regulars. They also decided to send a series of officers with specific orders to raise militias in the provinces systematically. They hoped to raise 12,000 militia in Upper and Lower Canada and 8,000 in the Atlantic provinces.

The irony of this period of growing tension is that both British North America and the United States had great difficulty in organizing adequate defenses against one another. The US far outnumbered British North America in population, but both sides were equal in military strength. The US had a perennial problem trying to decide whether to have a "regular" army and what the role of the militia should be. British North America relied primarily on varying numbers of British regulars, and its militia system was a shambles until 1808.

Part III
The War of 1812

James Madison, President of the United States 1809–17,
depicted in a period print. (Library of Congress)

Introduction

Off the coast of Virginia in 1807, during Great Britain's long war with France, the captain of His Majesty's Ship *Leopard* ordered the United States frigate *Chesapeake* to stop so he could search it for deserters from the Royal Navy. The Americans refused. The British let loose a broadside that killed or wounded 21 men. After replying with a single artillery shot to assert the dignity of the flag, the *Chesapeake* surrendered, whereupon a boarding party seized four deserters serving on the US vessel. This attack on a neutral warship outraged Americans, insulted their sovereignty, and served as a symbol of a wider crisis unfolding between Great Britain and the United States over free trade and sailors' rights.

Meanwhile, in the upper Mississippi Valley and western Great Lakes region, a Shawnee leader, Tecumseh, and his prophet brother, Tenskwatawa, spoke words of enraged bitterness and revitalization to the aboriginal peoples. Natives had lived through three decades of profound dislocation brought on by an expanding America that seemed to hold their rights in contempt if they conflicted with those of the land-hungry white population. Peaceful attempts to protect their interests had failed, and many tribal leaders now thought they had to go to war, as they had done in earlier times, to beat back the 'long knives' and secure a homeland for their children.

As relations degenerated towards war from 1807 to 1812, many Americans argued that the United States ought to seize the British provinces that lay to the north of the republic in order to get even with Britain, to realize America's destiny, or even to profit personally through territorial expansion. Others, such as President James Madison, desired conquest because these colonies were emerging as a competitor to the United States in the export of North American products. Annexation would benefit US expansion elsewhere too: in the west against the aboriginal tribes, who would be deprived of help from British officials and Canadian fur traders; and in the south, where filibusters and expansionists hoped that the subjugation of Canada would help them in realizing their goal of taking the Floridas from Britain's new European ally, Spain.

All these issues, along with a political crisis that threatened Madison's hold on power, came together in June 1812, when the United States declared war on Great Britain. A month later, US soldiers invaded Canada, heralding the onslaught of three years of war that would engulf the United States, Great Britain, its colonies, and many of the aboriginal nations of eastern North America.

In the following pages we will examine the War of 1812 on land and sea, study the still-debated causes and outcomes of the conflict, and explore some of the many interesting tales associated with the war.

The USS *Chesapeake* was not only involved in the incident of 1807 which outraged Americans, but also took part in one of the most famous naval engagements of the war, in June 1813, when it fought the HMS *Shannon*. Despite being a better-built ship, the inexperience of the *Chesapeake*'s crew led to the ship being boarded. (Topfoto)

A small war with complex causes

Sailors' rights

The *Chesapeake* affair symbolized how grave an issue 'impressment' was between Great Britain and the United States. The Royal Navy (RN) ratio of seamen per ton of ship was the smallest of the major maritime powers, and in its desperation to fill ships' companies in the war with France, it impressed men, a practice that amounted to little more than legalized kidnappings in port towns and from merchant vessels. Naturally, many victims deserted; as did other sailors who had volunteered for the RN but who later lamented their decision. Large numbers of these men fled to foreign ships, including American ones, for asylum and employment. At the same time, American and other foreign seamen, finding themselves down on their luck in some port far from home, joined the Royal Navy; often they also deserted.

All of these individuals, as well as Britons who had emigrated to the United States, were liable under British law to being seized for service in the navy. Consequently, the RN stopped merchant vessels to remove subjects and deserters, and they often also took US citizens and other individuals who had no history of prior service in the navy.

The number impressed is uncertain, but the United States issued a report stating that 6,057 men had been taken from American ships between 1803 and 1811. However, the list was full of duplications, and did not identify British-born sailors or individuals who had deserted from the RN after volunteering to serve.

Some officials also undermined the credibility of American claims of injustice by selling false citizenship documents, as happened in London, where one US diplomat provided certificates to deserters for a half-crown fee. Conversely, the British released illegally impressed people when their cases came to the attention of the authorities. Thus the issue was more complex than is commonly believed, but even with these ambiguities it nevertheless represented an affront to national sovereignty, and there can be no doubt that large numbers of Americans found themselves wrongly impressed.

When the *Leopard* fired on the *Chesapeake* and removed sailors (whom the US acknowledged were RN deserters), the tensions that had been brewing over impressment came to a head. Many Americans demanded a recourse to arms, asserting that it was one thing to take people from merchantmen, but quite another to attack a man-of-war. The British, desperate to prevent hostilities, repudiated the action, disciplined the officers responsible, and offered compensation. For his part, the American president, Thomas Jefferson, hoped to avoid a conflict, so the crisis passed, although passions continued to run high because impressment from merchant vessels did not stop.

At the same time, the United States Navy protected the country's neutrality whenever it could. On one occasion, in May 1811, the frigate USS *President* opened fire upon the smaller RN sloop *Little Belt*, which had been mistaken for a larger warship that had impressed some Americans. The sloop lost 32 killed and wounded, to only one person injured on the *President*. The US government apologized but exonerated the captain of the *President*. Nevertheless, the British did not pursue the matter because their attentions were focused on protecting themselves against Napoleon Bonaparte's dream of turning their island kingdom into a French vassal state.

This 1818 print shows Castle Williams in New York, built immediately after the *Chesapeake* affair of 1807. Coastal forts often had less artillery than the attacking squadrons, but shipboard guns were not as accurate because of the movement of the vessels. The earth or masonry walls of shore batteries could absorb shot better than wooden ships, and forts could return fire with heated shot to set vessels on fire. (National Maritime Museum)

Free trade

In addition to 'sailors' rights,' problems surrounding the issue of 'free trade' contributed to the American decision to go to war. As a neutral nation, the United States faced serious challenges in expanding its trade and gaining access to the world's markets while France and Britain made war against each other. Despite all this, US international trade actually grew dramatically before 1812, largely through opportunities created by these very wars. However, a watershed in the crisis occurred around 1805–07. Until that time, there had been problems enough: the United States had suffered from existing British and French restrictions, had fought the 'Quasi-War' of 1797–1801 with the French, and had seen hundreds of American ships seized by both European powers. Nevertheless, Britain essentially turned a blind eye to American ships that violated a British policy denying neutral vessels the right to replace belligerent ones in carrying goods between a belligerent's ports, so long as the Americans 'broke' the voyage by stopping in the US. (This then turned their cargo into 'American' exports.) In 1805, however, a British court decided that this was illegal, yet the British government decided not to enforce the decision, choosing instead to blockade part of the English Channel and North Sea but allow Americans to continue trading at non-blockaded ports.

Napoleon responded to the British actions with a series of decrees (beginning with the Berlin Decree of 1806). They were designed to destroy the economy of the United Kingdom by putting Britain under blockade and ordering the seizure of merchantmen – including American ones – carrying goods from the UK or its colonies. Bonaparte's

blockade was a sham because he could not enforce it, but the French did take large numbers of vessels entering their own ports and those of other European countries under French control. Britain retaliated with a series of Orders-in-Council, beginning in 1807. They declared all French and French-allied ports to be under blockade (which the RN only partially enforced) and ordered neutral ships apprehended unless (and as a concession) they put into British ports to pay duties on their cargoes. The objective was not so much to cut trade with France as to levy a tribute on merchants who traded with Britain's enemies. Napoleon responded with his Milan Decree in 1807, authorizing the confiscation of vessels that complied with the orders, and he later issued additional decrees to seize American ships that he claimed had violated either his own or US trade regulations.

Theoretically, both countries' policies were equally offensive to Americans, but Britain had the naval might to enforce them more effectively and hence became the focus of outrage. The US government rejected the authority of the decrees and the orders, arguing that blockades only could be lawful if fully enforced, which not even the Royal Navy could aspire to do. The Americans, however, did not want war, so they passed various laws themselves to restrict or halt trade with Britain, France, and, at one point, with the whole world. The thinking behind them was that European belligerents not only needed North American products to fight their wars, supply their manufacturers, and feed their people at home and in the West Indian colonies, but they also depended upon US merchant ships to move these goods – and European and colonial products – across the world's oceans. By restricting or denying access to these goods and services, the US would force the British and French to make the concessions America wanted, including further opening up the world's markets.

The most famous of the US laws was the Embargo of 1807, which fundamentally forbade trade with the entire world. It did not change London's views, but proved to be devastating to the US economy and

Eastern North America June 1812

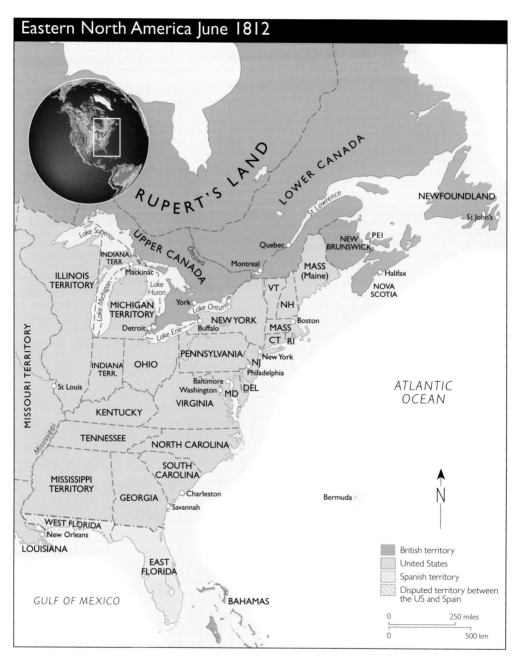

generated widespread opposition among Americans, who evaded its restrictions by smuggling goods across the porous border with British North America and through clandestine shipments from their own shores.

In 1809, just as James Madison succeeded Thomas Jefferson as president, Congress replaced the Embargo with the milder Non-Intercourse Act. It prohibited trade with France and Britain, reopened commerce with other countries, and promised to resume relations with whichever belligerent changed its hurtful policies. This legislation also proved to be ineffective, and in 1810, it was replaced by Macon's Bill Number Two, which re-established trade with everyone but allowed the president to impose non-importation on one of the European powers if the other repealed its restrictions. Without any serious ability to blockade Britain, Napoleon offered to repeal his decrees if either the UK revoked the Orders-in-Council or the US imposed non-importation on Britain. At the same time, however, he issued a new decree that saw France actually seize more American vessels in 1810 than the Royal Navy did. Somehow the normally astute Madison either fell for the ploy or went along with it, and in November, he imposed non-importation on Britain. This delighted Bonaparte, who hoped for an Anglo-American confrontation to relieve some of the pressure the British were exerting against him, but he continued to take American vessels despite his promises.

The USS *President vs* HMS *Little Belt* in a contemporary print. (National Maritime Museum)

Expansionism

In 1810–11, the British did not think they could comply with American demands on impressment or trade, believing that the Royal Navy was their best weapon in the struggle against France and so had to be used as effectively as possible. This required the British to maintain its manpower levels. Furthermore, the impact of American restrictions, although injurious, was not sufficient to force concessions, and the British were strong enough that they could look beyond the immediate wartime crisis to the possibility that coercive measures might translate into an expansion of their own maritime economy, at the expense of their competitors, once peace had returned. Furthermore, when faced with the Embargo and similar actions, they sought out alternative sources of goods, and naturally

US Dragoon officer, painted in 1816. The British and Americans only had small numbers of cavalry during the War of 1812, which they used mainly for scouting, patrolling, and delivering dispatches, with mounted charges being rare. Cavalry normally wore more elaborate uniforms than the other branches of the military. (Houghton Library, Harvard University)

found that the British American colonies offered enormous potential to meet the needs of the Empire. Through preferential trade and other measures, London fostered that potential at a time when those colonies had developed to the point where they could produce valuable surpluses (spurred on in part by the vacuum created by American trade restrictions). Between 1807 and 1811, for instance, Canadian exports of pine and fir timber rose 556 percent. To strengthen the British provinces further at the expense

of the United States, the British government issued an Order-in-Council in 1811 excluding American salted fish from the West Indian colonies and imposing heavy duties on other US imports. This was a blow to President Madison, who had assumed that the West Indies simply could not be fed without American fish, and thus it demonstrated the weakness of his trade policies as vehicles of coercion. At the same time, it underscored how much of a rival the British colonies had become, both in their own right and as a conduit for American smugglers seeking to avoid his restrictions.

Looking to the future, Madison worried that the Great Lakes-St Lawrence system through British territory even might turn out to be the main route that American goods from the northern interior would use to travel to Europe. The president therefore decided that those provinces had to be conquered. This would deny Britain access to North American produce entirely, except under conditions dictated by the United States (to say nothing of the impact annexation would have on the overall prosperity of the nation).

Many Americans supported expansion; for some, the expulsion of Britain from the continent represented a natural step in achieving the republic's destiny. Congressman John Harper articulated this idea in 1812, when he proclaimed that no less an authority than 'the Author of Nature' himself had 'marked our limits in the south, by the Gulf of Mexico [in what then was Spanish territory]; and on the north, by the regions of eternal frost.' For others, seizing Canada would be a fitting punishment to avenge their problems on the high seas.

Some leading expansionists wanted to profit personally from changing America's borders. Such were the aims of the entrepreneur and 'War Hawk' Peter B. Porter (who would command a brigade in the 1814 invasion of Canada). His views differed somewhat from Madison's because he thought both Upper and Lower Canada should be conquered but that only the upper province should be absorbed into the

American infantry, 1816, dressed in fundamental conformity to the tailoring requirement of the 1813 regulations, with minor variations that were typical of the era. Not all infantry wore the officially approved blue uniform; when scarcities of the correct cloth occurred, foot soldiers might find themselves sporting black, brown, or gray coats instead. (Houghton Library, Harvard University)

American union while the lower, largely francophone, colony should be turned into an independent state. This vision fitted with his business interests: on the one hand, he ran a carrying trade around Niagara Falls on the New York side of the border, and assumed that the conquest of Upper Canada would allow him to knock out or replace his competitors on the British side of the river; on the other hand, he did not want inland trade to move down the St Lawrence because he was a promoter of a canal system – the future Erie Canal – to move goods from the Great Lakes to the Hudson River and on to New York City. Having Lower Canada become a separate country would discourage the development of the St Lawrence route in order to keep the transportation system within the United States. It also would constrain entrepreneurs in Montreal and Quebec (who might compete against his interests) by ensuring their foreign status.

The Old Northwest

As debates over impressment, trade, and the destiny of British North America unfolded, other troubles on the western and southern frontiers helped to propel the United States to war. After the end of the American Revolution, in 1783, the aboriginal peoples in the Old Northwest (modern Ohio, Michigan, Indiana, and adjoining regions) saw a flood of hostile settlers stream into their territories. The newcomers not only wanted to take land, but the agricultural economy they brought with them changed the environment, as they cut down the forests, chased away the game, and rendered existing native subsistence patterns non viable. The mainly Algonkian-speaking peoples of the region (such as the Shawnees, Potawatomis, and Ottawas) responded to this challenge by forming a confederacy to fight for their homelands in the latter part of the 1780s; and at the battle of the Wabash in 1791, they inflicted the greatest defeat the US ever suffered at the hands of the natives. In 1794, however, the tribes lost the decisive battle of Fallen Timbers, and in 1795, surrendered most of Ohio and other tracts of land in return for a new boundary between themselves and the settlers. They hoped that an established border would allow them to evolve independently of unwanted intrusions in their remaining territories, but the lines proved to be temporary. Immediately after their creation, American authorities began to acquire more land through heavy-handed tactics, forcing the natives to continue moving west. In their desperation, the tribespeople again thought about uniting to defend their homes in the Old Northwest. In 1805, two Shawnee

brothers, the prophet Tenskwatawa and the political and military leader Tecumseh, began forming a pan-tribal confederacy. (Not all natives in the Great Lakes region were hostile to the US; some embraced neutrality, and small numbers of others allied themselves to the Americans.)

The British were implicated in the frontier crisis because the Crown had formed an alliance with the majority of tribespeople during the revolution and had supplied weapons and other assistance to them through the war years of the 1780s and 1790s. The British had hoped that native successes would allow them to help the tribes renegotiate the Anglo-American border of 1783 to create an aboriginal homeland on Upper Canada's south-western border, which, aside from the benefits it would provide to the tribes, would make the province more defensible. At the same time, Canadian fur traders moved freely through the region, conducting their business and helping maintain the British alliance.

As the clouds of war formed in the years before 1812, the British continued to cultivate native anger, recognizing that they would need aboriginal support to defend Canada. Yet they also tried to defuse frontier tensions in the hope of ultimately avoiding hostilities altogether. Naturally, their activities offended Americans, who were convinced that the British were plotting against them. These fears were only compounded by the first of the new round of battles for the frontier, when American forces clashed with the warriors of the western tribal confederacy at Tippecanoe in November 1811, some seven months before the outbreak of the Anglo-American war. This new crisis quickly amplified the cries for the conquest of Canada, to isolate the tribes from foreign aid and ensure that their opposition to American expansion could be more easily suppressed.

Far to the south, other expansionists thought that war against the natives and the conquest of Canada would help them achieve their own regional territorial ambitions. One of these 'prizes' was the land of the Creek nation, mainly within the Mississippi Territory, where tensions between natives and newcomers were similar to those in the Old Northwest. The Americans also wanted to annex the Spanish territories of East and West Florida. As it was, they had occupied much of West Florida before the outbreak of the War of 1812, but they assumed that hostilities with Spain's ally, Britain, would facilitate their designs on the remainder of these colonies.

Madison's political problems

The American declaration of war was also fuelled by James Madison's fears that he might lose the presidency in the election of late 1812. His perceived weakness in his handling of government in general, and of international affairs in particular, had generated widespread criticism and he faced the possibility of a challenger from within his own Democratic-Republican party, as well as Federalist Party opponents. (The Federalists advocated better relations with Britain over France.) The president thought he needed to take a stronger stand against the British in order to regain his party's confidence, which he assumed meant he had to either negotiate a settlement on American terms or go to war.

The negotiations that did take place were somewhat confused. Essentially, the British argued that revoking the Orders-in-Council would be wrong because Napoleon's actions had been fraudulent and therefore the US decision to invoke non-importation against the British made no sense, and even invited retaliation. Faced with factionalism within his own party, Madison would not admit to having made a mistake in accepting Bonaparte's offer because this would have confirmed the incompetence claimed by his political adversaries. He found himself in a corner in which the nation's interests and his own may have come into some conflict. With the realization that many leading supporters within his party opposed the continuation of ineffective trade policies, and in keeping with his developing annexationist views, Madison called Congress into an early session for November 1811 to prepare for war. His objectives were to unite his supporters and his critics and increase the pressure on the British to relent. If they did not, he would provide the country with the resources it would need to fight.

In the end, Madison embarked on a dubious war against Great Britain but skirted the challenges to his presidency, receiving his party's nomination in May 1812 and being reelected the following November.

'Free trade and sailor's rights' was not the simple cry of justice that popular history would have us believe. It was fraught with its own ambiguities and, perhaps more importantly, it was a cry co-opted to promote belligerency by annexationists who drove much of the government's thinking. Combined with the native crisis on the western border, and Madison's struggles to preserve his presidency, this led, in June 1812, to war. It was a small war when compared with the great conflict being fought over the European continent at the time, but nevertheless it was an important one in the histories of both North America and the British Empire.

Soldiers, sailors, and warriors

For a country contemplating war against the world's greatest naval power and against the tribes of the Old Northwest, the United States did not prepare well. In part, Americans were confident enough in their local superiority in North America to think that they did not need to invest heavily in their military, especially since Britain was not expected to be able to reinforce its colonies adequately because of the war in Europe. Many Americans also distrusted standing military forces, believing that a powerful army and navy might pose a threat to their own liberty; and they also possessed an unreasonable faith in the capabilities of the citizen militia. President Madison was typical of many in his discomfort with a professional military and of his embrace of the militia. Toward the end of the war, however, he realized his mistake first-hand when he witnessed the defeat of a force comprised largely of militia at the hands of British regular soldiers outside of Washington. 'I could never have believed that so great a difference existed between regular troops and a militia force, if I had not witnessed the scenes of this day,' he remarked.

Naval forces

Between the two branches of fighting service, the army and the navy, the United States Navy (USN) entered the conflict in better shape. With 7,250 sailors and marines in 1812, it was composed mainly of professional officers and experienced volunteer seamen, many of whom had seen action against the Barbary pirates of North Africa beginning in 1794 and in the Quasi-War with France of 1797–1801. Yet the navy suffered from inadequate funding and woolly political thinking in the prewar years, and thus was not as strong as it might have been by 1812. At the outbreak, the saltwater fleet had 13 operational vessels. Three of them were the famous 'super frigates,' *United States*, *Constitution*, and *President*; three were regular frigates; and, in descending order of size, there were five sloops and two brigs. There also were 165 coastal gunboats, 62 of

This plan from 1817 compares a British 38-gun frigate (top), armed principally with 18-pounder guns (firing 8kg balls) to an American 44-gun 'super frigate,' equipped primarily with 24-pounders (firing 11kg shot). (National Maritime Museum)

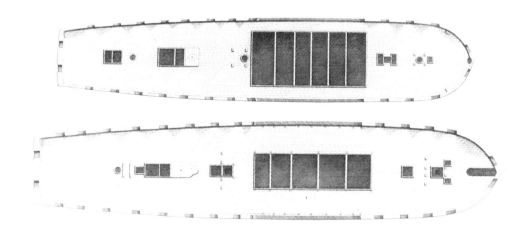

which were in commission. Of the vessels in reserve, the Americans repaired two frigates and cut down a third into a corvette in 1812–13. During the conflict, some captured British ships entered USN service and other vessels were built.

The Royal Navy was the world's most powerful maritime force, following Horatio Nelson's victory at Trafalgar in 1805. However, its size and successes masked serious problems. Most notably, France continued to pose a real threat at sea, which would prevent the RN from deploying significant resources to the western Atlantic unless and until the European situation improved (which the Americans did not expect to happen until they had conquered Canada, if indeed it happened at all). For instance, Napoleon only had 34 ships-of-the-line (main battleships) in 1807, having lost 30 in 1805–06, but he had increased that number to 80 by 1813 and had another 35 under construction. Meanwhile, Britain's ability to maintain equivalent vessels dropped from 113 to 98 between 1807 and 1814 as the years of war with France took their toll on the island kingdom of 12 million. In addition, the Royal Navy's global commitments forced it to send under-strength, ill-trained, and partially impressed crews to sea, often in badly built vessels. Yet in 1812, the sheer weight of the fleet promised to give the RN dominance in the western Atlantic, should Britain triumph over France.

Both sides also developed their freshwater capabilities on the Great Lakes and on Lake Champlain. The British entered the conflict with the advantage of their Provincial Marine, a transport service maintained by the army to move men and supplies in a region without adequate roads. It had two small ships and two schooners to serve Lake Ontario and the St Lawrence River as far down as Prescott, where the rapids shut off access to the rest of the river and the Atlantic beyond. To the west, on the other side of the great barrier at Niagara Falls, the Provincial Marine operated four vessels on Lake Erie, one of which had a shallow

enough draft to sail up the Detroit River to the upper Great Lakes. On Lake Champlain, however, a single derelict schooner protected British interests. At the outbreak of war, the Americans only had two gunboats on Lake Champlain, plus a brig on each of lakes Ontario and Erie. During the conflict, the two powers augmented their freshwater forces by taking merchant schooners into naval service, capturing enemy craft, and building new vessels at such a ferocious pace that historians have dubbed it 'The Shipbuilders' War.' For example, by August 1813, the British had increased their strength on Lake Ontario to six vessels carrying 97 guns and carronades, while the American squadron boasted 13 ships and schooners mounting 112 pieces of artillery.

Land forces

The land forces of the British and Americans in the war were fundamentally similar, although the Americans usually had a numerical advantage while the British had stronger leadership and better training. (The Americans did not begin to match these skills until the last year of hostilities.) Like other western armies, both the British and the Americans had a mix of line infantry, light infantry, artillery, and cavalry, along with various specialized troops, such as engineers. Both powers also relied heavily on part-time militiamen drawn from the civilian population. Indeed, the Americans would call out over 450,000 militia during the war, a number not much smaller than that of the total population of British North America. Additionally, both sides included elements which fell somewhere between the professionalism of the regulars and the amateurism of the militia, such as American volunteer corps and Canadian fencible regiments.

The land war was primarily an infantry struggle, fought by men organized into regimental or battalion formations that typically numbered 500–800 soldiers. The principal infantry firearm for both sides was the smoothbore, muzzle-loaded, single-shot, flintlock musket. Using paper cartridges containing a ball and powder (and sometimes extra buckshot, especially in American service), a soldier could load and fire his weapon two or three times each minute. In action, the musket could be reasonably accurate at 60 paces, and deadly at 175.[1] After that, its potency declined rapidly, to the point where there was little reason to fire at an enemy beyond 250 paces.

The most effective way of using muskets was to stand troops in tightly packed lines and fire massed volleys into the enemy at close range. Ideally, these volleys would shatter the enemy line so that the winning side could use its secondary weapon, the bayonet, to drive its adversaries from the field. There was some adaptation to the rough North American environment, such as thinning out the lines somewhat, but the fundamental principle of volley fire dominated the deployment and combat operations of both the United States and British armies.

As effective as these dense formations of infantry were – and it was these soldiers who would decide the big battles – they could not be used in all of the situations in which foot soldiers had to be engaged. Therefore, armies also needed light infantry soldiers if conditions called for skirmish and ambush skills and for guarding the line infantry's front, flanks, and rear. Normally, light infantry deployed in a very thin line, or chain, to allow their small numbers to cover a larger frontage than the formation they protected. This meant that they could not produce the volume of fire of line troops, which was their fundamental weakness. In battle, light infantry tried to preserve the main body from harassment by covering it so that it could approach the enemy in as fresh a state as possible. They might also try to harass the enemy line to blunt its fighting edge before the arrival of their own line. In retreat, light infantry might deploy to hold off pursuing troops long enough to allow the

main force to escape. In an advance, they might rush ahead to prevent the enemy recovering from a setback or to capture bridges and strong points.

Most light troops carried muskets, but some used rifles, which differed from muskets primarily in that their barrel

---

[1] A pace is about 30 inches (75cm).

interiors were not smooth but had spiral grooves cut into them; they were also intended to hold a tighter-fitting bullet. This meant that rifles could be more accurate than muskets and were dangerous at 350 paces or more. However, they took longer to load, fouled from gunpowder

The three men in this 1807 engraving would be expected to serve as warriors in native society. For battle, men often stripped down from the clothes seen here to their moccasins, leggings, breechcloths, and equipment. They also painted their bodies and prepared their hair in 'scalp locks,' which were often painted red and decorated with such spiritual objects as feathers and wampum. (National Archives of Canada)

Lieutenant's uniform of the rifle company of the Leeds Militia in Upper Canada, 1812. Although most uniforms were flamboyant, some light infantry uniforms, such as this black and green example, were designed to make soldiers less conspicuous because of the distinctive nature of their warfare. (City of Toronto Museums and Heritage Services)

residue more quickly, and were limited by other problems. This prevented them from becoming the dominant infantry weapon until technological advances solved these issues in the middle of the 19th century.

In the confusion of popular history, a commonly held view is that the British fought, fundamentally, in tightly packed lines and the Americans deployed in a more individualistic manner and used cover, because of their experience on the North American continent. The reality was that it was the British who had proportionately more light infantry in their regular force in the War of 1812, and all armies in the western tradition had long recognized the need for a good balance of line and light troops.

Aboriginal forces

The populations of the aboriginal nations were too small and the life of each individual within a community was of too great a value to allow for large numbers of casualties. Therefore, a fundamental principle of native warfare was to avoid losses, even to the point of giving up larger objectives to preserve lives in a war party. In addition, the personal freedoms enjoyed by members of native societies, combined with their conceptualizations of masculinity, meant that a warrior's participation in hostilities was voluntary. It depended upon his assessment of the opportunities available to him to win glory and prestige, and was sensitive to omens and signs that might lead him to withdraw from a campaign. These factors contributed to a style of native warfare distinct from white modes of fighting, resembling, at best, a kind of light infantry combat.

The main weapons carried by warriors were muskets, rifles, tomahawks, and knives, although spears, swords, and pistols were popular, and traditional clubs and bows still saw some use in 1812–15. Warriors preferred to ambush their adversaries or utilize other tactics that mimicked ambush in order to strike from an advantage, mask their movements to reduce casualties, upset their enemy's equilibrium, and thereby prevent the enemy from responding effectively. For example, a war party might conceal itself near a road until an enemy had passed, then attack from a position that blocked the line of retreat to demoralize its adversaries and thereby increase the odds of victory. Once engaged, natives often used war cries to try to unnerve their opponents further, and they kept up pressure by advancing in relays to prevent their foes from establishing a solid firing line. In a fixed firefight, warriors typically moved to a new position after each shot, so that an enemy would fire at a vacant spot (at least in theory) rather than one that was occupied. This was also designed to confuse their opponents about the size of the warrior force. If their enemies broke, the warriors gave chase, in the hope of killing and capturing as many of them as possible. If a war party had to retreat, it tried to minimize losses through a careful fighting withdrawal until it was out of harm's way.

Formidable as natives were in combat, they were not without their weaknesses. The threat of a high number of casualties could force them off a battlefield or even stop them from engaging in the first place. Their tactics also tended to work better in offensive rather than defensive engagements. Beyond these issues, natives took to the field not as pawns of the whites, but as allies, with their own goals, so their participation on campaign was conditional. Often British and American commanders failed to recognize this most basic of facts when they tried to have natives achieve some objective that did not meet aboriginal interests, and thus ended up complaining about the 'unreliability' of native war parties as they watched them withdraw from the field. For the Americans, however, especially in 1813 and 1814, their native allies provided them with their most effective light troops on the northern front, and for the British, aboriginals comprised a significant proportion of their forces in a conflict where the numerical odds were stacked against them.

America sets its sights on Canada

The declaration of war

On 5 November 1811, President James Madison delivered a message to Congress asking it to prepare for hostilities. Much of the ensuing debate was led by the War Hawks – mainly younger men from frontier regions who saw expansion, and the destruction of native resistance, as fundamental objectives for war, and who demanded a more aggressive approach to dealing with Great Britain than had been followed in previous years. In contrast, politicians who represented seaboard areas and shipping interests tended to oppose the slide toward belligerency. On 1 June 1812, Madison asked Congress to declare war, listing impressment, interference with trade, and British intrigue in the Old Northwest as causes, but remaining silent on the conquest of Canada because the point of the message was not to articulate objectives, but to blame Britain for hostilities. On 18 June, with votes of 79 to 49 in the House of Representatives and 19 to 13 in the Senate, the United States declared war on Great Britain.

In the final months of peace, the British had hoped to avoid a conflict that would see them trying to defend their colonies against heavy odds while they had their hands full in Europe. Furthermore, American trade restrictions, while not meeting Madison's objectives of bringing Britain to its knees, had hurt commercial interests in the United Kingdom and had generated calls for relief from its manufacturers and merchants. The problem lay in what concessions could be made. There was no reason to offer up territory, and British officials did not believe their activities among the tribes were so wrong because they considered them to be defensive in focus and because they worked

to keep a lid on frontier tensions so long as the United States restrained from hostilities. On the oceans, the Royal Navy's desperate manpower problems precluded relenting on impressment. What they could offer was the revocation of the Orders-in-Council, which they did on 23 June 1812. Nevertheless, word of this concession did not cross the Atlantic until after the United States had declared war, and it was not enough to inspire Madison to stop fighting.

The strategic situation

Americans confidently predicted that the conquest of Canada would occur quickly, if not painlessly. In August 1812, Thomas Jefferson wrote: '... the acquisition of Canada this year as far as the neighbourhood of Quebec, will be a mere matter of marching and will give us experience for the attack on Halifax the next, and the final expulsion of England from the American continent.' The *National Intelligencer* published an article in December 1811 expressing the Madison administration's view that the whole of Canada west of Quebec was 'in the power of the U. States because it consists of a long and slender chain of settlers unable to succour or protect each other, and separated only by a narrow water from a populous and powerful part of the Union,' while the fortified city of Quebec itself could be reduced through siege. All that would be needed, according to the newspaper, was an army of 20,000, only one-third of which needed to be regulars.

There were good reasons for the Americans to feel confident. All of British North America had only a half-million people, compared to 7.5 million for the United States, while the front-line province of Upper Canada was particularly vulnerable, with a population of 70–80,000. Many of these people were loyalists who had moved north as refugees from the American Revolution or their children, who might be expected to stand firm. However, many more settlers were recent American immigrants who had been attracted to the province because they could acquire their own land more easily than they could on the American frontier but who might not be hostile to annexation. This possibility was not lost on the British commander in Upper Canada, Isaac Brock, who thought it might be unwise to arm more than 4,000 of the 11,000 men of the militia. In Lower Canada, the majority were French-Canadians, whose ancestors had been conquered by the British in 1763 and who had shown only limited support for the Crown during the American Revolution. While their language, religious, and other rights were protected under British law, officials doubted that they would rally with enthusiasm to repel an invasion. The Atlantic provinces were more homogeneously British and were more isolated from attack, so the odds of their surviving seemed greater than in the Canadas.

Another card that seemed to play into the hands of the Americans was the state of the aboriginal population of the Canadas. Unlike those on the American frontier who followed Tecumseh and Tenskwatawa, these natives were undecided about what to do. Many assumed that the Americans would overwhelm the provinces and thus did not want to be punished for fighting on the losing side. Others were unhappy about how they had been treated by the Crown in the years leading up to 1812 over such issues as the alienation of land and the amount of independence they could exercise within the colony, so they had reasons to hold back when government officials tried to obtain their assistance. The internal aboriginal situation was so uncertain that the British were afraid that the tribes near the border might actually join the Americans once an invasion

occurred to buy peace with them. This would discourage militiamen from leaving their families unguarded to meet broader strategic objectives and might pose an insurmountable challenge to the small force of regulars in the colony.

In contrast to the natives of the lower Great Lakes, however, those within the British areas of the upper lakes had closer ties to the fur trade community, and officials assumed that at worst they would adopt a position of neutrality, but that there was a good possibility of encouraging them to oppose the Americans.

Another major reason why American leaders expected to conquer the British provinces easily was that the garrison in Upper and Lower Canada numbered only 7,000 soldiers in 1812 and could not be reinforced significantly while Napoleon menaced Britain. Furthermore, these troops needed to be concentrated to guard Montreal and Quebec. Montreal had to be maintained in order to keep the St Lawrence River open so that troops and supplies could be moved to the upper province; otherwise, that colony would be doomed. However, if Montreal could not be held, the troops deployed around it had to be able to retreat to Quebec, the strongest position in British North America. This had to be held, in the hope that a relief force, if available, could cross the Atlantic and rescue it before trying to recover lost territory up the St Lawrence River and into the Great Lakes region. This strategy, logical as it was, meant that Upper Canada, the more vulnerable colony, entered the war defended by only 1,600 regulars.

Yet the US army was not as formidable as was commonly believed. At the outbreak, it had an authorized strength of 35,600, but only 13,000 soldiers actually had been enlisted, and many of them were untrained recruits. Nevertheless, a concentrated blow against the upper province could be decisive, and as the conflict wore on, the Americans appeared to possess the capacity to increase the disparities in numbers dramatically and quickly.

Opening moves

On 4 April 1812, the United States implemented an embargo on international trade in order to get its merchant ships into American ports and prevent them from falling into British hands. At the outbreak of hostilities in mid-June, a squadron of five warships sailed from New York in anticipation of capturing an important merchant convoy, but became diverted on 23 June when it sighted the British frigate *Belvidera*. Her captain was suspicious enough not to let his guard down, and fled north as soon as the Americans opened fire. The Americans gave chase, and both sides inflicted casualties, but the *Belvidera* escaped to Halifax, saving the British commercial fleet in the process by diverting the Americans, and heralded the coming of war. The commodore at Halifax took his ships to sea in pursuit of the US squadron.

At about the same time, the American privateer *Dash* spotted a small Royal Navy schooner, the *Whiting*, lying at anchor in Hampton Roads, and quickly overwhelmed her crew, who were unaware that war had been declared, and were in fact on a mission to deliver diplomatic dispatches. The US government released the *Whiting*, but she did not make it back to England, being captured on the way by a French privateer,

symbolizing how Britain now had to fight two distinct but overlapping wars. (Rarely, however, would the Americans and French cooperate against their common enemy. One exception occurred in 1814, when the British frigate HMS *Majestic* beat off two French frigates, an American privateer, and other craft, capturing an enemy frigate in the process.)

On the northern front, the Americans put their armies in motion to make a simultaneous three- or four-pronged invasion of Canada across the Detroit, Niagara, and St Lawrence rivers, as well as against Montreal. The plan promised to divide the outnumbered defenders, thereby increasing the odds against them, and with the taking of Montreal, guarantee the fall of Upper Canada. However, the US army, led largely by over-the-hill political appointees and without a proper staff or adequate supply system, could not pull off the plan. Instead, the invasions came piecemeal over several months, the first occurring in July, when Brigadier-General William Hull led his force across the Detroit River into Upper Canada.

Halifax was the main Royal Navy station in British North America. The guns in this 1801 image are mounted on traversing carriages to maximize their field of fire. (National Archives of Canada)

The war on land and at sea

The Great Lakes –St Lawrence front

Most of the fighting in the War of 1812 occurred along the upper St Lawrence River and through the Great Lakes region because the conquest of British territory was the primary military objective of the United States.

America's other main territorial ambition in the war – the elimination of the western tribes as a roadblock to expansion – assumed that the fall of Canada would deprive natives of the trade, diplomatic, and military alliances that they needed to protect their interests.

As a result, American forces crossed into Canada in each of 1812, 1813, and 1814, bent on conquest, and won a number of important, even legendary, victories. Yet in only one of the eight invasion attempts did they achieve their objective of occupying British territory for more than a short (and contested) period; and that land, in south-western Upper Canada, was later handed back in the peace treaty.

Britain countered with land and sea offensives, directed from Canada and along the Atlantic and Gulf coasts of the United States. These efforts were designed, fundamentally, to cripple the ability of America to threaten the British colonies and to force an end to the conflict, as well as to avenge the suffering experienced by the Canadian population. If the British also managed to occupy some American territory in the process, then they thought the international border might be redrawn to make Canada more defensible, especially if a native homeland could be carved out of the Old Northwest. Nonetheless, their primary objective was to retain Canada, and the war for the British was essentially defensive.

1812

When William Hull's army crossed into Canada on 12 July, the senior officer in Upper Canada, Major-General Isaac Brock, sought to strike back at the invaders with energy. He believed he had to take bold action to reassure the settler population and demonstrate British strength to the aboriginal people, whose help he would need if the upper province were to have any chance of survival.

Fortunately for Brock, Hull's invasion began to falter almost as soon as it had begun. Instead of marching on the fort at Amherstburg to knock the British out of the Detroit region and intimidate the natives and settlers into submission, a nervous Hull dithered, engaged in some minor skirmishing, and worried that his army might be too weak to achieve its objectives. (Only one of his four regiments consisted of regulars; the others were militiamen.) In addition, on Lake Erie, the British captured a vessel carrying Hull's baggage, medical supplies, and important papers, which made him feel more vulnerable since his overland supply line ran through dismal swamplands threatened by Tecumseh's followers.

Meanwhile, to the north, on Brock's orders, soldiers, fur traders, and native warriors captured the American fort on Mackinac Island on 17 July without a fight, after quietly mounting an artillery piece overlooking the unsuspecting post and then demanding its surrender.

This bloodless victory was significant because it secured the important British fur trade operations in the north from a local American threat and helped to preserve southward connections through Lake Michigan to the tribes of the Mississippi region. It also inspired a good portion of the natives of the upper lakes to take up arms against the United States.

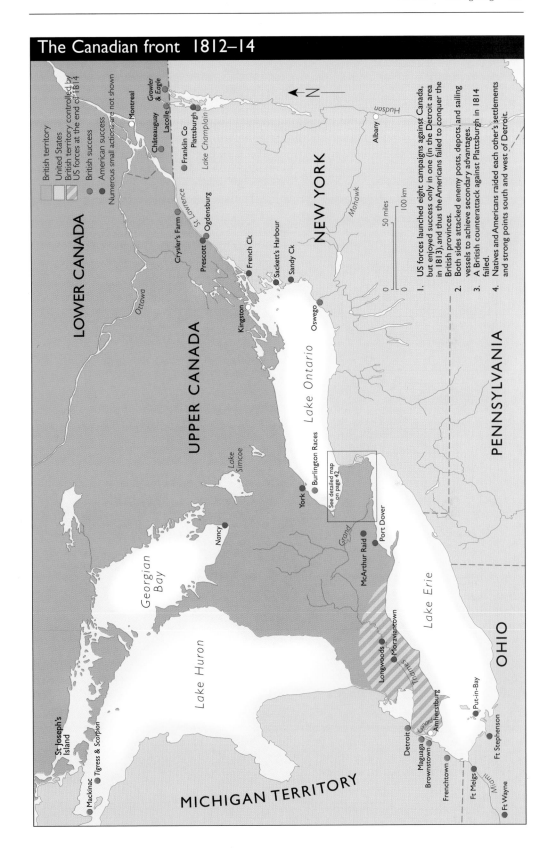

The Canadian front 1812–14

British territory
United States
British territory controlled by
US forces at the end of 1814
British success
American success
Numerous small actions are not shown

LOWER CANADA

UPPER CANADA

NEW YORK

PENNSYLVANIA

OHIO

MICHIGAN TERRITORY

Lake Ontario

Lake Erie

Lake Huron

Georgian Bay

Lake Simcoe

Lake Champlain

Hudson

Mohawk

Ottawa

St Lawrence

Thames

Grand

Miami

Montreal
Growler & Eagle
Châteauguay
Lacolle
Franklin Co
Plattsburgh
Crysler's Farm
Ogdensburg
Prescott
French Ck
Kingston
Sackett's Harbour
Sandy Ck
Oswego
Albany
York
Burlington Races
Nancy
McArthur Raid
Port Dover
Longwoods
Moraviantown
Put-in-Bay
Detroit
Maguaga
Brownstown
Amherstburg
Frenchtown
Ft Meigs
Ft Stephenson
Ft Wayne
St Joseph's Island
Mackinac
Tigress & Scorpion

See detailed map on page 42

0   50 miles
0   100 km

N

1. US forces launched eight campaigns against Canada, but enjoyed success only in one (in the Detroit area in 1813), and thus the Americans failed to conquer the British provinces.
2. Both sides attacked enemy posts, depots, and sailing vessels to achieve secondary advantages.
3. A British counterattack against Plattsburgh in 1814 failed.
4. Natives and Americans raided each other's settlements and strong points south and west of Detroit.

When Hull learned about the loss of Mackinac, he assumed that the tribes along the Detroit border would rise against him and perhaps fall upon the settlers on the American frontier. Therefore, on 8 August, he withdrew most of his men from Canada to secure his army inside Detroit, sent a plea for reinforcements so he could resume the offensive, and also ordered the garrison at Fort Dearborn (now Chicago) to withdraw, in anticipation of widespread aboriginal hostilities. At the same time, he learned that the campaign against Montreal, designed in part to divide British forces and assist his efforts, had been postponed. Closer to home, Hull received further frightening news that the western tribes had attacked a supply column on its way to Detroit at Brownstown

and had beaten off a force sent to meet it. He dispatched 600 men south to reopen communications, but British and native forces ambushed it at Maguaga on 9 August. The Americans did repulse the attack, but they failed to achieve their objective and suffered heavy casualties. As they retired to Detroit, the British Provincial Marine demonstrated its mastery on Lake Erie by subjecting them to a barrage along those parts of the road that ran past the shoreline. Now thoroughly demoralized, on 11 August, Hull pulled his remaining troops out of Canada, and a few days later, a

Mackinac, from an 1813 print, with the fur trade community in the foreground and the garrison behind. (William L. Clements Library)

Potawatomi force destroyed the garrison at Fort Dearborn as it complied with Hull's orders to evacuate that post.

Isaac Brock arrived on the Detroit River from Niagara on 13 August. Two days later, he demanded William Hull's surrender and tried to unnerve him by threatening massacre: 'It is far from my intention to join in a war of extermination,' he wrote, 'but you must be aware, that the numerous body of Indians who have attached themselves to my troops will be beyond control the moment the contest commences.' Hull still had enough nerve to reject the summons, and perhaps was wise enough to realize that the threat probably was an empty one, but after a cross-river artillery bombardment on the night of 15/16 August, followed by a British advance against the settlement, his resolve disappeared. Before Brock's men could get within range of the town, Hull lowered the Stars and Stripes over Detroit. To a mixed force of 1,300 regulars, militia, and natives, Hull surrendered 2,200 men, large quantities of weapons and supplies, the USN brig on Lake Erie, and the whole of the Michigan Territory.

This was a critical victory for Brock. He had secured his western flank, acquired desperately needed equipment for his poorly armed militia, and sent a powerful signal to bolster the faithful, encourage the wavering, and subdue the disloyal in both the white and native populations of Upper Canada. Most of the Iroquois of the Six Nations Tract along the Grand River, for instance, who had largely stood aloof before the capture of Detroit, swung behind the British, adding 400 valuable warriors to augment the Upper Canadian garrison.

With the approach of autumn, the Americans next mustered several thousand regulars, volunteers, and militia along the Niagara River for a second invasion of Upper Canada. Their plan was to cut the province in half, seize superior winter quarters, demoralize the population, and wipe away the disgrace of Hull's surrender. However, they suffered from poor training, bad equipment, inadequate supplies, and a deep

Mohawk chief John Norton (depicted in an 1805 miniature) commanded the Six Nations Iroquois at Queenston Heights. During the early stages of the battle, when his warriors kept the Americans from consolidating their position, his men 'returned the Fire of the Enemy with coolness & Spirit, – and altho' their fire certainly made the greatest noise, from the Number of Musquets, yet I believe ours did the most Execution.' Across the battlefield, volunteer rifleman Jared Willson thought 'hell had broken loose and let her dogs of war upon us. In short, I expected every moment to be made a "cold Yanky" as the soldier says.' (National Archives of Canada)

tension between the senior officers – Brigadier-General Alexander Smyth of the army and Major-General Stephen Van Rensselaer of the New York Militia. Consequently, when Van Rensselaer's men crossed the border, most of Smyth's troops sat out the confrontation.

The thrust came on the night of 12/13 October 1812. Batteries along the length of the Niagara River opened fire on British positions while Van Rensselaer's troops rowed across the waterway from Lewiston to Queenston. As they got out into the current, they came under fire and suffered heavily. Yet they persevered, reached the Canadian shore, secured their landing, and found a way to the top of Queenston Heights, a natural ridge that dominated the village of Queenston and the surrounding countryside. General Brock counterattacked, leading an outnumbered British and Canadian force up the steep heights in a frontal charge. The American line opened fire, Brock fell mortally wounded, and the charge faltered shortly afterward.

Brock's successor, Major-General Roger Sheaffe, ordered more troops and Iroquois warriors to converge on Queenston from Fort George in the north and from posts to the south. At the same time, small detachments of British soldiers at the landing kept the Americans out of the village of Queenston and continued to harass the boats ferrying men and supplies across the border. The Iroquois were the first reinforcements to arrive on the scene. They ascended the heights inland, out of range and sight of the Americans, then attacked from behind the cover of the forest and scrub. Although badly outnumbered, the warriors managed to keep their ill-trained enemy pinned down in open ground close to the riverside cliff of the heights. One key factor in their success was the absence of sufficient numbers of competent American light infantry to drive the tribesmen away from the US line standing exposed in the open. Thus the Americans fired heavy but ineffectual volleys at the warriors in the brush to their front, while the Six Nations returned fire with far fewer shots, but with more effect.

Iroquois efforts enabled Sheaffe to assemble 900 regulars, militia, volunteers, and additional warriors on top of the heights out of range of his enemy. He then led them across flat ground against American soldiers who had been badly shaken by the natives, had expended much of their ammunition, and who felt trapped because their compatriots – frightened by the aboriginal presence and British fire – refused to row back across the river, either to reinforce or to rescue them. Sheaffe's force marched forward, fired one volley, and charged.

Within 15 minutes it was over. The Americans had suffered another humiliation, losing as many as 500 killed and wounded and 960 prisoners-of-war. On the British side, there were only 104 killed and wounded. Within a week, another 1,000 dismayed American fighting men had deserted their camps on the New York side of the border and headed for home.

In November, Alexander Smyth led another US thrust across the Niagara River, near Fort Erie, at Red House and Frenchman's Creek, but cancelled the invasion shortly after encountering stiff British and native opposition. To the east, American forces made two half-hearted attempts against Montreal from Plattsburgh, but withdrew when they encountered resistance from defending forces.

The outcome of the 1812 Detroit, Niagara, and Montreal campaigns was not the one Americans had expected. The United States had lost every engagement of significance and had suffered huge losses in prestige, supplies, land, and men in proportion to the resources their opponents had applied in defending their territory. The British had even occupied sufficient American territory to allow many in the western tribal confederacy, as well as their British and Canadian friends, to think that the dream of an independent indigenous homeland might be achieved.

1813

Great Britain and the United States both took measures to increase their forces along the Canadian-American border over the winter of 1812/13, in anticipation of the second season's fighting. Despite their European commitments, the British managed to spare five additional infantry battalions, part of a cavalry regiment, and other reinforcements for the American war. Within the Canadian colonies, some militiamen were incorporated for full-time service and a few special units, such as the Provincial Dragoons, were raised. The Royal Navy took command of the Provincial Marine and added 470 officers and ratings to the

Some Americans thought the army should equip one-third of each infantry regiment with pikes (and shortened muskets slung over the pikemen's backs) because in close combat the extra reach of the pike would give the Americans a decided advantage over enemies using bayonets on the end of their muskets. However, the idea was not popular, and the only regiment that may have adopted the idea was the 15th Infantry during the advance against Montreal in 1812 and in the battle of York in 1813. Both navies, however, used pikes. For example, 200 British sailors at the amphibious attack on Oswego in 1814 carried them. This print is from *The American military library*, published in 1809. (Library of Congress)

freshwater ships, along with carpenters to build up the Great Lakes squadrons. In the United States, Congress authorized 20 new infantry regiments, approved an expansion of the navy, and sent hundreds of sailors to the Great Lakes from the Atlantic, where a developing British blockade of the eastern seaboard prevented much of the saltwater fleet from setting sail.

The first battle of 1813 occurred in the Detroit region, following several months of minor hostilities in which Americans and natives attacked each other's strong points and villages south and west of Lake Erie. The US sent an army to assert control in this contested area and to retake the territory that had been lost in 1812, but its advanced guard suffered defeat at Frenchtown (now Monroe) in the January snows at the hands of Brigadier-General Henry Procter. To the east, on 22 February, the British captured Ogdensburg in an effort to weaken the American threats to the St Lawrence lifeline that connected Upper Canada to the rest of the British Empire.

Meanwhile, in Washington, Secretary of War John Armstrong spent the winter planning a new strategy for the invasion of British territory. He thought the first target should be Kingston, and the naval squadron anchored there, because the British would not be able to hold Upper Canada if they lost their warships on Lake Ontario. However, the American commanders on the northern front – Major-General Henry Dearborn of the army and Commodore Isaac Chauncey of the navy – did not want to attack Kingston because they overestimated the strength of its fortifications. Instead, they thought that the more weakly defended York (now Toronto) should be seized. They argued that the capture of two warships in the town would swing the balance of power on Lake Ontario to the United States and facilitate the second and third phases of their proposed plan – the capture of the Niagara Peninsula, followed by offensive operations against either Kingston or Montreal late in the year. At first, Washington rejected the scheme, realizing that Armstrong's was the better strategy, but the federal government eventually accepted it for political reasons. The pro-war governor of New York, Daniel Tompkins, was seeking reelection in April 1813 but feared defeat through voter disenchantment with the lack of progress of the war. Thus a victory on the Canadian front was needed to help swing voters over to Tompkins. York was a good target because of its vulnerability and because its capture would have good propaganda value since it was the capital of Upper Canada.

The Americans sailed from Sackett's Harbour, at the south-east corner of Lake Ontario, and on 27 April, launched an amphibious assault against the town of York. They drove General Sheaffe out of the capital and seized a large quantity of supplies. However, they did not get the British ships:

The battle of York ended when the British retreated from their fortifications and blew up a magazine full of gunpowder, inflicting 250 casualties upon the Americans in the explosion. Among those mortally wounded was US Brigadier-General Zebulon Pike, depicted in this c.1815 print. One witness to the blast said that he 'felt a tremulous motion in the earth resembling the shock of an earthquake, and looking toward the spot ... saw an immense cloud ascend into the air ... At first it was a great confused mass of smoke, timber, men, earth, &c., but as it rose in a most majestic manner it assumed the shape of a vast balloon.' (National Archives of Canada)

one had left shortly before the attack, and the British had burned the other before retreating. Through delays brought on by bad weather, the battle actually took place too late to have a legitimate influence on the election; however, Tompkins' supporters simply circulated victory proclamations to an unsuspecting electorate before the assault occurred and Dearborn kept the New York troops in his army at home to vote for the governor, with the result that he squeaked back into power by 3,606 votes. The Americans occupied York for a week, and then returned to Sackett's Harbour, before implementing the second phase of the Dearborn-Chauncey plan.

On 25 May, the guns of Fort Niagara and the US Lake Ontario squadron began a two-day bombardment of Fort George at the mouth of the Niagara River. On 27 May, the American army landed near the

This early 19th century print shows a corner of the American Fort Niagara at the mouth of the Niagara River in the right foreground. In the left background is British Fort George with its naval station by the waterfront. In reality they were further apart than depicted here, but were well within range of each other's artillery. (National Archives of Canada)

now-destroyed fort. About 1,000 soldiers, militiamen, and warriors met the 4–5,000 Americans, but were repulsed after losing one-third of their force in the fighting. Defeated, they abandoned not only Fort George but also Fort Erie and the other posts along the Niagara River to retreat to Burlington Heights (now Hamilton). So far, the plan seemed to be working as US forces occupied the former British posts and rebuilt Fort George to secure their Upper Canadian toehold. At that point, the province was on the brink of being cut in half, with Procter's and Tecumseh's forces to the west facing the possibility of their already poor supply lines being severed completely. As it was, the retreat from Fort Erie had allowed the Americans to sail naval vessels, previously trapped by British artillery on the Niagara River, west to join the squadron being built on Lake Erie that would challenge the Royal Navy later that year. In addition, an attempt by the British to destroy Sackett's Harbour while the USN squadron was away at the western end of Lake Ontario failed on 29 May, further demoralizing Upper Canada's defenders.

On the Niagara Peninsula, General Dearborn followed up his success at Fort George by sending an expedition to knock the British out of Burlington Heights and force them to retreat to Kingston. Dearborn's thinking was influenced in part by information that the Grand River Iroquois were worried that the Americans might make a punitive attack against their settlements since there was now nothing to prevent them from such a strike. Concerned to preserve their territory, the Six Nations considered abandoning the British and buying American forgiveness by falling upon the redcoats if they retreated eastward. Thus, as Dearborn dispatched 3,700 infantry, artillery, and cavalry toward Burlington, Iroquois warriors assembled near the British camp but, with the exception of a handful of men, refused to

have anything to do with the redcoats when Crown officials tried to secure their help. On 5 June, the Americans camped at Stoney Creek for the night to rest before the assault.

Recognizing the combined American and aboriginal threats and worrying about the fate of the Canadian population, the British made a desperate decision. Rather than await the Americans, they would launch a surprise attack against their enemy with 700 men at 2.00 a.m. on 6 June. The ensuing battle of Stoney Creek was a violent and confused affair: friend shot at friend, and the two American brigadier-generals walked into the hands of British troops because they could not distinguish blue from red uniforms in the dark. After sharp fighting, the British withdrew, but they had achieved their objective because their enemies cancelled their plans and retired to a camp on the Lake Ontario shoreline at Forty Mile Creek. The Grand River people, although still nervous, cautiously decided to maintain their alliance with the British, which quickly solidified as events unfolded over the following weeks.

Sackett's Harbour (as represented in an 1815 print) was the main American naval base on Lake Ontario. (US Naval Historical Center)

A short time later, a small party of pro-British Iroquois ambushed an American patrol and chased it into the camp at Forty Mile Creek. At about the same time, the Royal Navy squadron, which had sailed west from Kingston to support the army, bombarded the site. Although both acts were fundamentally ineffective, the Americans abandoned much of their equipment and fled to Fort George, with native warriors and Canadian militia pursuing them to capture stragglers and supplies. General Dearborn assumed that the British were about to launch a counteroffensive, so he evacuated all of the newly won positions except Fort George. The British, under the command of Major-General John Vincent, reoccupied the vacant posts and began to put pressure on Fort George. At the same time, additional aboriginal reinforcements from Iroquois and Algonkian communities in Lower Canada arrived, followed by more warriors from the west and the north, until Vincent had over 800 tribesmen in his lines. Combined with his own troops, he was well equipped to annoy the Americans.

Dearborn responded to the developing challenge by organizing a secret expedition to destroy an important forward British position near Beaver Dams. About 600 infantry, cavalry, and artillery moved from Fort George south toward Queenston before swinging inland against the target, in an effort to confuse his opponents as to the destination. However, a Canadian, Laura Secord, overheard American officers discussing their plan and rushed off to warn the British, who detached men to watch the various routes along which their enemy might come. As the column continued its march, aboriginal scouts spotted it and alerted a native force of 465 that had been deployed along one of the roads. The tribesmen ambushed the soldiers on 24 June. As at Queenston, the Americans suffered from inadequate light infantry, and despite holding their own for three hours in the fierce battle, they surrendered, having suffered 100 casualties, compared to 50 on the native side.

The Niagara front 1812–14

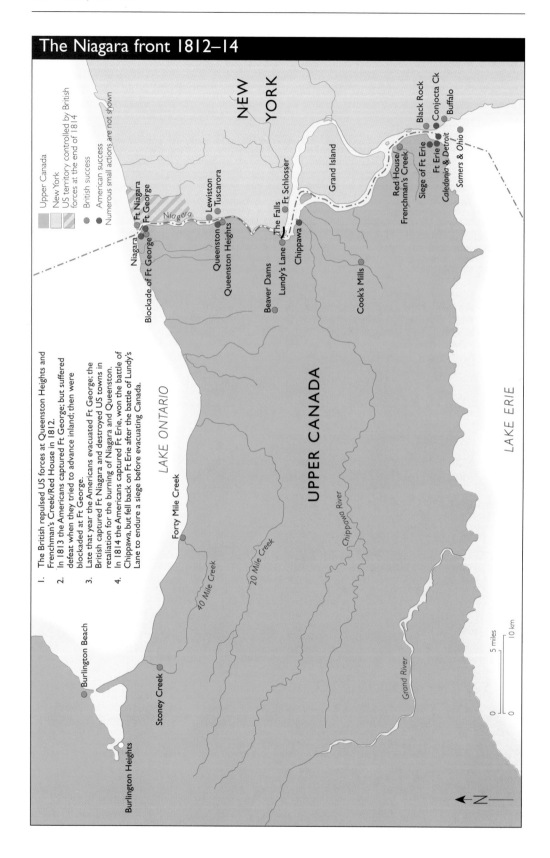

1. The British repulsed US forces at Queenston Heights and Frenchman's Creek/Red House in 1812.
2. In 1813 the Americans captured Ft George; but suffered defeat when they tried to advance inland; then were blockaded at Ft George.
3. Late that year the Americans evacuated Ft George; the British captured Ft Niagara and destroyed US towns in retaliation for the burning of Niagara and Queenston.
4. In 1814 the Americans captured Ft Erie, won the battle of Chippawa, but fell back on Ft Erie after the battle of Lundy's Lane to endure a siege before evacuating Canada.

Upper Canada
New York
US territory controlled by British forces at the end of 1814
British success
American success
Numerous small actions are not shown

NEW YORK

UPPER CANADA

LAKE ONTARIO

LAKE ERIE

Burlington Beach
Burlington Heights
Stoney Creek
Forty Mile Creek
40 Mile Creek
20 Mile Creek
Chippawa River
Grand River

Niagara
Ft Niagara
Ft George
Blockade of Ft George
Lewiston
Tuscarora
Queenston
Queenston Heights
The Falls
Lundy's Lane
Beaver Dams
Chippawa
Ft Schlosser
Grand Island
Cook's Mills
Red House/
Frenchman's Creek
Siege of Ft Erie
Ft Erie
Caledonia & Detroit
Somers & Ohio
Black Rock
Conjocta Ck
Buffalo

5 miles
10 km

N

ABOVE Oliver Perry's victory on Lake Erie captured the imagination of Americans, with the result that artists and engravers created many images of the battle. This particular post-war print is typical of the battle scenes created in the 19th century. (National Archives of Canada)

BELOW A contemporary print of the 1813 battle of Moraviantown. (National Archives of Canada)

British infantry, 1813. On active service, the grenadier on the left normally wore a shako, like the soldier beside him, and both probably wore grey overalls instead of white breeches. Note the belt around the waist of one man, to keep his equipment from moving around – a non-regulation feature representative of the alterations soldiers made for comfort and efficiency. (National Army Museum)

Following this victory, a new commanding officer in Upper Canada, Major-General Francis de Rottenburg, advanced closer to Fort George to constrict the American foothold in the province further. He did not have enough men to retake the post, so he intended to blockade the Americans inside the fort until cold weather brought the campaigning season to an end. (The size of the forces fluctuated during the blockade, but generally the British were outnumbered, at roughly 2–3,000 against 4–5,000 Americans.) De Rottenburg's task was made easier by orders sent from Washington, in light of the recent defeats, telling General Dearborn to avoid action unless necessary and to work on much-needed training. At the same time, in one of his last acts before leaving the Canadian front in disgrace, Dearborn recruited Iroquois warriors from reservations in New York to help address his light infantry deficiency, and what success the Americans did enjoy afterward in pushing back British and native pickets in front of Fort George was largely a result of their efforts. Through the summer that followed, fairly large sorties and raids occurred from time to time, in addition to the almost daily low-level harassment of the American position.

During part of the blockade, the RN's Lake Ontario squadron cruised the mouth of the Niagara River and the south shore of Lake Ontario to intercept supplies and destroy American depots. In general, the naval war on Lake Ontario was a kind of see-saw affair, in which both sides took advantage of small opportunities but avoided a major battle because the consequences of defeat would be devastating for whichever side lost control of the lake. However, there were some encounters. A more important one occurred in early August, when the squadrons tried to catch each other at a disadvantage as part of the operations focused on Fort George. However, the Americans backed off when the British captured two schooners and two others sank in a sudden squall in an engagement known as the Burlington Races.

As the summer wore on, the British found it increasingly difficult to maintain their blockade because of supply problems and widespread sickness in the hot, humid weather. By early October, with General Vincent back in command, they withdrew to comfortable quarters at Burlington Heights, thinking that it was too late in the year for the Americans to pose much of a threat. Yet the invaders showed some energy by making a demonstration toward Burlington, only pulling back when they realized how well entrenched the British were; instead they contented themselves with burning barrack buildings closer to Fort George.

Later, the Americans were no longer in a position to take an aggressive stance on the Niagara Peninsula because they withdrew the majority of troops to participate in a two-pronged offensive against Montreal. One army marched north from Lake Champlain, while the other journeyed down the St Lawrence in 300 small boats (and made a daring night-run past the British batteries at Prescott). While the British had concentrated a significant portion of their Canadian garrison to protect Montreal, the city lacked good fortifications, and because of its location at the junction of the Ottawa and St Lawrence rivers, its capture would isolate Upper Canada completely. This offensive – the largest American operation of the war, with over 11,000 soldiers – represented a most dangerous threat to the survival of Upper Canada.

One of the American forces, commanded by Major-General Wade Hampton, crossed the border south of Montreal, but on 16 October, at Châteauguay, 3,564 of his soldiers suffered defeat at the hands of a mere 339 well-positioned defenders, consisting mainly of Canadians and natives under Lieutenant-Colonel Charles de Salaberry. Then, on 11 November, the other American thrust, led by Major-General James Wilkinson, came to an inglorious end when 1,169 men under Lieutenant-Colonel Joseph Morrison defeated 3,050 invaders in the open fields of Crysler's Farm, along the banks of the St Lawrence. Hampton and Wilkinson lost all their fighting spirit in the aftermath of these disasters and ordered their armies into winter quarters. Thus ended the gravest threat to Canada posed by the Americans in the war.

Despite their failures in the York-Niagara and Montreal campaigns of 1813, the Americans did enjoy military success in south-western Upper Canada. After the Frenchtown disaster in January, they built Fort Meigs, south of Lake Erie, as a depot and jumping off point to recapture Michigan and invade Upper Canada. Henry Procter and Tecumseh besieged the fort in late April and early May, but could not take it (although losses among the US defenders were very high compared with those on the British side). The British and natives were also repulsed at another post in the region, Fort Stephenson, in one of the small number of instances during the war when they outnumbered their adversaries; and a second attempt to capture Fort Meigs in late July also failed. The result was that the British, and the western tribesmen who followed Tecumseh, retired to Canada and the initiative passed to the Americans.

On 10 September, the American and British squadrons on Lake Erie met for their long-anticipated duel at Put-in-Bay. The British had six vessels, while the Americans had nine better prepared craft, a testimony to their ability to move men and material more efficiently than the British. (American communications routes were much shorter and lay behind the front lines, unlike those of their opponents, which extended all the way through the contested Great Lakes and across the ocean.) Despite the disparities between the squadrons, the battle was a close-fought and bloody affair, but in the end, as the American commander Oliver Hazard Perry famously recorded: 'We have met the enemy and they are ours: two ships, two brigs, one schooner, and one sloop.'

With this defeat, Procter's already tenuous link to the east was cut. Therefore, he destroyed the military works at Detroit and Amherstburg and retreated east toward Burlington, despite outraged protests from Tecumseh and other native leaders who wanted to stand and fight. Meanwhile, Perry ferried an American army across the lake and, with 3,500 men, including 250 American-allied warriors from the Ohio country, under the command of Major-General William Henry Harrison, the Americans pursued Procter. They caught the British and their allies at Moraviantown and defeated some 1,000 men on 5 October. Among those slain was Tecumseh, and with his death and the recent defeats, the native dream of an independent homeland effectively ended. In the weeks that followed, the majority of aboriginal survivors either went home and made peace with the Americans or limped east to seek shelter behind the British lines in Burlington.

The western victories were significant for the Americans and brought their only campaign success on the northern front during the conflict, giving them control of part of Upper Canada and all of Lake Erie.

With their triumph at Moraviantown, the road lay open to strike the Six Nations of the Grand River. These people, hearing stories of atrocities committed by Americans against natives, fled to join the many white settlers and aboriginal refugees from the west in camps behind the British post on Burlington Heights. Even there they did not feel safe, worrying that their redcoated allies would retreat to York, or even to Kingston, because General Harrison stood poised to use the Grand River to get behind Burlington Heights and cut them off.

The British did not leave, partly because they worried that this might cause the natives to go over to the Americans and turn upon the settlers. Fortunately for them, Harrison was satisfied with his achievements on the Thames and chose not to consolidate with a strike eastward. Instead, he retired to Amherstburg, dismissed most of his volunteers, and sent the bulk of his regular force to join the army being formed for the ill-fated Montreal campaign.

There was one more outbreak of fighting along the Canadian border before the close of 1813. With the movement of US troops east to attack Montreal, and the expiration of many militiamen's terms of service, the American garrison at Fort George dropped to less than 600 men by early December. At that point, and with the passing of Harrison's threat to Burlington, the British resolved to recapture the post; their opponents, suffering steady harassment, decided to consolidate their forces on their own side of the border. Before withdrawing, the American commander, Brigadier-General John McClure, turned the people of the town of Niagara out of their houses on a frigid December day and burned down their homes, ostensibly to prevent the British from quartering their troops there over the winter and to improve Fort Niagara's defensibility. The next day, American artillery at Lewiston destroyed part of the village of Queenston by firing red-hot shot (heated canon balls) to set its buildings on fire. The new British commander in Upper Canada, Lieutenant-General Gordon

Drummond, arrived on the peninsula soon afterward, determined to avenge the destruction of these settlements.

Drummond's men crossed the Niagara River and made a surprise night assault on the sleeping garrison of Fort Niagara on 19 December. After a short, sharp fight, the fort fell. The British seized vast quantities of supplies, and killed, wounded, or captured over 400 Americans, losing only 11 of their own. Drummond then cleared the Americans out of the region completely: over the next few days, the settlements along the New York side of the river fell to the torch and the Americans and their native allies suffered a series of small defeats. Once he had captured Buffalo (and destroyed four vessels of the US Lake Erie squadron wintering there), Drummond thought he might continue westward, make a surprise attack on the rest of the American Lake Erie squadron, destroy it, and perhaps even retake Detroit. However, a January thaw melted the ice on the rivers he needed for a quick strike, so Drummond abandoned the idea and retired to the Canadian side of the river, maintaining a garrison on American territory only at Fort Niagara, which the British retained until the return of peace, in 1815.

The United States emerged from the second year of the war in a better position than they had had in 1812. With a number of victories behind them, they had also regained most of the lost territory in the west, occupied a small part of south-western Upper Canada, and seemed to have killed off the possibility of an aboriginal homeland being created at their expense in the Old Northwest. However, their main objective – the conquest of at least all of Upper Canada – had not been accomplished. The British, Canadians, and natives had performed well, despite the odds against them. This had bought the colony another year's grace, but the question now was what would happen with the coming of spring.

1814

Across the Atlantic, the military events of 1812 and 1813 had improved Britain's position in Europe and presented the possibility that far more resources could be applied to the American war in 1814 than had previously been available. In 1812, Napoleon invaded Russia, but rather than conquering the country, endured a disastrous rout in the brutal northern winter. The French emperor suffered additional defeats in 1813 and 1814; then, in March 1814, British and allied armies marched into Paris. Bonaparte abdicated in April, whereupon Britain dispatched significant numbers of reinforcements across the Atlantic.

As the 1814 campaigning season approached with the end of the cold weather, the Americans knew they had to take advantage of the few months that lay ahead before fresh British troops reached Canada. They recognized that the conquest of all the British provinces was no longer viable, but they hoped to secure a good bargaining position in peace negotiations and, if possible, annex Upper Canada.

Logically, their 1814 strategy should have concentrated on the early capture of Kingston or Montreal, with the aim of cutting off the upper province; yet once again they chose to direct their efforts in the west, in part because the battles of Lake Erie and Moraviantown had given them dominance there, a position they enhanced by reoccupying Buffalo after Gordon Drummond abandoned it during the winter.

At the same time, the US government decided not to concentrate its strength on the northern border against one target, but chose to divide it and make two thrusts. One army was to cross the Niagara River from Buffalo, to roll up the Niagara Peninsula, and continue as far east as possible, ideally seizing all of Upper Canada. Hopefully, Britain would relinquish the province in a treaty; at the very least, this would give the Americans something to bargain with if the British were to occupy New England or other parts of the Atlantic region. The second thrust was to sail north from Detroit to retake Mackinac, which had been lost in 1812. The number of men involved in the latter expedition was small, but it was

enough to deprive the commanding officer on the Niagara front of a force that might very well have tipped the balance toward the Americans.

Before these plans could be put into effect, there were a number of confrontations along the Canadian border as the opposing sides tried to achieve advantages in preparation for the upcoming campaigns. In February, the British raided American communities along the St Lawrence River to take supplies. In March, an American army marched against Montreal, but withdrew when it could not dislodge a small force at Lacolle. In May, the British captured Oswego, but another attempt that month to seize naval supplies at Sandy Creek resulted in defeat, and a planned attack on the US Navy base at Sackett's Harbour had to be cancelled for lack of men.

The American expedition against Mackinac called for the recapture of the post and the destruction of enemy military and fur trade operations in the north. The objectives were to regain their lost fort, knock the northern tribes out of the war, and cut the flow of supplies to the native peoples on the Mississippi, who had been fighting the United States despite the defeat of their aboriginal compatriots in Tecumseh's alliance. (See Black Hawk's War, page 250.) Earlier, the Americans had expected that their successes in south-western Upper Canada would have cut the supply line to the west. However, the British had overcome the loss of Lake Erie by sending goods to Mackinac from Montreal, both via the traditional fur trade route that extended up the Ottawa River and along other waterways to Lake Huron, and by moving material west through Kingston to York, then north along a road and water route to Georgian Bay and points to the west.

About 1,000 regulars, militia, and sailors on five vessels of the US Lake Erie squadron, under the command of Lieutenant-Colonel George Croghan of the army and Captain

The amphibious assault on Oswego in 1814, from an 1817 print. (National Maritime Museum)

Arthur Sinclair of the navy, sailed north in July 1814. On their way, they captured two small commercial vessels and burned British fur trade posts. They landed on Mackinac Island on 4 August, planning to advance against the fort. Its commandant, Lieutenant-Colonel Robert McDouall, marched out with 140 soldiers and perhaps as many as 300 militiamen and native warriors and drove the Americans off the island. Defeated, the American commanders sent two vessels south with their casualties and took the other three to Georgian Bay, where they destroyed a fur trade schooner, the *Nancy*, which a small Royal Navy detachment had been operating (although the crew of the *Nancy* got away). Then, one of the three American vessels sailed back to Lake Erie, while the schooners *Tigress* and *Scorpion* headed west to blockade Mackinac. The crew of the *Nancy* set out for Mackinac

in two bateaux and a canoe, accompanied by some natives and fur traders, slipped past the blockade, and obtained permission to try to seize the US schooners. Reinforced with four boats and 50 soldiers, they surprised and captured the *Tigress* in fierce hand-to-hand fighting on 3 September. Three days later, they sailed their prize up to the unsuspecting *Scorpion*, opened fire, then boarded and captured the second vessel. Thus in small-scale fighting, the British kept control over the crucial northern regions as the first snows of the winter of 1814/15 began to blow, and retained the ability to supply their allies in the Mississippi country.

The main American offensive into Canada in 1814 came from Buffalo, with a force that was far better trained and led than any the United States had deployed in the war up to that point. Two years of frustration had led to the replacement of poor quality and incompetent senior officers with better men, and the army as a whole had benefited tremendously from weeks of rigorous training in anticipation of the campaign. On the morning of 3 July, Major-General Jacob Brown led 5,000 soldiers and 600 warriors across the Niagara River against Fort Erie. The 170-man garrison only put up token resistance and then capitulated. When the British commander on the Niagara front, Major-General Phineas Riall, heard about the invasion – but not about the fall of the fort – he rushed south to Chippawa to repel Brown. He also sent some of his native allies and light troops further south to watch American movements and harass any attempt to move north.

On 4 July, one of Brown's brigades, commanded by Brigadier-General Winfield Scott, advanced north with the objective of seizing the bridge across the Chippawa River; Riall's skirmishers harassed their enemy, destroyed the bridge and some nearby buildings that might have provided cover for the Americans, then retired to the north bank of the Chippawa. Scott, faced with the loss of the bridge and a British battery opposite, pulled back and camped for the night along the south bank of Street's Creek.

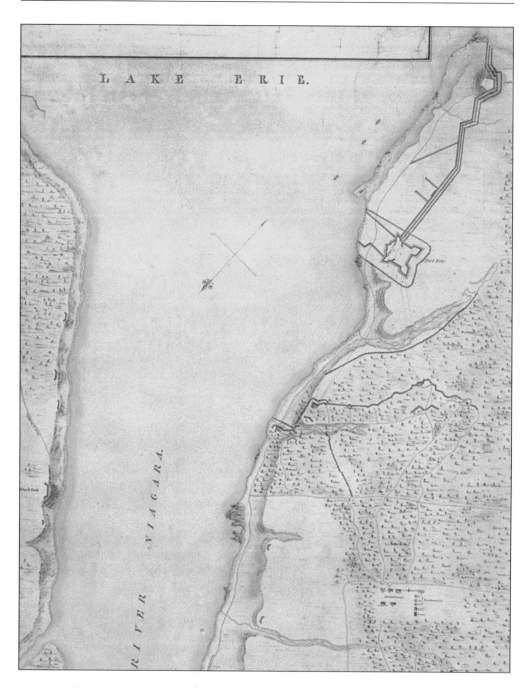

The blockade of Fort Erie, 1814, from a contemporary map. The Americans captured the post in July, and then extended it to accommodate their forces with a long earth wall between the original post and the hill at the top of the map, in time to withstand the British blockade of August–September. The earth 'traverses' in the fort were designed to reduce the devastation of a bombardment. The British lines can be seen below the fort in the forest. (National Archives of Canada)

There the American right flank anchored on the Niagara River, while their left rested 1,400 paces across a field on the edge of a forest. During the night and the next day, the other two brigades in the army arrived in the camp. Riall underestimated the size of the force opposing him, in part because he did not realize that Fort Erie had capitulated, so he assumed that part of Brown's army was investing the place, and in part because some of the American troops arrived in their camp after his patrols had performed their reconnaissance. On 5 July, with about 2,000 men, he decided to attack a force he believed to be a similar size, when in fact the Americans numbered 3,500.

Riall sent his light infantry, Canadian militia, and native allies through the woods to attack the American left; he organized the rest of his regulars to advance across the open plain beside the Niagara River, but without the Americans realizing what he planned to do because the topography hid his crossing of the Chippawa. General Brown, unaware of Riall's movements, already had decided to put an end to some minor harassment he had been suffering from bands of warriors in the forest, and he sent one of his brigades, consisting of regulars, volunteers, and native allies, into the bush to clear out the skirmishers. In the ensuing melee, the brigade inflicted heavy casualties upon the warriors but was repelled when it came up against the light force that had been deployed as part of the larger attack. From the sound of the heavy fire in the forest, Brown assumed that he was probably about to be attacked in force, and he deployed to meet the soon-to-become-visible British troops advancing across the plain. Jacob Brown and Phineas Riall clashed in a classic linear battle. The combined fire of the American artillery and musketry halted the British. A stationary, close-range firefight ensued for the next 20 minutes, then Riall acknowledged defeat, and ordered a retreat. The total number of killed, wounded, captured, and missing may have been as high as 600 on the British side and 350 on the American.

After the battle, both armies returned to their former positions: the British on the north side of the Chippawa River, the Americans on the south side of Street's Creek. Riall then fell back to the mouth of the Niagara River on 8 July, where the British were well entrenched, occupying Forts George and Niagara, as well as a new work,

Fort Mississauga, then under construction. Brown marched to Queenston, where he established a camp, probed the British works to the north, and awaited the arrival of the US Lake Ontario squadron to push his adversaries out of the peninsula completely. Afterward, he hoped to use the ships to move his army against York and Kingston. However, while he waited, he had to be cautious because the British not only had troops in his front at the three forts, but also had men at Burlington Heights and the mouth of Forty Mile Creek who might try to swing behind his rear.

Despite pre-arranged plans, Commodore Isaac Chauncey did not sail his squadron to Brown's assistance, but instead sent a variety of excuses to account for his inaction, even declaring that the navy had a higher calling than that of merely supporting the army! Without Chauncey, and facing losses in men because of sickness, while the British began to receive reinforcements from Europe, Brown decided to retire south to Chippawa. The British marched against the Americans, and the two armies met at dusk on 25 July at Lundy's Lane, not far from Niagara Falls. There 2,800 Americans fought 3,500 men opposite them to a bloody standstill in the confusion of the dark, with the opposing lines pouring devastating volleys into each other from as little as 15 paces apart. The next day, the Americans pulled back, not stopping until they reached Fort Erie. The British, badly bloodied, could not pursue them, which gave Brown time to enlarge and strengthen Fort Erie to house his entire force. At the same time, the US squadron finally arrived, which prevented the British from advancing south because of the threat it posed in their rear and because it stopped supplies being sent from Kingston.

Lieutenant-General Gordon Drummond, who had resumed command on the Niagara Peninsula, moved against Fort Erie early in August and put it under blockade. Unlike Francis de Rottenburg before Fort George in 1813, he intended to retake the post rather than just keep the Americans holed up inside. This proved to be a poor decision because Brown's force was still strong by comparison and because the Americans were able to ferry supplies and reinforcements to the fort from Buffalo with little difficulty (because a British attempt against the town, initiated from Fort Niagara, had been repulsed). Drummond launched an ill-fated assault against Fort Erie on the night of 14 August. It was meant to be a surprise, but the Americans were waiting, and the attack cost Drummond 905 killed, wounded, prisoners, and missing, to only 84 on the American side. The British, frustrated and facing supply problems, sickness, and bad weather, decided to abandon the blockade. While they were preparing to leave, the Americans sortied from the fort on 17 September, spiked three of Drummond's six siege guns, and destroyed ammunition, at a cost of 511 killed and wounded to 606 British killed, wounded, and captured. Drummond retired toward the end of September.

Meanwhile, an American raid along the Lake Erie shoreline by 1,500 men under Duncan McArthur, designed to help Brown in Fort Erie, faltered when it came up against British and Iroquois resistance at the Grand River. Nevertheless, the raiders destroyed mills, farms, and supplies that Drummond had hoped would meet some of his army's needs over the coming winter.

In October, the Americans marched north from Fort Erie in one final attempt to achieve a significant territorial gain. However, after British troops bloodied their advanced detachments at Cook's Mill, word reached the Americans that control of Lake Ontario had fallen decisively to the British, not in a dramatic battle, but by the launch in September of the enormous 104-gun warship HMS *St Lawrence*. The now powerful RN squadron put the USN under blockade at Sackett's Harbour shortly afterward. With the loss of the lake, the Americans returned to Fort Erie. On 5 November, they blew it up and retired to Buffalo. The 1814 American Mackinac and Niagara campaigns had come to a failed end. Despite most people's

predictions in 1812, with the exception of the small portion of south-western Upper Canada lost in 1813, Canada had survived the third year of the war.

The saltwater war 1812–15

Shortly before declaring war, the American government had deployed warships on the Atlantic Ocean to guard merchantmen on their return home, seize British commercial vessels, and hunt down Royal Navy warships. It was at that early point that the Americans had chased the *Belvidera* to Halifax and this had led the British squadron to sail forth in response. On 16 July, the British sighted and captured the American brig *Nautilus* without a fight. Two days later, they came into contact with the USS *Constitution* and set off in pursuit, but the frigate escaped after a dramatic three-day chase. On 13 August, the American frigate *Essex* overwhelmed the smaller Royal Navy sloop *Alert* in a short engagement off the Grand Banks of Newfoundland. These first encounters defined the fundamental character of high seas confrontations between the two navies for the rest of the war: in most situations, larger and better-armed ships defeated opponents in combat, captured them without a fight, or lost them in a chase.

Occasionally the two navies met on essentially equal terms. The most famous of these incidents occurred in June 1813, when the USS *Chesapeake* sailed out of Boston to meet HMS *Shannon*. The *Shannon* had a smaller crew, but her captain had devoted years to developing his men's gunnery skills. The *Chesapeake* was a better-built frigate, but the crew included a large number of newcomers, some experienced, some not. In 15 minutes of horror, culminating in hand-to-hand fighting as a boarding party descended on the *Chesapeake*, 146 Americans and 83 Britons fell dead or wounded. The US ship surrendered, to spend the rest of her days in the Royal Navy.

The most famous warship in the conflict was the USS *Constitution*. After she had made

The USS *Constitution*, or 'Old Ironsides,' from a *c.*1813–15 print. In 1831, Commodore William Bainbridge, who was wounded twice during the frigate's battle with HMS *Java*, reflected on his service on this famous American vessel: 'The ship! Never has she failed us! Never has her crew failed in showing their allegiance and belief in the country they served, or the honor they felt, in belonging to the ship that sheltered them, and on whose decks they fought, where many gave their lives. To have commanded the Constitution is a signal honor; to have been one of her crew, in no matter how humble a capacity, is an equal one. Her name is an inspiration.' (National Maritime Museum)

the dramatic escape from a British squadron mentioned above, she defeated the frigates *Guerrière* and *Java* in August and December 1812 respectively, and inflicted so much damage that both British ships had to be sunk – an unusual event in naval warfare of the time. Although blockaded in port for most of 1813 and 1814, the *Constitution* managed to escape for one cruise in early 1814 and captured a schooner, HMS *Pictou*; then, in February 1815, she met two smaller British warships, the corvette *Cyane* and the sloop *Levant*, defeating both in a single action, and managed to get the *Cyane* back to the United States after being chased by a squadron of Royal Navy warships.

An important aspect of the naval conflict was the effort made by the British and American governments to use their warships against merchantmen. The British, in particular, also organized convoys to diminish threats to their commercial vessels. One well-known instance of commerce raiding occurred in the summer of 1813, when the USN brig *Argus* ventured into the home waters of the United Kingdom, where merchant vessels were vulnerable because convoys typically broke up near the end of their journeys and made for their various ports of call, and because the RN's strength was deployed to blockade enemies rather than guard the British Isles. Thus the *Argus* took 19 merchantmen in three weeks, until she was captured by HMS *Pelican* in an engagement on 14 August. In another, similar, incident, the USS *Essex* wreaked

The ocean war between the USN and the RN 1812–15

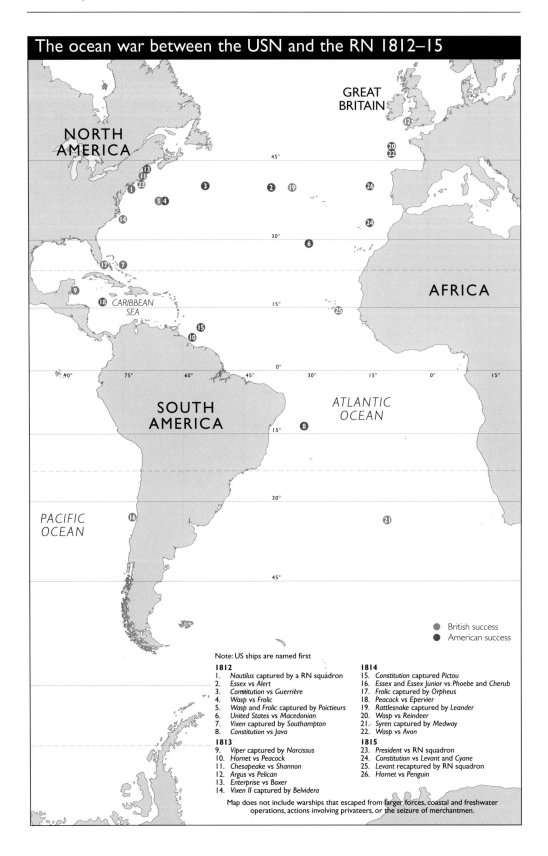

GREAT
BRITAIN

NORTH
AMERICA

AFRICA

CARIBBEAN
SEA

ATLANTIC
OCEAN

SOUTH
AMERICA

PACIFIC
OCEAN

● British success
● American success

Note: US ships are named first

1812
1. Nautilus captured by a RN squadron
2. Essex vs Alert
3. Constitution vs Guerrière
4. Wasp vs Frolic
5. Wasp and Frolic captured by Poictieurs
6. United States vs Macedonian
7. Vixen captured by Southampton
8. Constitution vs Java

1813
9. Viper captured by Narcissus
10. Hornet vs Peacock
11. Chesapeake vs Shannon
12. Argus vs Pelican
13. Enterprise vs Boxer
14. Vixen II captured by Belvidera

1814
15. Constitution captured Pictou
16. Essex and Essex Junior vs Phoebe and Cherub
17. Frolic captured by Orpheus
18. Peacock vs Epervier
19. Rattlesnake captured by Leander
20. Wasp vs Reindeer
21. Syren captured by Medway
22. Wasp vs Avon

1815
23. President vs RN squadron
24. Constitution vs Levant and Cyane
25. Levant recaptured by RN squadron
26. Hornet vs Penguin

Map does not include warships that escaped from larger forces, coastal and freshwater operations, actions involving privateers, or the seizure of merchantmen.

havoc on the British South Pacific whaling industry when she captured about half of the ships engaged in the business. In this war against commercial shipping, the USN seized 165 British vessels (and a few troop transports), while the Royal Navy captured 1,400 American merchant vessels and privateers. The RN took some of the privateers into its own service, although it also lost a handful of small schooners and tiny dispatch vessels to larger enemy privateers.

Both Great Britain and the United States licensed privateers to seize enemy ships for profit in a kind of legalized piracy. Some of these privately owned vessels were fast-sailing, heavily crewed craft that preyed upon slow, lightly manned merchantmen. Others were regular ships that would attempt to pick up enemy vessels if opportunities arose during their normal round of business. Privateering was a perilous business: of 526 known American privateers, 148 were captured and others were lost to British action, but only 207 ever took a prize. British privateers, mainly from the maritime provinces of North America, scooped up several hundred prizes, especially among coastal trading craft. At the same time, privateers from the United States captured 1,344 merchantmen from the richer pickings of the British Empire. However, of the vessels taken by American privateers and warships, at least 750 were either recaptured by the British, handed back by neutral powers, or lost at sea, often being burned by their captors once valuable goods had been removed because there was little chance of getting the ships home in the face of RN patrols. Other captured ships had to be used as 'cartels' to return prisoners, and many vessels captured by American privateers were ransomed back to their owners.

The event that had the greatest impact on the ocean war was the Royal Navy's blockade of the American coast, which began informally in 1812 with the modest resources available in the western Atlantic at that time. As more warships took up station off American ports – from roughly 20 in 1812 to 135 at the end of the conflict –

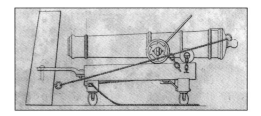

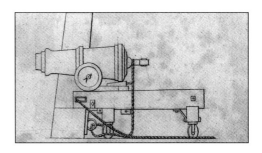

Both navies used guns (top) and carronades (below), shown here in a period print, on experimental carriages. Guns had more range than carronades of the same caliber, but carronades needed less space, smaller crews, and less gunpowder. (Ann Ronan Picture Library)

the RN cut off more and more ports from the outside world. In February 1813, the blockade covered the Atlantic coast between the Delaware and Chesapeake bays (where public sentiment had supported the war more than in other coastal regions). However, New England was exempted, because the British hoped to increase dissension between the north-eastern states that opposed hostilities and the rest of America, and because the British army fighting Napoleon in Spain and Portugal needed American grain to survive, which New Englanders happily supplied in American ships licensed and protected by the British. In March 1813, the Royal Navy expanded the blockade to include Savannah, Port Royal, Charleston, and New York, then extended it again by mid-November to the entire coast south of Narragansett Bay. In May 1814, with Napoleon defeated in Europe and the end of the British army's Iberian supply problems, the RN blockaded New England.

One consequence of the blockade was that the USN could not get its warships out to sea with ease. For example, the super

The *Grand Turk* of Salem, Massachusetts (right), a purpose-built, 14-gun privateer took about 30 prizes, yet the heavily outgunned British packet *Hinchinbrook* (left) beat off an attack in May 1814, as represented in this print from 1819. (National Maritime Museum)

frigates *United States* and *Macedonian*, accompanied by a smaller warship, set sail to prey upon British West Indian shipping in 1813 but had to flee back to port when a Royal Navy squadron intercepted them. Both frigates then sat out the rest of the war, as did the largest and most dangerous ships the USN built during the conflict – six new super frigates and four even larger ships-of-the-line. Provisioned and maintained from bases in Newfoundland, Nova Scotia, Bermuda, and the West Indies (and often replenished by profit-seeking American civilians in coastal waters), the blockading ships not only locked up much of the US saltwater navy in port, but also dissuaded many privateers from leaving home. Despite the tightening noose, some vessels did manage to escape the blockade to fight the RN or raid British commerce.

Most importantly, the blockade devastated America's international trade. Between 1811, the last full year of peace, and 1814, the value of American exports and imports fell from $114 million to $20 million and the customs revenues needed to finance the war

Attacking the United States 1813–15

Beginning in February 1813, British naval and army commanders used modest reinforcements from Europe to launch destructive raids against the Chesapeake region, close to Washington. For the most part, they met only ineffectual resistance as they destroyed military, naval, maritime, and industrial targets and captured a large number of sailing vessels. They also burned or took property when the locals opened fire or otherwise resisted them or did not offer the British ransoms against the seizure or destruction of their possessions (although those who remained quietly at home generally were left in peace and were paid for supplies requisitioned to support these British operations). Raids took place elsewhere along the Atlantic coast too, particularly in areas where the population undertook hostile acts against the blockaders. Among the several dozen operations, most of which were successful, six boats from a blockading naval force rowed up the Connecticut River in April 1814 to torch seven privateers, 12 large merchantmen, and 10 coastal vessels, while Stonington, Connecticut, endured the miseries of a naval bombardment a month later because the British thought the town was sheltering men who planned to sail booby-trapped vessels up to Royal Navy warships in order to blow them up.

With the fall of Napoleon in 1814, the British expanded their operations against the American Atlantic coast, undertaking larger initiatives as well as raids. In August, they landed 4,000 men near Washington and on 22 August, Royal Marines and sailors struck at the American gunboat flotilla on the Patuxent River; over the following day the Americans lost a privateer, 17 gunboats, and 13 merchant schooners, either captured, or destroyed by retreating US forces. On 24 August, part of the British force, numbering 2,600, easily defeated 6,000 militia, sailors, and regulars at Bladensburg in a very short battle, leaving

fell from $13 million to $6 million (despite a doubling of the rates). At the same time, the cost of trade within the United States increased dramatically as people abandoned the efficient coastal lanes for slow overland routes. By 1814, only one out of every 12 merchant ships in the United States even dared to leave port, dramatically exemplifying the economic impact of the war on the republic's economy. For the British, in contrast, international trade grew in the same period, from £91 million in 1811 to £152 million in 1814, despite American actions that brought death, destruction, and heartache to ship owners, seamen, and their families.

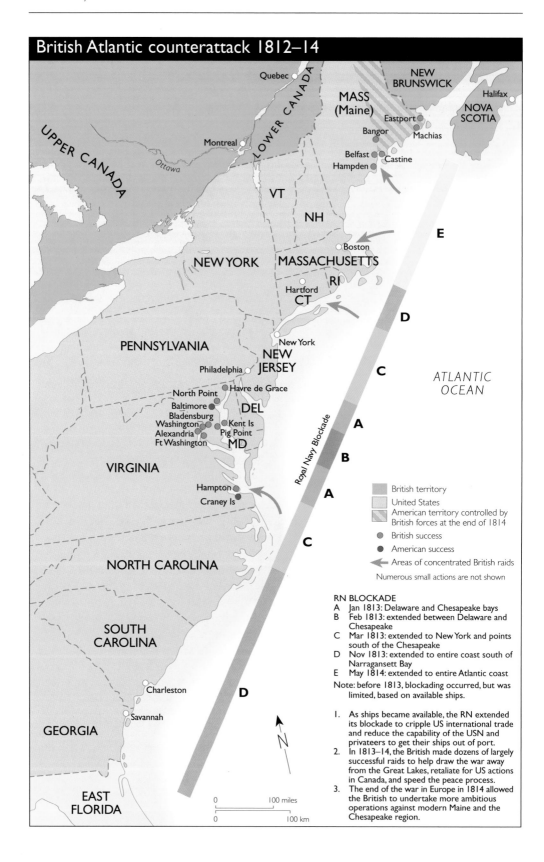

British Atlantic counterattack 1812–14

ATLANTIC OCEAN

Royal Navy Blockade

British territory
United States
American territory controlled by
British forces at the end of 1814
● British success
● American success
← Areas of concentrated British raids
Numerous small actions are not shown

RN BLOCKADE
A   Jan 1813: Delaware and Chesapeake bays
B   Feb 1813: extended between Delaware and
    Chesapeake
C   Mar 1813: extended to New York and points
    south of the Chesapeake
D   Nov 1813: extended to entire coast south of
    Narragansett Bay
E   May 1814: extended to entire Atlantic coast
Note: before 1813, blockading occurred, but was
limited, based on available ships.

1. As ships became available, the RN extended
    its blockade to cripple US international trade
    and reduce the capability of the USN and
    privateers to get their ships out of port.
2. In 1813–14, the British made dozens of largely
    successful raids to help draw the war away
    from the Great Lakes, retaliate for US actions
    in Canada, and speed the peace process.
3. The end of the war in Europe in 1814 allowed
    the British to undertake more ambitious
    operations against modern Maine and the
    Chesapeake region.

0   100 miles
0   100 km

This contemporary print presents a fanciful composite of the 1814 attack on Washington. The destruction of the US gunboat flotilla is in the lower foreground, the battle of Bladensburg is in the upper right, and the burning of the public buildings and navy yard are on the left. (Library of Congress)

an American officer, Joseph Sterett, to remark: 'We were outflanked and defeated in as short a time as such an operation could well be performed.' Among those in retreat was James Madison.

Meanwhile the president's wife, Dolley (or Dolly), saved as much as she could from the presidential mansion, including one of the nation's iconographic artifacts, a portrait of George Washington attributed to Gilbert Stuart. As the British continued their march on the capital, the commandant of the Washington navy yard burned its extensive facilities as well as a frigate and a sloop, while other people blew up a nearby fort at Greenleaf's Point. The victorious redcoats entered the capital unopposed and set fire to the White House, Capitol, Treasury, and War Office, as well as various military facilities.

They also took large quantities of munitions and weapons before starting back to their ships the next day. Meanwhile, other British soldiers and sailors were moving upriver against Fort Washington. Expecting a fight, they were surprised when the Americans blew up the fort and retreated. The British then took Alexandria on 27/28 August and seized 21 prize vessels as well as other goods. As the squadron withdrew, the Americans set up shore batteries to destroy the British ships, but the raiders experienced little trouble taking them on and making it back to sea by early September.

The British then moved against Baltimore, home of much of the privateering fleet and hence a city that deserved, in the minds of many officers, to be either destroyed or compelled to pay an enormous tribute in order to be spared. The navy sailed to the mouth of the Patapsco River on 11 September to land troops, before continuing on to attack Fort McHenry. The army came ashore the next day and marched against the city. On the way, an advanced

ABOVE The White House, after being burned by British forces, from a contemporary print. When opposition politicians in London condemned the torching of public buildings in Washington, Prime Minister Lord Liverpool offered the justification that American forces on the Canadian front had 'displayed a ferocity which would have disgraced the most barbarous nations. In one instance, a town [Niagara] was, in the middle of December, committed by them to the flames, and the inhabitants then driven … into the open country amidst all the severities of a Canadian winter. On another occasion, when the town of York, the capital of Upper Canada, was occupied by the Americans they burnt the public buildings, and took possession of the property of the governor as such. It was a retaliation for this excess that the public buildings at Washington were destroyed.' (Library of Congress)

BELOW The 1814 battle of Plattsburgh, from a contemporary print. (National Maritime Museum)

guard fell into an ambush, and although it drove the Americans away, the commanding officer, Major-General Robert Ross, the victor of Bladensburg, was mortally wounded in the action. The redcoats continued, ran into a large force blocking the way to the city, but pushed it aside at the battle of North Point. On 13 September, the British advanced further, but halted when they came up against the well entrenched Americans, who outnumbered them by three to one. Believing that their only hope lay in a surprise night attack, the British decided to wait until midnight before striking. On the American side, some pessimists burned the ropewalks that supplied the city's ships and schooners along with a new USN frigate. The Royal Navy began a 25-hour bombardment of Fort McHenry and another battery with artillery and rockets on 13 September from such evocatively named bomb and rocket vessels as *Volcano*, *Aetna*, *Meteor*, and *Devastation*. However, the fleet could not get close enough to its targets, in large part because the people of Baltimore had sunk 24 merchant vessels to block the way. At the same time, a squadron of American gunboats threatened its rear. The

fleet commander, Vice-Admiral Sir Alexander Cochrane, decided to pull back, and he sent word to those on shore that a withdrawal probably would be wise because the odds were too great. The officers on the scene called off the planned landward assault and marched back to the ships on 14 September. Despite losing the actions outside of the city, the Americans had good reason to be jubilant. Fort McHenry had held out and Baltimore had been saved.

On the northern frontier, the governor of British North America, Sir George Prevost, invaded New York with reinforcements from Europe. He marched south late in the summer of 1814 with 10,000 men, intending to capture the border community of Plattsburgh on Lake Champlain and secure Lower Canada's vulnerable underbelly. However, the United States Navy had built up a formidable squadron on the lake. Prevost knew this would have to be destroyed before he could move since he did not think it would be safe to operate with such a force in his rear. He ordered the British squadron on the lake into action on 11 September, although its commanding officer did not think it ready but hoped that support from Prevost directed against American shore batteries would give him victory. The British naval force – a frigate, a brig, two sloops, and 15 gunboats with 90 guns – met the US squadron carrying 88 guns spread between two sloops, a brig, a schooner, and 10 gunboats and galleys (with additional support from the shore batteries). About an hour after the lake battle began, Prevost ordered his army to advance on Plattsburgh itself, but he left the batteries alone. About half an hour later, the British squadron was defeated, and its commander, George Downie, lay dead under an overturned 24-pounder. Prevost, unwilling to move with the American squadron threatening his back, cancelled the attack and withdrew to Canada, to the outrage of the officers under his command and the delight of the Americans, who rewarded their commander, Thomas Macdonough, with praise and a promotion.

Two regiments of black troops, including the 5th West India Regiment pictured in this 1815 image, served in the New Orleans campaign. Other blacks, such as in Upper Canada, fought in regular, volunteer, and militia units. Many free blacks within the US helped to defend their country, but some slaves, such as several hundred from the Chesapeake region, joined the British. Most blacks, with little reason to trust either side, avoided participation in the war. (National Army Museum)

The British, however, enjoyed success elsewhere in the north, when troops from Nova Scotia occupied the Maine district of Massachusetts. They first took Moose Island, on 11 July 1814, then Castine, on 1 September. Two days later, they attacked Hampden and dispersed a militia and naval force. During that action, the Americans burned a corvette to prevent her capture. On 5 September the British marched into Bangor and took a large number of merchant vessels. They then seized Machias. The occupiers treated the local population, which capitulated on 13 September, with respect, and reopened trade with the outside world.

Toward the end of the war, far to the south, the British attacked the American Gulf coast. Until that time, the south had been a backwater in the Anglo-American crisis, but the United States had been engaged in two parallel conflicts in the region. In 1812, Spain, a country recently allied to Britain, ruled East and West Florida but was unable to pay much attention to these colonies because it was busy trying to expel the French army from its own motherland. In October 1810, President Madison proclaimed the annexation of West Florida and sent troops to occupy much of the colony; then, in 1813, he took more land. In 1812, filibusters from Georgia invaded East Florida but enjoyed only minimal success. (Later, in 1819, the United States purchased Florida from Spain.) North of Florida, the aboriginal people who made up the Creek nation tore themselves apart in a civil war in 1813–14. The conflict stemmed from deep internal tensions over whether or not to sell land and adapt to white ways; it brought American intervention when traditionalists began to attack the white

settlers. The conflict devastated the Creek population and ended with survivors either fleeing to Spanish territory or signing away half their territory to the United States. During the American conflicts with the Spanish and Creeks, the British made half-hearted efforts to intervene to support their own objectives, but at best they played marginal roles.

In the final year of the fighting, the British hoped to seize the lower portions of

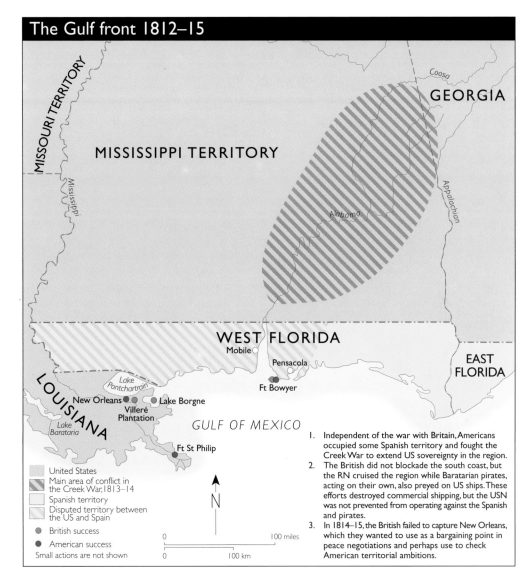

The Gulf front 1812–15

MISSOURI TERRITORY

MISSISSIPPI TERRITORY

GEORGIA

Coosa

Appalachian

Alabama

Mississippi

WEST FLORIDA

Mobile

Pensacola

Ft Bowyer

EAST FLORIDA

LOUISIANA

Lake Pontchartrain

New Orleans   Lake Borgne

Villeré Plantation

Lake Barataria

GULF OF MEXICO

Ft St Philip

United States

Main area of conflict in the Creek War, 1813–14

Spanish territory

Disputed territory between the US and Spain

British success

American success

Small actions are not shown

N

0   100 miles

0   100 km

1. Independent of the war with Britain, Americans occupied some Spanish territory and fought the Creek War to extend US sovereignty in the region.
2. The British did not blockade the south coast, but the RN cruised the region while Baratarian pirates, acting on their own, also preyed on US ships. These efforts destroyed commercial shipping, but the USN was not prevented from operating against the Spanish and pirates.
3. In 1814–15, the British failed to capture New Orleans, which they wanted to use as a bargaining point in peace negotiations and perhaps use to check American territorial ambitions.

the Mississippi River to use as a bargaining chip in peace negotiations – or even to affirm Florida's independence from the United States and perhaps create a separate state in the lower Mississippi because the ethnic diversity of the region and the American government's tenuous authority there suggested that the map could be redrawn. The first major British act was to send an inadequately small force on a failed expedition to capture Fort Bowyer at Mobile Point in September 1814, in preparation for a larger assault against New Orleans. The expedition against this main target, however,

had to wait until the blistering summer and hurricane seasons were over. After assembling troops in Bermuda and the West Indies, the British sailed to New Orleans, arriving near their target in December with a force of 7,500 men.

Anticipating the attack, Major-General Andrew Jackson dispatched a flotilla of gunboats to Lake Borgne to guard one of the approaches to New Orleans. Royal Marines in small ships' boats attacked them on 14 December and captured all of the USN vessels. This helped the British land near the city, with assistance from Spanish and

Portuguese fishermen, who held little regard for the American government. However, unusually cold weather, combined with the deep swamps and difficult terrain, made the advance on the city very difficult, created serious supply problems, and contributed to a large number of deaths through illness and exposure. Then, on 23 December, Jackson led a combined naval and land attack against the British in their camp at the Villeré Plantation outside of the city. The redcoats held their own in the confused night action and the Americans pulled back.

This painting, probably from the 1820s, shows small British boats rowing to capture American gunboats on Lake Borgne. Gunboats typically were 40–60 feet (12–18m) long and were armed with one or two 18-, 24-, or 32-pounder guns, firing respectively 8, 11, and 15kg shot. (National Maritime Museum)

Jackson then fortified the approach to New Orleans at the Rodriguez Canal, which he equipped, in part, with artillery, powder, and shot supplied by the local Baratarian pirates who had allied themselves to their erstwhile enemies in the face of the British invasion. Meanwhile, the commander of the British expedition, Major-General Sir Edward Pakenham, ordered the destruction of a schooner, the *Carolina*, which had participated in the attack on Villeré plantation, with red-hot shot. On 28 December, he performed a reconnaissance in force against Jackson's line, but was forced to withdraw, despite coming close to breaking one of the American flanks. Then, on 1 January 1815, he bombarded the Americans, hoping to silence their guns, but with little effect because the British did not have enough ammunition and because their

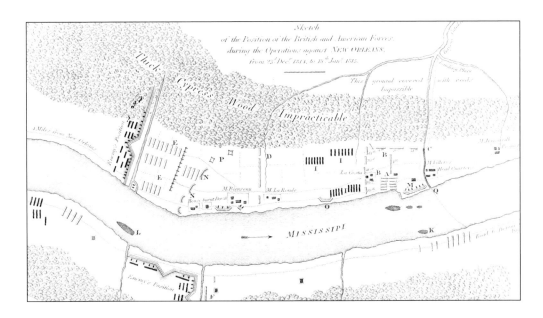

An 1815 British map showing their operations against New Orleans that ended in disaster. (National Maritime Museum)

guns became bogged down in the soggy ground. American artillery fire did considerable damage in return. A week later, on 8 January, the British made their famous but notoriously ill-executed frontal assault against Jackson. They carried one of Jackson's batteries at bayonet point, but the main assault collapsed into disaster, and Pakenham fell in the action. The British withdrew, having suffered their worst defeat in the war, and, like the Americans, having fought the battle in ignorance of news that diplomats had agreed to terms of peace on 24 December.

In the short New Orleans campaign, the British suffered 2,450 killed, wounded, missing, and captured, to only 350 losses on the US side. They nevertheless maintained their fighting spirit and later made two more attacks against American posts – one that failed, against Fort St Philip near New Orleans, and one that succeeded, against Fort Bowyer, which capitulated on 11 February and which the British took in preparation for a move against Mobile. The next day, however, word of the peace treaty arrived, and the soldiers and sailors shifted their attention to the task of preparing to go home.

Black Hawk's war

In 1833, the Sauk war chief, Black Hawk, looked back over his life and dictated his memoirs, which were translated into English for publication. There are a few problems with them, such as some obvious interventions by the translator or publisher, along with numerous chronological lapses, but they provide a fascinating first-hand account of one warrior's life around the time of the War of 1812.

Black Hawk was born in 1767 at Saukenuk, the principal tribal town, on the east bank of the Mississippi River. At the age of 15, he took up the ways of the warrior and wounded his first enemy. Shortly afterward, he joined his father in a campaign against the Osages, a tribe that lived to the south-west of his own people, and was 'proud to have an opportunity to prove to

him that I was not an unworthy son, and that I had courage and bravery.' Excited with 'valor and ambition,' Black Hawk 'rushed furiously upon another, smote him to the earth' with his tomahawk, ran his lance through his body, and took his scalp, while his father watched, said nothing, but 'looked pleased.' Upon returning home, he joined the other warriors in his first triumphal scalp dance, then continued fighting to protect his tribe's access to hunting lands from other aboriginal challengers and to avenge the killing or capture of members of his nation.

A new period of challenge began in 1804, when American officials assumed control of the fur trade community of St Louis following the 1803 Louisiana Purchase in which the United States acquired sovereignty over the vast territories on the west side of the Mississippi River from France. Although Sauk territory had fallen within the boundaries of the United States previous to that time, American influence had been minimal. However, in 1804, the newcomers invited four Sauk leaders to St Louis, where they used alcohol to befuddle them into signing a fraudulent treaty, alienating an enormous amount of Sauk (and Fox) land as a condition for restoring peace with the settler population following an outbreak of low-level hostility between natives and the

Black Hawk (from a print done in the wake of the Black Hawk War). He found American and British modes of combat to be deficient, noting in disgust: 'Instead of stealing upon each other and taking every advantage to *kill the enemy and save their own people*, as we do (which with us is considered good policy in a war chief), they march out in open daylight and *fight*, regardless of the number of warriors they may lose! After the battle is over they retire to feast and drink wine as if nothing had happened; after which, they make a *statement in writing* of what they have done – *each party claiming the victory!* and neither giving an account of half the number that have been killed on their own side.' (Peter Newark)

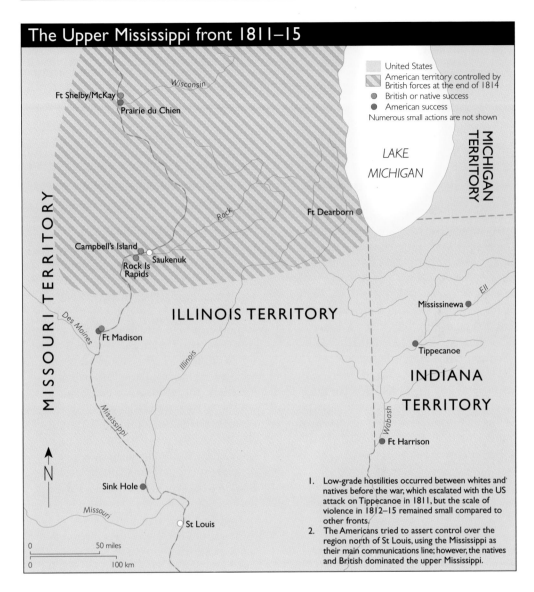

The Upper Mississippi front 1811–15

United States

American territory controlled by British forces at the end of 1814

● British or native success

● American success

Numerous small actions are not shown

Wisconsin

Ft Shelby/McKay

Prairie du Chien

LAKE MICHIGAN

MICHIGAN TERRITORY

MISSOURI TERRITORY

Rock

Ft Dearborn

Campbell's Island

Saukenuk

Rock Is Rapids

Mississinewa

Ell

ILLINOIS TERRITORY

Des Moines

Ft Madison

Illinois

Tippecanoe

INDIANA TERRITORY

Mississippi

Wabash

Ft Harrison

N

Sink Hole

Missouri

St Louis

1. Low-grade hostilities occurred between whites and natives before the war, which escalated with the US attack on Tippecanoe in 1811, but the scale of violence in 1812–15 remained small compared to other fronts.

2. The Americans tried to assert control over the region north of St Louis, using the Mississippi as their main communications line; however, the natives and British dominated the upper Mississippi.

0   50 miles

0   100 km

---

newcomers. The Sauks were allowed to remain in the ceded territory until the US sold it to settlers. This treaty, combined with tensions arising from increasing settlement, led Black Hawk and many in his nation to maintain friendly relations with the British in Canada in the hope that the British might help the Sauks to overturn the treaty and secure the independence of their homeland. However, another Sauk group, the peace band, chose the path of neutrality and accommodation, partly because the growing American presence was changing their trade and other relationships, and partly because

its members did not believe they could oppose the United States successfully.

Black Hawk then learned about the efforts by Tecumseh and Tenskwatawa to form their pan-tribal confederacy, remembering ruefully how 'runners came to our village from the *Shawnee Prophet* ... with invitations for us to meet him on the Wabash. Accordingly a party went from each village. All of our party returned, among whom came a *Prophet*, who explained to us the bad treatment the different nations of Indians had received from the Americans by giving them a few presents and taking their land from them. I remember well his saying, "If you do not join your friends on the Wabash, the Americans will take this very village from you!" I little thought then that his words would come true! Supposing that he used these arguments merely to encourage us to join him, we agreed that we would not.'

Despite his coolness to the Shawnee brothers, Black Hawk remained hostile to the Americans and rejected the legitimacy of the 1804 treaty. Naturally, he participated in the slowly escalating opposition to the United States, which exploded into war in 1811 at Tippecanoe. Once the Anglo-American war had broken out in 1812, Black Hawk led a war party in an attempt to take Fort Madison near his village, but it failed. In early 1813, he responded to a call by British officials to lead 200 men away from his homeland to the Detroit frontier, where he saw action at Frenchtown and at forts Meigs and Stephenson. When he returned to the Mississippi early in 1814, he learned how the conflict had transpired there during his absence. In many ways, this was a classic frontier struggle with both the natives and settlers organizing small-scale raids against each other and attacking non-combatants. Perhaps the best news from Black Hawk's perspective was the burning and evacuation of Fort Madison by its American garrison in September 1813 following a summer of aboriginal harassment. This 'pleased' him because 'the white people had retired from our country.'

As the 1814 campaigning season opened in the spring, the locus of American strength in the west was St Louis. To the north, the British occupied the fur trade village of Prairie du Chien and used it to encourage and supply native allies along the Mississippi who continued to oppose the Americans (unlike many of the tribesmen of Tecumseh's alliance, who had been knocked out of the war after the battle of Moraviantown). The fighting that ensued repeated the patterns of raids and harassment set earlier, and also saw a more energetic American response to try and subdue the tribes and evict the British.

The Americans sent troops up the Mississippi in fortified gunboats to intimidate the tribes, and, in June, they entered Prairie du Chien without resistance because the small garrison had abandoned the village in the face of their advance. They then built Fort Shelby but surrendered it after a short British siege in July. (The victors renamed the post Fort McKay.)

Black Hawk fought in the 1814 Mississippi campaign, including an engagement at Campbell's Island in July and the battle of the Rock Island Rapids in September. At the latter, he defeated Major Zachary Taylor, the future president, who retreated downriver after the fighting. At the former, high winds drove one of the American vessels aground. Black Hawk declared: 'This boat the Great Spirit gave us!' and led an assault against it. He remembered: 'We approached it cautiously and fired upon the men' who had come ashore from the stricken vessel. Faced with the attack, the Americans 'hurried aboard, but they were unable to push off, being fast aground.' Black Hawk continued: 'We advanced to the river's bank, under cover and commenced firing at the boat. Our balls passed through the plank and did execution, as I could hear them screaming in the boat! I encouraged my braves to continue firing. Several guns were fired from the boat, without effect.' Then he prepared a bow and arrows 'to *throw fire to the sail*, which was lying on the boat; and after two or three attempts succeeded in setting the sail on fire. The boat was soon in flames!' Then one of the other vessels in the flotilla attempted to rescue the stranded soldiers. Black Hawk recalled that it 'swung in close to the boat on fire, and took off all the people except those killed and badly wounded. We could distinctly see them passing from one boat to the other, and fired on them with good aim. *We wounded the war chief in this way!'*

At this point, another American vessel came by and dropped anchor to assist the beleaguered boat, but the anchor did not take hold and the gunboat drifted ashore while the first rescue boat abandoned the fight. With another vulnerable target, Black Hawk's band 'commenced an attack' and 'fired several rounds' but the crew did not shoot back. Thinking his enemy was afraid or had only a few men on board, he ordered his men to rush the stricken craft. 'When we got near, they *fired*, and killed two of our people, being all that we lost in the engagement.' Then: 'Some of their men jumped out and pushed off the boat, and thus got away without losing a man!' This show of bravado impressed Black Hawk, who declared: 'I had a good opinion' of the boat commander because he 'managed so much better than the other,' and in fact Black Hawk noted that it 'would give me pleasure to shake him by the hand.'

Word of the war's end reached the upper Mississippi in May 1815, when an American vessel from St Louis carried the news up to Prairie du Chien. The British invited their aboriginal allies to a council and told them that they had to end their hostilities. An angry and defiant Black Hawk held up a black wampum belt that had been given to him early in the conflict and declared: 'I have fought the Big Knives, and will continue to fight them till they are off our lands. Till then my father, your Red Children can not be happy.' He then led his followers against the Americans, with the most notable action of 1815 being a skirmish known as the 'battle' of the Sink Hole. Other Sauks, however, signed a treaty with the United States in 1815. A year later, Black Hawk acknowledged the wider peace and he too agreed to stop fighting.

After the war, whites pressured the Sauks to move to the west side of the Mississippi. Black Hawk told the story of one friend that symbolized the tensions of the era, recalling how, on an island in the Rock River, he 'planted his corn; it came up well – but the white man saw it! – he wanted the island, and took his team over, ploughed up the corn, and re-planted it for himself. The old man shed tears; not for himself, but the distress his family would be in if they raised no corn.' In 1831, with Black Hawk's band continuing to oppose removal, troops surrounded Saukenuk, opened fire with artillery, and then moved in. The village, however, was empty; its people had fled across the Mississippi during the previous night. The Americans torched their homes and desecrated their graves, perhaps knowing how important sites associated with the spiritual world were to the Sauks.

A cowed Black Hawk agreed to live in the west, but when the Americans failed to live up to promises to provide food in compensation for the loss of crops at Saukenuk, he and other leaders brought 1,000 or more Sauks, Foxes, and other native men, women, and children home again in April 1832. The so-called 'Black Hawk War' ensued, but it amounted to little more than a brutal series of tragedies for a short time and culminated in the butchering of the majority of Black Hawk's followers when they tried to swim back across the Mississippi River under fire. Black Hawk gave himself up to the Americans, who toured him through the eastern United States to demonstrate their power and thereby prevent further troubles. It was upon his return to the Mississippi that he dictated his memoirs.

Black Hawk lived out his remaining days quietly in the shadow of the sadness of all that his people had lost, passing away in 1838. Shortly afterward, a white man broke into his grave and stole his remains. They were put on display in a museum, and then were lost in a fire.

Mississippi region natives in 1814. Note the military-style 'chief's coat' on one man, presented by British authorities to aboriginal leaders. He also wears 'chief's medals' around his neck as tokens of alliance. Note as well the black man beside him. Tribes in 1812 often adopted outsiders – native, white, and black – into their ranks. (National Archives of Canada)

Propaganda and protest

Propaganda

Both sides used propaganda to advance their cause, boost morale among their people, and win approval on the international stage. One example of this was the reluctance of the United States to speak openly about expansion as a reason for war, preferring instead to condemn Britain and the tribes for affronting American rights on the Atlantic and in the Old Northwest. Likewise, the British played down maritime tensions and concentrated on issues related to defending their colonies and assisting the natives in protecting their homelands. Troops from both armies committed crimes against civilians (although on a comparatively small scale), but each side made a point of expressing indignity when their enemy was the perpetrator, even to the point of gross exaggeration. Bald-faced lies were another element of this propaganda war. After the battle of York in 1813, for example, Americans read broadsides proclaiming that their soldiers had dispersed 1,000 warriors in the action, when in fact native combatants opposing them numbered only 40–60 men.

Much of the propaganda war focused on the natives. US newspapers regularly condemned such 'Indian atrocities' as scalping and the desecration of the dead; yet the reality was that both the natives and the Americans scalped and committed indignities upon the other. In 1812, for instance, US Brigadier-General Alexander Smyth offered $40 bounties for native scalps, while a year later, another American officer, George McFeeley, saw a Kentuckian who 'had two Indian scalps that he had taken at Frenchtown' and who 'fleshed them with his knife, salted them, and set them in hoops in true Indian style.' American propaganda also roundly condemned native enemies for

killing prisoners after the battle of Frenchtown on the Raisin River, which generated the war cry, 'Remember the Raisin!' to motivate their troops in the Old Northwest. However, their newspapers (and subsequent historians) remained silent about American acts of brutality, such as the murder, scalping, and disfigurement of a captured British soldier and Canadian militiaman a few months later, in which the militiaman had not been killed before being butchered. For their part, the tribespeople expressed bewilderment at the dissonance between words and deeds, such as occurred in 1813, when British officers reprimanded some warriors for mutilating an American corpse. An Ottawa chief, Black Bird, replied with the complaint that their enemy had disinterred aboriginal dead and chopped up the bodies, then declared: 'If the Big Knives when they kill people of our color leave them without hacking them to pieces, we will follow their example.'

Protest

Many people opposed their leaders' decisions in the War of 1812. Among natives, individuals generally were free to stand aside from a community decision to engage in hostilities or at least determine the extent to which they would support the general consensus, even to the point of being able to desert in the face of enemy fire without

RIGHT Scalp, c.1812, consisting of skin and hair stretched to a wooden hoop with sinew. Many natives believed that spiritual power was concentrated in the scalp and that enemy scalps could be 'adopted' into a family grieving the loss of a loved one in order to strengthen its spiritual power and to serve as proof that the lost person had been avenged. (City of Toronto Museums and Heritage Services)

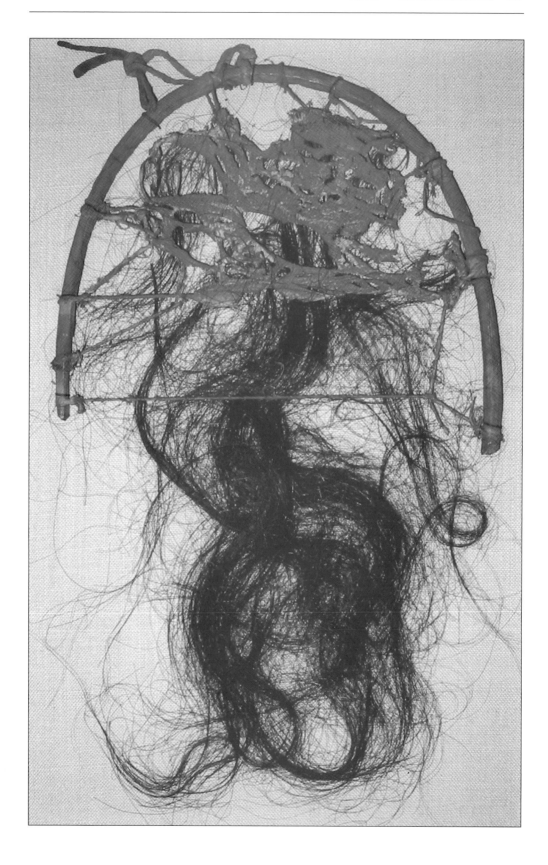

Cartoonists on both sides produced crude propaganda to sell to patriotic consumers. This 1812 American image denounces the British for purchasing scalps, something that the British did not do. In fact, they offered bounties to their native allies for prisoners to discourage the killing of captured enemies. (Library of Congress)

serious repercussions. Within the white world, militia service was not voluntary: men were obliged to turn out when called, although the regular armies on both sides were composed of volunteers. Yet American, British, and Canadian society allowed people considerable freedom to frustrate the wishes of officialdom or speak in opposition to their government. Thus, for example, in 1812, the legislative assembly of Upper Canada could reject Isaac Brock's request to suspend some civil liberties in order to allow the army to defend the province more effectively. In New England, the Revd Elijah Parish could comfortably denounce James Madison for going to war against Britain, which he saw as the bulwark against Napoleonic absolutism, with the words: 'If we engage in this war, then we take the side with the despot; we enlist

under his fatal banner ... and must share in his approaching destruction.'

The ability of the state to exert its authority was also limited enough that many who violated laws, such as militiamen who went home when they became dissatisfied, usually suffered no serious repercussions. Treason – helping the enemy – of course, could bring the death penalty, but even then there were far fewer prosecutions than there were incidents. Often, assisting the enemy was overlooked when territory was occupied, as happened when the British army marched

on Washington in 1814 and people sold livestock, offered to guide the way to the capital, and provided intelligence to the redcoats. Afterward, however, individuals might find themselves ostracized by their friends and acquaintances.

On the British side, the most dramatic event that involved cases of aiding the enemy was the 'Bloody Assize' of May and June 1814. Held in Ancaster, on the Niagara Peninsula, a court tried 19 residents of Upper Canada who had been captured while serving with the Americans. Charged with high treason, four were acquitted, one admitted his guilt, and 14 were found guilty on the evidence brought against them. Before imposing the death sentence, the judges held back the executions for a month to give the men the opportunity to supplicate royal mercy. After the time had passed, eight died at the end of a hangman's noose. The other seven were reprieved pending further consideration (three based on the recommendations of the judges involved and four as a result of petitions from the condemned men's friends and families). One of these seven escaped custody and fled to the United States, three died during an outbreak of disease in jail, and the remaining three received pardons on condition that they leave the British Empire for the rest of their lives.

For Americans, the most memorable story of potentially traitorous activity was that of the Hartford Convention of December and January 1814/15. Held in the Connecticut state capital, it arose from New England's frustrations with the war. Washington's defensive efforts in the region were inadequate, and the states felt they needed to keep control of their own militia forces despite federal government attempts to direct their operations. Madison's tax increases were proving worrisome, and the British blockade and raids, as well as the occupation of part of the region itself, created enormous consternation. As the convention met, some New England newspapers called for secession from the American Union and the signing of a separate peace with Britain. The federal government was so worried about the convention that it sent troops to Hartford in case there was an attempt to take New England out of the republic. However, most of the delegates were far more moderate than the press, and, despite the misunderstandings of the Madison administration and subsequent popular memory, it was not a seditious enterprise. Its final report did not pose a challenge to the republic, being instead a plea for change to restore New England's declining powers within the Union. As one politician, Josiah Quincy, noted when asked what he thought its outcome would be, the worst consequence he could come up with was 'A great pamphlet!'

John Strachan's war

John Strachan, born to a modest Scottish family in 1778, crossed the Atlantic in 1799 to find work as a tutor in Upper Canada. Toward the end of his contract, he sought holy orders in the Church of England and was ordained deacon in 1803 and priest in 1804. He served the church at Cornwall on the St Lawrence River, married a wealthy young widow, Ann Wood McGill, and established the best school in the backwoods colony, for which he received an honorary doctorate of divinity from the University of Aberdeen. In 1812, he moved to the provincial capital of York to take up duties as rector of the parish, headmaster of the York District Grammar School, and chaplain to both the garrison and the provincial parliament.

His own sense of loyalty was both conservative and steadfast, so the content of his first major war sermon to the colony's parliament was no surprise. In a long and impressive address, he tried to resolve the problems of being both a soldier and a Christian, largely by affirming that the Christian was a moral and restrained combatant when fighting for a just cause. He entered political controversy by supporting the suspension of some civil liberties because of the crisis, which most of the politicians in his congregation did not want to do, and he addressed other issues that troubled the people of Upper Canada as they faced the imminent prospect of foreign invasion.

Shortly afterward, Strachan was overjoyed to learn about the surrender of Detroit and the capture of the Northwestern American army, leading him to declare: 'The brilliant victory … has been of infinite service in confirming the wavering & adding spirit to the loyal.' This was a real concern to him because the British cause had seemed to be almost hopeless at the outbreak and because so many people in the province were, as he

Silhouettes of John Strachan and his wife, Ann, in 1807. (Toronto Reference Library)

wrote, 'recently from the States and by no means acquainted with the obligations which they contract when they come to live under this government' and so 'a signal advantage gained over the enemy was therefore necessary to keep them to their duty.'

Strachan's war efforts were not confined to pulpit pronouncements. He encouraged the young women of York's leading families to embroider flags for the local militia regiment and he organized a subscription to provide shoes and clothing for militiamen serving on the Niagara Peninsula. He even helped to alleviate problems created by a wartime shortage of coinage and small-denomination paper money by organizing the York Association, where merchants could deposit bullion and army bills (the *de facto* currency of the province) in return for small denomination notes to facilitate commerce, and then used the interest the association earned for poor relief. Then, inspired by a suggestion from a young woman in his congregation, Elizabeth Selby, he founded the Loyal and Patriotic Society of Upper Canada at the end of 1812. It raised a substantial £21,500 in British North America, the West Indies, and the United Kingdom to relieve distressed militiamen and their families, subsidize the cost of bread because wartime inflation caused hardships for the poor, and engage in other charitable acts during the conflict. After the war, the society used its surplus to establish a general hospital in York.

As garrison chaplain, Strachan not only welcomed soldiers and their families to his church, but he held additional services for them (such as occurred when there were too many people to fit into his small clapboard house of worship), and carried out marriages, churchings, baptisms, and burials. During the conflict, the army established military hospitals in York, and Strachan visited the sick and wounded twice each week. During weekday visits he usually spoke privately to the patients, asked after their health, and 'dropped something concerning their spiritual welfare.' He also gave out religious tracts, Bibles, and prayer books, but never had enough to keep up with the demand for these publications (which says something about the views and literacy of common British soldiers that clash with the general image of them as 'the scum of the earth'). On Sunday visits he also read prayers and delivered 15–20 minute homilies. Since ambulatory patients followed him through the hospitals to hear his sermons, he felt that he had to preach something different in each ward, with the result that he sometimes gave five distinct addresses during a single visit, which he found fatiguing. As casualties mounted and as space to care for them became scarce, Strachan agreed to turn his church over to the army in 1814 to be used

as a hospital. Faced with ministering to large numbers of patients, a great many of whom Strachan wrote were 'sadly mangled' from their battlefield injuries, and having to bury as many as six or eight souls a day during particularly grim periods, he lamented: 'I wish that those who are so ready stirring up wars would traverse the field of battle after an engagement or visit the hospitals next day and they would receive a lesson that might be very beneficial to them in future.'

Strachan's most dramatic contributions during the war occurred at the time of the battle and occupation of York, in late April and early May 1813. During the fighting, he evacuated wounded men from one of the

batteries until it fell to the Americans and the British regulars retreated from the capital. Once the battle was over, he joined senior militia officers to negotiate a capitulation with the Americans. They surrendered those soldiers remaining in the community, consisting mainly of wounded men and the militia, and turned over government supplies to the invaders. In return, the US commanders agreed to respect private property, allow the civil government to function without hindrance, and let surgeons and others attend to the British wounded.

Despite these terms, American troops, including some officers, broke into homes, molested and robbed the townspeople, and pillaged Strachan's church. They also locked up the British and Canadian wounded to languish without food, water, or medical attention for two days. On the day after the battle, an outraged Strachan stormed up to the enemy leaders, Major-General Henry Dearborn and Commodore Isaac Chauncey, to demand that they abide by the conditions of the capitulation. At first these officers tried to brush the priest aside, but he stood his ground and eventually they agreed to post sentries in the town, release the

The barracks at York, where John Strachan served as garrison chaplain, as depicted in 1804. (National Archives of Canada)

wounded into his care, and feed the prisoners. Over the next two days he moved the injured to private homes, procured food, clothing, medicines, and dressings for them, and even provided what treatments he could. Looting continued, however, and at one point, Strachan rescued one of his parishioners from a gang of Americans who were about to shoot her while robbing her home. With these ongoing violations of the terms of surrender, Strachan called a meeting of the town magistrates to produce a list of grievances to give to the American commanders. Dearborn 'promised everything,' as Strachan recorded, and increased the town guard, but robberies continued and in another violation of the agreement, US forces torched the governor's home and the parliament buildings before leaving after their short occupation.

The war years proved to be profoundly traumatic for the Strachan family. In 1812, one of Ann and John's children died, plunging them into a deep grief. A few months later, John received a letter telling him that his mother had passed away in Scotland. After the battle of York, he sent Ann and their children to Cornwall because he thought they would be safer there, but the decision brought personal horror when American soldiers moved through the town and a gang of them robbed, assaulted, and probably raped Ann, who was pregnant at the time, and who was left in such a state of emotional and physical collapse that her family and friends despaired of her life. Thankfully, she recovered and gave birth to a baby girl in early 1814, but then, just after the return of peace, the Strachans' home in York was gutted by fire.

Word of the end of hostilities and the survival of Upper Canada within the British Empire reached York in February 1815. In early April, the people of the town attended a special service of thanksgiving at which John Strachan preached the sermon. He looked to the postwar period with hope: 'Since the return of Peace, a great change is observable among our inhabitants, many are desirous of religious instruction who used to be cold and indifferent.'

In looking back over the war with America, as well as Britain's larger conflict with France, Strachan searched for divine purpose in the conflicts that had engulfed his world and which he said had resulted in Britain's triumph over its enemies, something that few had expected in 1812, when the United States 'with horrid joy' grasped at expansion at the very moment when Britain was mired in the European crisis. Despite Britain's own failings, he believed that King George's subjects at home and in the colonies had 'abundant cause to give thanks to Almighty God for the successful issue of the contest; that we are a free and happy people; have never bowed to a foreign yoke; and have preserved in all its vigour our most excellent constitution.'

Strachan's wartime service brought him public recognition that led him into the corridors of power in the backwoods province, where he tried to impose a High Tory ideology that had been shaped by his wartime experiences. His objective was to create an ordered and deferential society on the frontier, based on the twin pillars of an established Church of England and the British constitution. However, the colony was too diverse for this in religious terms to be acceptable, and the times were too liberal and democratic for his old-fashioned notions of civil society to develop. Gradually, even officials in York and London turned their backs on him, and by the 1830s he had become a political anachronism.

Fortunately for Strachan, his church began to be reinvigorated by ideas that emanated from the Oxford Movement, which suggested a new and independent role for Anglicanism, less tied to the state but more attached to its older traditions and roles. After his consecration as bishop of the newly created diocese of Toronto in 1839, he worked tirelessly for his church until his death in 1867 – the same year that some of the British North American colonies came together to form a new nation within the British Empire, the Dominion of Canada.

The peace of Christmas Eve

The Treaty of Ghent

During the winter of 1814/15, both sides assumed that fighting would resume in the spring. They strengthened their forts and fleets and otherwise made their plans. However, these efforts became pointless as word arrived that the war had ended. Much of eastern North America had heard the news by February 1815, although some isolated posts, such as Prairie du Chien, had to wait until the spring to learn of the return of peace. After three years of hostility, people moved quickly to return their lives to normal. For example, the RN commander at Kingston, Sir James Lucas Yeo, accepted an invitation from his old rival, Commodore Isaac Chauncey, to visit Sackett's Harbour with his fellow officers, who, in their hurry to get back to England, took the fastest route home, via New York City. Sadly, the good news took longer to reach some of the more distant parts of the world, with the result that far away in the Indian Ocean on 30 June 1815, the USS *Peacock* fired upon the small East India Company brig *Nautilus*, killing and wounding 14 people, despite the fact that officers from the British vessel had come aboard the *Peacock* with news that the war was over.

Efforts to end the conflict had begun almost as soon as it had broken out, when the American *chargé d'affairs* in London suggested an armistice in return for a renunciation of impressment (the Orders-in-Council having been revoked at the outbreak), but the British were unwilling to concede on that issue. Shortly afterward, when the British captured Detroit and news of the repeal of the Orders reached North America, Sir George Prevost arranged an armistice with the American commander on the northern front, Henry Dearborn, to

enable the United States government to reconsider its plans. However, the administration of James Madison decided to continue the war, having set its sights on the conquest of Canada. In March 1813, Russia offered to mediate a peace, but the British government rejected the opportunity because it might compromise British interests in Europe. However, in January 1814, both powers agreed to negotiate with each other directly and settled on the then-Dutch city of Ghent as the meeting place, having rejected their initial choice, Gothenburg in Sweden, as too isolated. Diplomats from the two nations first met in August 1814.

Both sides used the changing see-saw in fortunes across the Atlantic to push for as many concessions as possible, although the fundamental difference between the two powers was that the primary British objective was to maintain the 1812 status quo by retaining Canada and asserting Britain's maritime rights, except, if possible, to force the United States to accept the creation of a native homeland in the Old Northwest. The Madison administration essentially wanted to alter the status quo dramatically, by annexing Canada, changing Britain's naval policies and practices, and eliminating aboriginal resistance in the west. At times, such as when the news of the fall of Washington reached Ghent but not the withdrawal of British forces from Baltimore, British diplomats naturally tried to get more from the Americans – such as land cessions and a demilitarization of the Great Lakes – to improve Canada's security. The Americans made forlorn attempts to win Upper Canada through diplomacy while their army was failing to do so militarily.

Both sides wanted the war to end if national dignity could be maintained. The main British objective of keeping Canada had been met as of 1814, and they feared it might be endangered if the war were to continue; at the same time, the fragile peace established in Europe showed enough signs of disintegration that the troops recently sent to North America were needed back on the Continent. Furthermore, British taxpayers cried out for relief, having borne the costs of fighting wars and subsidizing allies for 20 years. The Americans realized that their own objectives in going to war could not be achieved, and thought the best they could probably get was the preservation of the status quo that they had been fighting so hard to upset. Conquest was proving impossible, and in fact the British controlled more US territory than the Americans occupied in Canada. The Orders-in-Council had been revoked before the outbreak of hostilities, and while the British would not relent on impressment and other policies, the end of the European war promised to render concern for at least some of these issues academic. At the same time, the United States faced bankruptcy, recruitment for the army had fallen below the rate at which men were being lost, and federal officials did not appreciate just how weak was the secessionist movement in New England. Thus, American diplomats dropped their demands for a resolution of Anglo-American maritime problems and for restitution for damages done during the blockade and coastal raids, along with their claim for compensation for, or the return of, slaves who had sought freedom with the British, and for the cession of Canada. Both parties also agreed to make peace with the native peoples and restore to them the rights they had enjoyed in 1811 – a move that had far more impact on the United States than it did on Great Britain because of the aboriginal situation in the Old Northwest. All captured territory, except for some islands in Passamaquoddy Bay, off Maine, that the British had seized, were to be returned to their 1812 owners, and other issues, such as conducting a scientific survey of the Canadian-American border to determine an exact boundary line, were left to be settled in the future. The Americans also agreed to assist the British in suppressing the slave trade. On 24 December 1814, the diplomats signed the peace treaty, with most of its articles being based on the principle of *status quo ante bellum*, and then joined together to celebrate the coming of Christmas in Ghent cathedral.

On 26 December, London business interests had learned enough to shift their investments in anticipation of renewed trade with the United States, and on 27 December the Prince Regent (the future George IV) ratified the document. Across the Atlantic, the US Senate unanimously ratified the treaty on 16 February 1815, and at 11.00 p.m. the next night the war officially ended with an exchange of ratifications. In Britain, the government learned about the events in Washington on 13 March, and with the coming of spring, both sides withdrew their forces from the territories of their former enemy and began to send prisoners-of-war home. Within the aboriginal world, negotiations took place through 1815 and 1816 to end the fighting between the tribes and the respective white powers they had fought against, also to bring hostilities to a close among the tribes that had fought against each other.

Perceptions of victory

As word filtered across the Atlantic that peace had returned, most Americans, like their British counterparts who had heard the news earlier, sighed with relief as the associated burdens and uncertainties lifted and they could look to a future with greater promise. Most Americans seemed to forget why their country had gone to war, the failure of their soldiers, sailors, and diplomats to achieve their objectives, and instead embraced the memories of successes at Plattsburgh, Baltimore, and especially New Orleans to bolster an interpretation of the peace that affirmed the independence and dignity of their country, going so far as to proclaim that they had won a 'second war of independence.' Some pronounced their enthusiasm for the outcome with a surprising degree of hyperbole: Congressman George Troup declared the Treaty of Ghent 'the glorious termination of the most glorious war ever waged by any people.' For his part, President James Madison told Congress, on 18 February 1815, that the war had been a success.

As time passed, the legends of American victory grew. The famous Democratic-Republican party newspaper *Niles Register*, on 14 September 1816, crowed: '... we did virtually dictate the treaty of Ghent to the British,' ignoring completely that it had been a scramble just to get the status quo of 1812, let alone achieve any war aims, while vague affirmations that Britain had come out of the war with a new-found respect for the United States helped to solidify such views. This attitude has remained dominant in the American public consciousness, as can be seen in today's brochures and web presentations from 1812 historic sites as well as in textbooks and the popular media, and even in much academic writing. Other Americans in 1815 saw things differently. While some thought of the war fundamentally as a draw, many Federalist party supporters who had opposed the Madison administration noted how the government had failed to achieve its goals. These views, less helpful in building national identity and patriotism, have been embraced by far fewer Americans, both then and in subsequent decades.

An assessment of objectives set in 1812 and realized in 1814 points to a British victory, although perhaps one that is not clear in the modern mind, partly because the war occurred in an age when diplomatic negotiations, the preservation of dignity, and compromise marked treaties, rather than the images of unconditional surrender that have come to dominate our consciousness. Furthermore, a successful defensive war has less impact on the popular imagination than a conflict that changes national boundaries. On maritime issues, the British understood

that their prewar policies risked conflict with the United States, but they believed that they could not abandon these policies because of the imperative to defeat Napoleon. Yet, as the possibility of hostilities loomed larger, they rescinded the Orders-in-Council to avoid a confrontation before learning of the US declaration, and so the revocation of the Orders had nothing to do with the war itself.

Britain would not, however, negotiate a compromise on impressment or other maritime policies, such as excluding American ships from trade routes it wanted to keep for exclusive British use, and thus the peace treaty was silent on these points and did not challenge British policies or practices. That impressment evaporated as a problem between the two powers was due entirely to Britain's triumph over France and had nothing to do with American actions, and the United Kingdom came out of the war fully prepared to implement any restrictions it wished if future tensions required them. More importantly, Britain defended its North American colonies successfully, and thus the Canadian experiment in building a distinct society was not brought to a violent and premature close through American conquest, but continued, as it does today. This was the most significant outcome of the War of 1812. For Britain, the retention of these colonies (and their subsequent identity as a nation within the Empire) gave it access to North American products outside of the control of the United States, and also contributed to the overall strength of the Empire; it also provided the mother country with absolutely critical support in both 1914 and 1939 when Canada went to war (while the United States stayed out of the great conflicts of the 20th century until 1917 and 1941 respectively).

While the case for a fundamental British victory over the United States is the most logical one that can be made, there were other participants in the conflict whose stories muddy the waters. Although their fights had only the most peripheral links to the war, the contemporary struggles of

DEFENCE OF FORT M.HENRY.

The annexed song was composed under the following circumstances—
A gentleman had left Baltimore, in a flag of truce for the purpose of getting released from the British fleet, a friend of his who had been captured
at Marlborough.—He went as far as the mouth of the Patuxent, and was
not permitted to return lest the intended attack on Baltimore should be
disclosed. He was therefore brought up the Bay to the mouth of the Patapsco, where the flag vessel was kept under the guns of a frigate, and
he was compelled to witness the bombardment of Fort M'Henry, which
the Admiral had boasted that he would carry in a few hours, and
that the city must fall. He watched the flag at the Fort through the
whole day with an anxiety that can be better felt than described, until
the night prevented him from seeing it. In the night he watched the Bomb
Shells, and at early dawn his eye was again greeted by the proudly waving
flag of his country.

Tune—ANACREON IN HEAVEN.

O! say can you see by the dawn's early light,
  What so proudly we hailed at the twilight's last gleaming,
Whose broad stripes and bright stars through the perilous fight,
  O'er the ramparts we watch'd, were so gallantly streaming?
And the Rockets' red glare, the Bombs bursting in air,
Gave proof through the night that our Flag was still there;
    O! say does that star-spangled Banner yet wave,
    O'er the Land of the free, and the home of the brave?

On the shore dimly seen through the mists of the deep,
  Where the foe's haughty host in dread silence reposes,
What is that which the breeze, o'er the towering steep,
  As it fitfully blows, half conceals, half discloses?
Now it catches the gleam of the morning's first beam,
In full glory reflected new shines in the stream,
    'Tis the star spangled banner, O! long may it wave
    O'er the land of the free and the home of the brave.

And where is that band who so vauntingly swore
  That the havoc of war and the battle's confusion,
A home and a country, shall leave us no more?
  Their blood has washed out their foul footsteps pollution.
No refuge could save the hireling and slave,
From the terror of flight or the gloom of the grave,
    And the star-spangled banner in triumph doth wave,
    O'er the Land of the Free, and the Home of the Brave.

O! thus be it ever when freemen shall stand,
  Between their lov'd home, and the war's desolation,
Blest with vict'ry and peace, may the Heav'n rescued land,
  Praise the Power that hath made and preserv'd us a nation!
Then conquer we must, when our cause it is just,
And this be our motto—"In God is our Trust;"
    And the star-spangled Banner in triumph shall wave,
    O'er the Land of the Free, and the Home of the Brave.

The best-known patriotic legacy of the war is *The Star Spangled Banner*. This is the first known printing of the lyrics, probably made right after the bombardment of Fort McHenry. The words are by Francis Scott Key, who set them to the music of a British song, *To Anacreon in Heaven*. In 1889 the USN began using *The Star Spangled Banner* at flag-raising ceremonies, a practice copied by the army. In 1931, Congress made it the US national anthem. (Maryland Historical Society)

Spanish Florida and the Creek nation in resisting US expansion failed. Much more closely related to the war between Great Britain and the United States were the ordeals of natives in the north and west, who divided roughly into Canadian-resident natives, who largely (if conditionally) supported the British, American-resident natives, who allied with the Americans, and those who lived within the borders of the United States but fought against the Americans. This last group was the largest and potentially the most vulnerable. The Treaty of Ghent included an article that stated that all these peoples were to have their territorial and other rights of the prewar period returned. This was far less than the native homeland that the majority of natives of the Old Northwest wanted, but the one campaign the Americans had won

on the Canadian front was on the Detroit frontier. This made it difficult to argue for a homeland without a corresponding willingness on the part of the British to continue waging war to achieve that goal. Such a course of action was simply not in the interests of either Britain or Canada, and the natives, as the junior partner in the alliance, like junior partners throughout history, had their interests sacrificed to those of the dominant party. Nevertheless, the article was not insubstantial.

The problem with the treaty, however, was that it did not preclude the United States from working to alienate native lands and reduce aboriginal rights after having restored them to their 1811 status. Ironically, those natives who had fought as allies of the US, such as the Iroquois in New York, received no better treatment from the Americans after 1815 than those who had opposed the United States.

Native people in Canada also suffered, as settlement pressures accelerated the alienation of their lands, although this occurred at a slower pace and without the degree of violence and dislocation that marked the experience of the tribes south of the Canada-US border.

The world's longest undefended border?

The end of the War of 1812 brought permanent peace between Great Britain and the United States, and politicians at cross-boundary events today like to speak of the world's longest undefended border, claiming that it has existed since 1815. The reality is somewhat different. Military planners in 1815 did not know that peace would last, so they prepared for another conflict, and both sides agreed that the reason the Americans had failed to conquer Upper Canada was that they had not severed the St Lawrence supply line by capturing either Kingston or Montreal. Thus, both sides

strengthened fortifications, focusing particular attention on the St Lawrence. The British, for example, built a massive citadel in Kingston in the 1830s and added several Martello towers to the town in the 1840s. Most ambitious of all, they built the Rideau Canal to create an alternative water route to the vulnerable St Lawrence, hoping that in a future war it would allow them to keep supply lines open to the upper province. The Americans improved their forts and built roads to facilitate future invasion attempts. They also worked to cut the ties between the British in Canada and the tribes of the Old Northwest, mainly through removing the natives farther west. In part, these efforts were little more than prudent planning by the British and American governments, rather than serious preparations for conflict, but both powers thought of the other as a potential enemy in the decades that followed.

The British built the Rideau Canal in the 1820s–30s to bypass the St Lawrence River above Montreal in case the Americans should seize control of the waterway in another war. This 1839 image shows the locks and defensive blockhouse on the canal at Merrickville. (National Archives of Canada)

Nevertheless, neither power wanted war, and in general their diplomats tried to ease tensions whenever problems arose. Both countries also wanted to avoid unnecessary expenditure on military preparedness; thus in 1816–17, the British minister to Washington, Sir Charles Bagot, and the acting US secretary of state, Richard Rush, negotiated a naval disarmament for the northern border. Accepted in 1817, the Rush-Bagot Agreement limited each power to maintaining a small number of armed vessels across the Great Lakes and on Lake Champlain. Most of the 1812-era warships were put into 'ordinary' for future use or were sunk, broken up, or sold to civilians. Yet, in spite of that agreement and general aspirations to avoid hostilities, both sides still eyed each other suspiciously from time to time and, in fact, both violated Rush-Bagot during periods of tension. However, a

After the end of hostilities, both sides secured their warships for future use, as can been seen in this 1815 image of Kingston, Upper Canada. Note the roof over one of the ships and how others have had their masts removed for storage. From left to right, note: Fort Henry, the top of a blockhouse (behind the workers), Navy Bay and its naval dockyard, the town waterfront, and the civilian community. (National Archives of Canada)

breach never occurred, and in 1917, over a century after the end of the War of 1812, the United States joined France, Britain, Canada, and the other colonies of the Empire on the Western Front in the great struggle against Germany and its allies.

Legacies

The War of 1812 was a small conflict compared with the great Napoleonic wars that were its contemporaries and that contributed to its genesis. This has meant that the British largely have forgotten the conflict. In the United States, memories survived, but to a large degree were subsumed by those of a more congenial war, the one with Mexico in 1846–48, in which the United States expanded into Texas, California, and other regions due to a military establishment that had been improved dramatically in light of the experiences of 1812–15. Afterward, the great national crisis of the Civil War shook Americans and eclipsed the conflicts with Britain and Mexico in the public consciousness. In Canada, the War of 1812 was the most acute crisis of the

19th century, and it dominated the popular imagination, resulting in a series of impressive centennial celebrations in 1912–14. Even today, with Britain, Canada, and the United States being firm friends, and with their shared experiences of the wars of the 20th century, Canadians still hold the War of 1812 to be one of the great moments in their country's history.

The Stoney Creek Monument was built by the 'people of Canada' through the efforts of the Women's Wentworth Historical Society and was 'unveiled by electricity' by Queen Mary from Buckingham Palace in 1913 on the centennial of the battle. Part of the monument's text reads: 'Here the tide of invasion was met and turned by the pioneer patriots and soldiers of the King of one hundred years ago. More dearly than their lives they held those principles and traditions of British liberty of which Canada is the inheritor.' (Battlefield House Museum)

Further reading

Primary sources

Manuscript Sources:

The Bostonian Society
Doc. 973.38 Letter of Rev. John Tucker, 1768

Boston Public Library, Manuscript Division
Ch.B. 12.72 Diary of an American soldier, 4/19/1775-5/13/1775
Ch.F.7.78 Major-General Frederick von Steuben Militia Rules
Ch.F.7.85 General Putnam's condemnation
Ch.F.8.55a Lieutenant-Colonel Jean Baptiste Tennant's comments on the Continental Army
G.33.10 Diary of American Service at Quebec and Saratoga
G.33.37 Salem Selectmen
G.380 Major-General Benjamin Lincoln Papers
G.380.20 Journal Siege of Charleston
Ms.R.1.4 General Orders for British Army, 1775
Ms.9.AM General Orders for the British Army during Yorktown Campaign
Mss. Acc. 568 Benjamin Gould
Mss. Acc. 1328 Commission for Alexander Innes as Inspector-General of Loyalist Troops, 1777

British Library
Lord Auckland Papers
Bouquet Papers
Haldimand Papers
Hardwicke Papers
Munro Collection
Napier Papers
Newcastle Papers
Townshend Papers
Add 11813 Captain William Parry (RN) Louisbourg

Add Mss 45662 Journal of Richard Humphrys
Add Mss 15535 Plans of Military Operations in NA
Add. Mss. 32413 Lt William Digby Journal
Add. Mss. 32627 Journal of Alescambe Chesney
Add. Mss. 57715 Siege of Charleston
Add. Mss. 57716 Siege of Savannah

Massachusetts Historical Society, Boston
Journal of Isaac Bangs
Journal of Benjamin Dunning
Major John Hawks Orderly Books
Journal of David Holden
Diary of Timothy Nichols
Diary of Nathaniel Ober
Journal of David Sanders
Samuel Shaw Papers
James Wolfe's Journal (McGill University)

National Army Museum, London
5701-9 Accounts of Brandywine, Germantown, and the siege of Gibraltar
6707-1 Lt. T. Hamilton Journal
6806-41 1st Marquis Townshend Papers
6807-131 Journal of Augustus Gordon
6807-51 Orders given by Major General Wolfe
7204-6-4 Letters of Lord Howe, General Burgoyne and Lord George Germain
7204-6-2 "Journal of unknown individual"
7311-85 Williamson Papers
7803-18-1 Journal of Charles Lee
8001-30 Captain Phillip Townsend
8010-32 Nicaragua Expedition
8010-32-1 Lieutenant-Colonel Stephen Kemble
8010-32-3 Major James MacDonald

Public Records Office, London
Amherst Papers
Cornwallis Papers

Printed Sources:

"Journal of Braddock's Campaign," *JSAHQR*, LVII

"Journal of Beausejour" (Sackville, N.B., 1937)

"Journal of the Expedition to the River St. Lawrence," London, 1760 (Sergeant-Major)

"Journal of the Siege of Oswego," *Military History of Great Britain, for 1756, 1757* (London, 1757)

London Gazette (1775–83)

Military Guide for Young Officers containing a System of the Art of War (London, 1776)

"General Orders in Wolfe's Army," *Manuscripts Relating to the early History of Canada* (Quebec, 1875)

Naval and Military Memoirs of Great Britain 1727–1783 (London, 1790)

The Northcliffe Collection (Ottawa, 1926)

Planches Relatives à l'Exercise de L'infanterie suivant L'Ordinnace du Roi du premier Juin 1776 (Lille, 1776)

Regulations for the Order and Discipline of the Troops of the United States (Philadelphia, Pennsylvania, 1779)

"Reflections on the General Principles of War and on the Compositions and Characters of the Different Armies in Europe," *Annual Register* (1766)

Allaire, A., *Diary of Anthony Allaire* (New York, 1968)

Amherst, J., *Journal of Jeffrey Amherst* (Toronto, 1931)

Amherst, W., *Journal of William Amherst* (London, 1928)

Anburey, T., *With Burgoyne from Quebec: An Account of the Life at Quebec and of the Famous Battle at Saratoga* (Toronto, 1963)

Andre, J., *Major Andre's Journal: Operations of the British Army under Lieut. Generals Sir William Howe and Sir Henry Clinton* (Tarrytown, New York, 1930)

Balderston, M., & Syrett, D., *The Lost War: Letters from British Officers during the American Revolution* (New York, 1975)

Barker, J., *The British in Boston: Being a Diary of Lt John Barker* (Cambridge, Mass., 1924)

Barrett, A., *The Concord Fight: An Account* (Boston, Massachusetts, 1901)

Black Hawk, A. LeClair (trans.), Patterson J. & Jackson D. (eds.), *Life of Black Hawk* [1833] (Urbana, 1990)

Bougainville, L. A. de, *Adventure in the Wilderness* (Norman, Oklahoma, 1964)

Bradstreet, J., *Impartial Account of Lt Colonel Bradstreet's Expedition to Fort Frontenac* (London, 1759)

Brannan, J. (ed.), *Official letters of the military and naval officers of the United States during the war with Great Britain* (Washington, 1823)

Clinton, H., *The American Rebellion: Sir Henry Clinton's Narrative of his Campaigns, 1775–1782* (New Haven, Connecticut, 1954)

Closen, L., *The Revolutionary Journal of Baron Ludwig von Closen* (Chapel Hill, North Carolina, 1958)

Collins, V. (ed.), *A Brief Narrative of the Ravages of the British and Hessians at Princeton in 1775–1776* (Princeton, New Jersey, 1906)

Congreve, W., *An elementary treatise on the mounting of naval ordnance* (London, 1811)

Cruikshank, E. (ed.), *The documentary history of the campaigns on the Niagara Frontier, 1812–14*, 9 vols (Lundy's Lane, 1902–08)

Dalrymple, C., *Military Essay containing reflections of the raising, arming, clothing and Discipline of British Cavalry and Infantry* (London, 1761)

Dearborn, H., *Revolutionary War Journals of Henry Dearborn* (New York, 1969)

Deux-Ponts, C., *My Campaign in America: Journal Kept by Count William de Deux-Ponts* (Boston, Massachusetts, 1868)

Doughty, A. G. (ed.), *The Siege of Quebec and the Battle of the Plains of Abraham*, 6 vols (Quebec, 1901)

Duane, W., *American military library* (Philadelphia, 1809)

Dudley, W., Crawford, M. J. et al (eds.), *The naval War of 1812: a documentary history*, 4 vols (Washington, 1985–)

Dundas, Sir D., *Principles of Military Movement* (London, 1788)

Evelyn, W., *Memoir and Letters of Captain W. Glanville Evelyn of the 4th Regiment* (Oxford, 1879)

Ewald, J., *Diary of the American War: A Hessian Journal* (New Haven, Connecticut, 1979)

Fletcher, E., *The Narrative of Ebenezer Fletcher* (New York, 1970)

Gellner, J. (ed.), *Recollections of the War of 1812: three eyewitnesses' accounts* (Toronto, 1964)

Graves, D. (ed.), *Merry hearts make light days: the War of 1812 journal of Lieutenant John Le Couteur, 104th Foot* (Ottawa, 1993)

Graves, D. (ed.), *Soldiers of 1814: American enlisted men's memoirs of the Niagara campaign* (Youngstown, 1996)

Greenman, J., *Diary of a Common Soldier in the American Revolution, 1775–1783* (DeKalb, Illinois, 1978)

Hadden, J., *Hadden's Journal and Orderly Books: A Journal kept in Canada and upon Burgoyne's March* (Albany, New York, 1884)

Hamilton, C. (ed.), *Braddock's Defeat: Journal of Captain Robert Chomley's Batman; Journal of a British Officer; Halkett's Orderly Book* (Norman, Oklahoma, 1959)

Haskell, C., *Diary of Caleb Haskell*, (Newburyport, Massachusetts, 1881)

Hulton, A., *Letters of a Loyalist Lady*, (Cambridge, Massachusetts, 1927)

Jones, C. (ed.), *Siege of Savannah by Count D'Estaing* (New York, 1968)

Kemble, S., *Journals of Lieutenant-Colonel Stephen Kemble and British Army Orders 1775–1778* (Boston, Massachusetts, 1972)

King, T., *Narrative of Titus King* (Boston, 1938)

Klinck, C. & Talman, J. (eds.), *The journal of Major John Norton, 1816* (Toronto, 1970)

Knox, H., *Historical Journal of Campaigns in North America, 1757–1760*, 3 vols (Toronto, 1914)

Latour, A. G. Smith (ed.), *Historical memoir of the war in West Florida and Louisiana in 1814–15, with an atlas* [1816] (Gainesville, 1999)

Lister, J., *The Concord Fight: Narrative of Ensign Jeremy Lister* (Cambridge, Massachusetts, 1931)

Loudon, J., *General Orders 1757* (New York, 1899)

Lowry, J., *A Journal of Captivity* (London, 1760)

Mackenzie, F., *Diary of Frederick Mackenzie: Being a Daily Narrative of his Military Service*, 2 vols (Cambridge, Massachusetts, 1930)

Malcomson, R. (ed.), *Sailors of 1812: memoirs and letters of naval officers on Lake Ontario* (Youngstown, 1997)

Martin, J., *Private Yankee Doodle Dandee: Being a Narrative of Some of the Adventures, Dangers, and Sufferings, of a Revolutionary Soldier* (Boston, Massachusetts, 1962)

Moultrie, W., *Memoirs of the American Revolution so far as it related to the States of North and South Carolina and Georgia*, 2 vols (New York, 1802)

Munro, I., *Narrative of the Military Operations on the Coromandel Coast Against the Combined Forces of the French, Dutch, and Hyder Ally* (London, 1789)

Munro, I., *The Munro Letters* (Liverpool, 1988)

Myers, M., *Reminiscences 1780 to 1814: including incidents in the War of 1812–14* (Washington, 1900)

Pargellis, S. (ed.), *Military Affairs in North America* (New York, 1936)

Pouchot, P., *Memoir of the Late War in North America between the French and the English* (Roxbury, Massachusetts, 1864)

Quaiffe, M. (ed.), *The Siege of Detroit in 1763* (Chicago, 1958)

Recicourt, L., "American Revolutionary Army: A French Estimate in 1777," *Military Analysis of the American Revolutionary War* (Millwodd, New York, 1977)

Rice, H. & Brown, A. S. K. (eds.), *The American Campaigns of Rochambeau's Army*, 2 vols (Princeton, New Jersey, and Providence, Rhode Island, 1972)

Rogers, R., *Journals of Major Robert Rogers* (Albany, 1883)

Saavedra, D., *Journal of Don Francisco Saavedra de Sangronis during the Commission which he had in his Charge from 1780 until 1783* (Gainesville, Florida, 1989)

Sautai, M., (ed.) *Montcalm at the Battle of Fort Carillon* (Ticonderoga, New York, 1928)

Scheer, G., & Rankin, H., *Rebels and Redcoats* (New York, 1957)

Simcoe, J., *Journal of the Operations of the Queen's Rangers, from the End of the Year 1777 to the Conclusion of the Late American War* (Exeter, 1787)

Tallmadge, B., *Memoir of Colonel Benjamin Tallmadge* (New York, 1858)

Tarleton, B., *A History of the Campaigns of 1780 and 1781, in the Southern Provinces of North America* (London, 1787)

Tomlinson, A., *Military Journals of Two Private Soldiers* (Poughkeepsie, New York, 1855)

Uhlendorf, B. (trans.), *The Siege of Charleston: Diaries and Letters of Hessian Officers* (Ann Arbor, Michigan, 1938)

Uhlendorf, B. (trans.), *Revolution in America: Confidential Letters and Journals 1776–1784 of Adjutant General Major Baurmeister of the Hessian Troops* (New Brunswick, New Jersey, 1957)

Webb, T., *Military Treatise on the Appointments of the Army* (Philadelphia, 1759)

Wilson, J., "A rifleman at Queenston," *Buffalo Historical Society Publications* 9 (1906)

Wolfe, J., *Instructions to Young Officers* (London, 1768)

Wood, W. (ed), *Select British documents of the Canadian War of 1812*, 4 vols (Toronto, 1920–28)

Wright, E., *Fire of Liberty* (New York, 1983)

Yorke, P. C. (ed.), *Life and Correspondence of Phillip Yorke, Earl of Hardwick* (Cambridge, 1913)

Secondary sources

Allen, R., *His Majesty's Indian allies: British Indian policy and the defence of Canada, 1774–1815* (Toronto, 1992)

Allen, R. S., *Loyal Americans: The Military Role of the Provincial Corps* (Ottawa, 1983)

Altoff, G., *Amongst my best men: African-Americans and the War of 1812* (Put-in-Bay, 1996)

Anderson, F., *A People's Army: Massachusetts Soldiers and Society in the Seven Years' War* (Chapel Hill, North Carolina, 1984)

Anderson, F., *Crucible of War: The Seven Years' War and the Fate of Empire in British North America, 1754–1766* (New York, 2000)

Atwood, R., *The Hessians* (Cambridge, Massachusetts, 1980)

Balisch, A., "Infantry Battlefield Tactics in the 18th Century," *Studies in History and Politics* (83–84)

Barbuto, R., *Niagara 1814: America invades Canada* (Lawrence, 2000)

Benn, C., *Historic Fort York* (Toronto, 1993)

Benn, C., *The Iroquois in the War of 1812* (Toronto, 1998)

Benn, C., "A Georgian parish" in W. Cook (ed.), *The parish and cathedral of St James'* (Toronto, 1998)

Black, J., *War for America: The Fight for Independence* (Stroud, 1991)

Bowler, R. A., *Logistics and the Failure of the British Army in America* (Princeton, New Jersey, 1975)

Bowler, R. (ed.), *War along the Niagara: essays on the War of 1812 and its legacy* (Youngstown, 1991)

Brumwell, S., *Redcoats: The British Soldier and War in the Americas, 1755–1763* (Cambridge, 2002)

Burt, A., *The United States, Great Britain, and British North America from the Revolution to the establishment of peace after the War of 1812* (New Haven, 1940)

Calloway, C., *Crown and calumet: British-Indian relations, 1783–1815* (Norman, 1987)

Chartrand, R., *Uniforms and equipment of the United States forces in the War of 1812* (Youngstown, 1992)

Chartrand, R. & Embleton, G., *British forces in North America 1793–1815* (London, 1998)

Christie, I. & Labaree, B., *Empire or Independence* (Oxford, 1976)

Collins, G., *Guidebook to the historic sites of the War of 1812* (Toronto, 1998)

Conway, S., *The War of American Independence* (London, 1995)

Cruikshank, E., "Blockade of Fort George," *Niagara Historical Society Transactions* 3 (1898)

Curtis, E., *The Organization of the British Army in the American Revolution* (New Haven, Connecticut, 1926)

Duffy, C., *The Military Experience in the Age of Reason* (London, 1987)

Dull, J., *The French Navy and American Independence: A Study of Arms and Diplomacy, 1775–1787* (Princeton, New Jersey, 1975)

Dull, J., *A Diplomatic History of the American Revolution* (New Haven, Connecticut, 1985)

Eccles, W. J., *Essays on New France* (Toronto, 1987)

Everest, A., *The War of 1812 in the Champlain Valley* (Syracuse, 1981)

Fortescue, Sir J., *History of the British Army*, Vol. II (London, 1908)

Fredriksen, J. (comp.), *Free trade and sailors' rights: a bibliography of the War of 1812* (Westport, 1985)

Fredriksen, J. (comp.) *War of 1812 eyewitness accounts: an annotated bibliography* (Westport, 1997)

Gardiner, R. (ed.), *The Naval War of 1812* (London, 1998)

George, C. (ed.), *Journal of the War of 1812* (1995–)

Gipson, L. H., *The British Empire Before the American Revolution*, (V–VIII) (New York, 1936–1970)

Glover, R., *Britain at Bay: defence against Bonaparte 1803–14* (London, 1973)

Graves, D., *Red coats and gray jackets: the battle of Chippawa* (Toronto, 1994)

Graves, D., *Where right and glory lead! The battle of Lundy's Lane, 1814*, revised edition (Toronto, 1997)

Graves, D., *Field of glory: the battle of Crysler's Farm 1813* (Toronto, 1999)

Gray, W., *Soldiers of the king: the Upper Canadian militia 1812–1815* (Erin, 1995)

Guy, A. J., *Economy and Discipline: Officership and Administration in the British Army 1714–63* (Manchester, 1984)

Harper, J. R., *78th Fighting Fraser's in Canada* (Montreal, 1966)

Heidler, D. & J., *Old Hickory's war: Andrew Jackson and the quest for empire* (Mechanicsburg, 1996)

Heidler, D. & J. (eds.), *Encyclopedia of the War of 1812* (Santa Barbara, 1997)

Hickey, D., "The Monroe-Pinkney treaty of 1806: A Reappraisal," *William and Mary Quarterly 44* (1987)

Hickey, D., *The War of 1812: a forgotten conflict* (Urbana, 1989)

Hickey, D., "The War of 1812: still a forgotten conflict?" *Journal of Military History* 65 (2001)

Higginbotham, D., *The War of American Independence: Military Attitudes, Policies, and Practices 1763–1789* (New York, 1971)

Higginbotham, D., *War and Society in Revolutionary America* (Columbia, South Carolina, 1988)

Hitsman, J., *Safeguarding Canada, 1763–1871* (Toronto, 1968)

Hitsman, J., (revised D. Graves) *The incredible War of 1812* (Toronto, 1999)

Horsman, R., *Expansion and American Indian policy 1783–1812* (Norman, 1992)

Houlding, J. A., *Fit for Service: Training of the British Army* (Oxford, 1981)

Hughes, B. O., *Open Fire: Artillery Tactics from Marlborough to Wellington* (Chichester, Sussex, 1983)

Kennett, L., *French Armies in the Seven Years War* (Durham, North Carolina, 1967)

Kennett, L., *French Forces in America* (Westport, Connecticut, 1977)

Kert, F., *Prize and prejudice: privateering and naval prize in Atlantic Canada in the War of 1812* (St Johns, 1997)

Leach, D. E., *Arms for Empire: A Military History of the British Colonies in North America, 1607–1763* (New York, 1973)

Leach, D. E., *Roots of Conflict: British Armed Forces and Colonial Americans, 1677–1763* (Chapel Hill, North Carolina, 1986)

Lord, W., *The dawn's early light* (New York, 1972)

Lynch, J., *Bourbon Spain 1700–1808*, (Oxford, 1989)

Mackesy, P., *War for America*, 2nd edition (London, 1993)

Mahan, A., *The influence of sea power upon the War of 1812*, 2 vols (Boston, 1905)

Malcomson, R., *Lords of the lakes: the naval war on Lake Ontario 1812–1814* (Annapolis, 1998)

Malcomson, R., *Warships of the Great Lakes, 1754–1834* (London, 2001)

Marston, D., 'Swift and Bold: The 60th Royal American Regiment and Warfare in North America, 1755–1765' (Unpublished M.A. Thesis, 1997, McGill University)

Marston, J. G., *King and Congress the transfer of political legitimacy, 1774-1776* (Princeton, New Jersey, c.1987)

Martin, T., *A most fortunate ship: a narrative history of Old Ironsides*, revised edition (Annapolis, 1997)

Middleton, R., *Bells of Victory: Pitt-Newcastle Ministry and conduct of the Seven Years' War* (Cambridge, 1985)

Morris, J., *Sword of the border: Major General Jacob Brown 1775–1828* (Kent, 2000)

Nordholt, J. W. S., *The Dutch Republic and American Independence* (Chapel Hill, North Carolina, 1982)

Nosworthy, B., *Anatomy of Victory: Battle Tactics 1689–1763* (Hippocrene, New York, 1992)

Owsley, F., *Struggle for the Gulf borderlands: the Creek War and the battle of New Orleans 1812–1815* (Gainesville, 1981)

Owsley, F., *Filibusters and expansionists: Jeffersonian Manifest Destiny, 1800–1821* (Tuscaloosa, 1997)

Pargellis, S., *Lord Loudon in North America*, (New Haven, 1933)

Parkman, F., *Montcalm and Wolfe* (New York, 1995)

Petrie, D., *The prize game: lawful looting on the high seas in the days of fighting sail* (Annapolis, 1999)

Pfeiffer, S. & Williamson R. (eds.), *Snake Hill: an investigation of a military cemetery from the War of 1812* (Toronto, 1991)

Pratt, J., *Expansionists of 1812* (Gloucester, Massachusetts, 1957)

Quimby, R., *The US Army in the War of 1812: an operational and command study*, 2 vols (East Lansing, 1997)

Richards, F., *The Black Watch at Ticonderoga and Major Duncan Campbell* (Glen Falls, New York, 1930)

Riley, J., *The Seven Years War and the Old Regime in France: Economic and Financial Toll* (Princeton, New Jersey, 1986)

Roosevelt, T., *The Naval War of 1812* (New York, 1882)

Royster, C., *A Revolutionary People at War: The Continental Army and American Character* (Chapel Hill, North Carolina, 1979)

Schweizer, K., *England, Prussia and the Seven Years War: Studies in Alliance Policies and Diplomacy* (Lewiston, New York, 1989)

Shy, J., *A People Numerous and Armed: Reflections on the Military Struggle for American Independence* (Oxford, 1976)

Skaggs, D. & Altoff, G., *A signal victory: the Lake Erie campaign 1812–1813* (Annapolis, 1997)

Skelton, W., "High army leadership in the era of the War of 1812: the making and remaking of the officer corps," *William and Mary Quarterly* 51 (1994)

Smith, P. H., *Loyalists and Redcoats: A Study in British Revolutionary Policy* (Chapel Hill, North Carolina, 1964)

Stacey, C. P., *Quebec, 1759: The Siege and Battle* (Toronto, 1959)

Stagg, J., *Mr Madison's war: politics, diplomacy and warfare in the early American republic 1783–1830* (Princeton, 1983)

Stagg, J., "Enlisted men in the United States Army, 1812–1815," *William and Mary Quarterly* 43 (1986)

Stagg, J., "Between Black Rock and a hard place: Peter B. Porter's plan for an American invasion of Canada in 1812," *Journal of the Early Republic* 19 (1999)

Stagg, J., "Soldiers in peace and war: comparative perspectives on the recruitment of the United States Army, 1802–1815," *William and Mary Quarterly* 57 (2000)

Stanley, G., *The War of 1812: land operations* (Ottawa, 1983)

Sugden, J., *Tecumseh: a life* (New York, 1997)

Sutherland, S., *His Majesty's gentlemen: a directory of British regular army officers of the War of 1812* (Toronto, 2000)

Syrett, D., *The Royal Navy in American Waters*, (Aldershot, 1989)

Tucker, S., *The Jeffersonian gunboat navy* (Columbia, 1993)

Turner, W., *British generals in the War of 1812: high command in the Canadas* (Montreal, 1999)

Ultee, M. (ed.), *Adapting to Conditions: War and Society in the Eighteenth Century* (Alabama, 1986)

Updike, F., *The diplomacy of the War of 1812* (Baltimore, 1915)

Weigley, R., *Towards an American Army* (New York, 1962)

Whitehorn, J., *While Washington burned: the battle for Fort Erie* (Baltimore, 1992)

Whitehorn, J., *The battle of Baltimore* (Baltimore, 1997)

Wilder, P *The battle of Sackett's Harbour* (Annapolis, 1994)

Wright, R. K., *The Continental Army* (Washington, DC, 1983)

Zaslow, M. (ed.), *The defended border: Upper Canada and the War of 1812* (Toronto, 1964)

Index